fundamentals of coaching basketball

fundamentals of coaching basketball

Glenn Wilkes
Head Basketball Coach
Stetson University

wcb
Wm. C. Brown Company Publishers
Dubuque, Iowa

wcb group

Wm. C. Brown, Chairman of the Board
Mark C. Falb, Executive Vice President

wcb

Wm. C. Brown Company Publishers, College Division

Lawrence E. Cremer, President
Raymond C. Deveaux, Vice President/Product Development
David Wm. Smith, Vice President/Marketing
David A. Corona, Assistant Vice President/Production Development and Design
Marcia H. Stout, Marketing Manager
Janis M. Machala, Director of Marketing Research
Marilyn A. Phelps, Manager of Design
William A. Moss, Production Editorial Manager

Book Team

Judith A. Clayton/Edward G. Jaffe, Editors
James M. McNeil, Designer
John F. Mulvihill, Production Editor
Mary M. Heller, Visual Research Editor

Aileene Lockhart, Texas Woman's University, Consulting Editor

Printed in the United States of America
10 9 8 7 6 5 4 3 2

contents

Part Two Team Offensive Formations and Plays

Part Three Team Defensive Formations and Techniques

Part Four Organization and Techniques for Better Coaching

key to diagrams

◯   Offensive player

✕   Defensive player

– – – – ▶   Direction of pass

〜〜〜▶   Direction of dribble

+–+–+–+–+▶   Shot

————┤   Screen

⌒———▶   Fake in one direction and cut

Fundamentals of Coaching Basketball, written by Dr. Glenn Wilkes, is a clear, concise insight into understanding and teaching this beautiful game of basketball, as presented by a master who continues to give back to his profession by providing us, his students of the sport, a superb textbook.

Fundamentals of Coaching Basketball should be of great interest not only to the undergraduate students as a textbook guideline but to all people at all levels interested in basketball. This book stresses the supreme importance of teaching and understanding the fundamentals of basketball and how to become proficient in all of them. It indicates a most thorough knowledge of every aspect of the game, conveyed in simple language.

In addition, Coach Wilkes has carefully analyzed and expressed the methods he uses in teaching his style of play, plus the many variations employed by his coaching counterparts across the United States, which enables the reader to understand the many options available for all situations.

This unique textbook presents organization, philosophy, and a clear teaching style, assisted by the 400 quality descriptive illustrations.

Hubie Brown
Atlanta Hawks (NBA)
Kentucky Colonels (ABA)

preface

Fundamentals of Coaching Basketball is designed primarily as a textbook for basketball coaching classes in colleges and universities. The book's first objective is to provide students with an easy-to-understand overview of basketball and its coaching techniques. I have tried to keep the needs and limitations of students in mind in preparing the text. No attempt is made to cover advanced techniques in great detail.

Most basketball books are written for the coach who already is coaching actively. These books are usually rather specific. Their authors cover particular offenses or defenses that they have used successfully, or they may cover a specific technique in great detail, such as attacking the zone defense, teaching pressing defenses, or developing a team offense. Teachers of basketball coaching courses usually find they must use several books, develop an extensive outside reading list, and depend a great deal on personal knowledge. This book does not intend to be that specific; rather it intends to present a general coverage of basketball, consolidating the basic information needed by the beginning coach into one volume.

Fundamentals of Coaching Basketball is organized into four parts. It is essential that a student coach first get to know the basics of offensive and defensive execution before going on to the actual in-game plays. Part One, therefore, covers shooting, passing, dribbling, and the other fundamental skills. Part Two is devoted to various offensive patterns, while Part Three presents team defensive formations. Part Four discusses the organizational techniques that are an integral part of coaching success.

A number of teaching aids are presented with the text. Discussion questions, projects, and suggested readings are included at the end of each chapter. The accompanying Instructor's Manual lists course objectives and a suggested course outline. It also presents numerous test questions that can be used for evaluation of student achievement.

Although this book has been written with basketball coaching students in mind, it also can be a helpful reference manual for the experienced coach. The extensive coverage of virtually every phase of the game includes numerous offensive play patterns, defensive techniques, and teaching drills that can be used on any level of play.

I am well aware that any knowledge I have gained about basketball has come from studying and listening to many successful coaches. I would like to express my appreciation to those coaches who have so willingly shared their basketball coaching techniques with me. Also, any success I have enjoyed as a coach has come largely through the efforts of the many quality players I have been privileged to coach. And to them I say thanks.

I wish to thank the reviewers of this book, whose comments and suggestions were a great help to me. They are Coach Joe Gottfried of the University of South Alabama, Professor Jon Davison of the University of Dubuque, Dr. Jerry Krause of Eastern Washington University, Professor Ralph Miller of Oregon State University, and Professor James Maloney of Temple University.

I would like to thank the Los Angeles Lakers, Atlanta Hawks, Houston Rockets, and the Seattle Supersonics of the National Basketball Association for sending photographs for use as illustrations in this book. I am also indebted to Fred Cooper and the Stetson University Sports Information Office for photographs. I owe a special thank-you to my secretary, Cecelia Jackson, for typing this manuscript and for assisting me in countless other ways.

G. W.

Head basketball coach at Stetson University since 1957, Glenn Wilkes has compiled an enviable record there of 377–265 and has an outstanding overall record of 500–295. Among collegiate coaches, he ranks in the top ten in number of wins.

Through his writing and public speaking Wilkes has imparted his knowledge of basketball to a wide audience. He has written numerous articles on basketball and has authored three other books: *Winning Basketball Strategy, Basketball Coach's Complete Handbook,* and *Basketball.* He has lectured at numerous clinics throughout the nation and in Europe and South America. He also directs basketball schools for boys and girls and founded and directs one of the most successful coaching clinics in the nation.

Wilkes earned his AB at Mercer University and his MA and EdD degrees at George Peabody College.

fundamentals of coaching basketball

part one

Basic Foundation for Coaching Success

chapter one

Philosophy of Coaching

A coach's own philosophy is the basic foundation for basketball coaching success. All coaches must develop their own philosophy based on personal career experience and the knowledge they have gained throughout their education. Newell and Benington state, "a sound and definite philosophy is synonymous with good coaching," and, "a coach's philosophy is the foundation upon which he predicates his success."[1] This philosophy must encompass all aspects of coaching, from the technical knowledge required to build successful teams and essential motivational and disciplinary techniques, to the total school and community relationship that must be a part of a winning program. This philosophy must be the coach's own, not one copied from someone else. You will find it virtually impossible to function effectively in a coaching role if you attempt to use someone else's coaching philosophy—particularly if you do not believe completely in that philosophy.

Just what do we mean by a coaching philosophy? In simple terms, we mean *what the coach genuinely believes is what's important to coaching success.* This determines exactly how you as the coach teach, including what emphasis you place on the various aspects of the game, the offense and defense you run, the type of discipline you enforce, and how you handle the various other essential elements of coaching. Although all coaches must have definite beliefs about how the game should be coached, few commit these beliefs to paper. It is best to write down your philosophy. This requires a great deal of thought about exactly what you believe about the game. But it's worth it. A written philosophy will come to your aid again and again as you meet the many challenges of coaching. Your philosophy must be flexible—review it yearly and update it as your beliefs change with experience.

1. Pete Newell and John Benington, *Basketball Methods.* New York: The Ronald Press Company, 1962, p. 8.

Aspects of Coaching Philosophy

In building a total coaching philosophy, consider the following aspects:

Technical

1. System or style of play
2. Team offense
3. Team defense
4. Practice organization
5. Teaching methods
6. Fast-break offense
7. Importance of the "little things"
8. Conditioning

General

1. Emphasis on winning
2. Discipline
3. Motivation
4. School-community relations
5. Coach-player relationships
6. Place of academics
7. Team spirit

My Own Philosophy of Basketball Coaching

After more than twenty-five years of coaching, I have developed my own definite coaching philosophy. Certain things, I believe very strongly, are essential for coaching success. My philosophy began with my experience as a player and grew into a complete set of beliefs now based on years of experience and experimentation with various techniques. In the following paragraphs, I outline most of these specific beliefs as they relate to my overall coaching philosophy.

Technical

1. Basketball is a fast-moving game that should be enjoyed by both players and spectators. For maximum excitement, it should include aggressive defense, the fast break, and an offense based on team play.

2. Team offense should involve a few selected plays, a passing game offense with a limited set of rules, and the controlled fast break. The offense should be built from the inside-out rather than from the outside-in. By this we mean the emphasis first should be placed on getting the ball inside to players close to

Figure 1.1 Basketball is a fast-moving, exciting game enjoyed by millions throughout the world.

the basket. The ball inside results in both higher percentage shots and more fouls on the opponents.

3. Successful teams in all sports are good defensively. Proper emphasis must be placed on defensive play, and defense should receive at least as much practice time as does offense. Emphasize keeping the ball away from the inside.

4. The man-for-man defense is my team's basic defense. At least one type of zone defense and at least two types of pressing defenses make up the total defensive plan. I also believe in a system that lets the team change defenses from the bench throughout a game.

5. Practices should be well organized and run on schedule. Few drills should last more than ten minutes. Drills should simulate game conditions whenever feasible and should involve as many players as possible. I don't like to see players standing around or waiting in long lines. The length of practice should be two hours in early season tapering down to an hour and a half in mid-season and even less in late season. Occasional days off are very helpful to team morale and enthusiasm.

6. As the coach you are a teacher. Constantly try to improve your teaching techniques. Develop a "coaching voice" and be able to project it so all players can hear you. Positive instruction is far better than negative. Instead of saying "Don't throw the ball away," say, "Let's concentrate on making good passes." Use enthusiasm in teaching—it's contagious. Praise as often as possible, and, when criticism is necessary, make certain it is constructive. Never embarrass a player.

7. A controlled fast break with assigned responsibilities is essential to a total offensive plan. It is superior to a "run-and-gun" type fast break in which more emphasis is placed on getting the quick shot rather than on the type of shot. The controlled fast break includes assigned lane responsibilities, a secondary or transition break in the event the primary break does not materialize, and an easy flow into the regular offensive pattern if no shot is obtained from either.

8. If you are playing against a superior team, eliminating most fast-break opportunities and using a control-type offense increases your chances of winning.

9. The "little things" in basketball often mean the difference between victory and defeat. Recovering jump balls, using the blockout technique on a defensive free throw, executing a great last-second play, or having a good out-of-bounds defense are examples of "little things" that can separate great teams from good ones and good teams from mediocre. Our Stetson team lost a heartbreaking one-point game to Nevada/Las Vegas in a recent season because a player grabbed the rim on a dunk shot, resulting in a technical foul. We lost a game to Florida State one season because the inside player on the defensive free throw failed to block out, letting the opponent in the second lane tip in a missed free throw for a winning field goal. Never overlook the "little things."

10. Basketball requires players to be in superb physical condition, and the responsibility for a player's physical condition should be shared equally by coach and player. You must work your players hard enough in practice sessions and give guidance in off-season conditioning programs. However, the greatest responsibility for off-season conditioning lies with the player. I believe strongly that a player must *maintain* good physical condition to be truly fit.

11. A well-supervised weight program in the off-season is an integral part of a conditioning program. A player gains strength, flexibility, and endurance from a quality weight program. Begin this program shortly after the last game of the season and continue through fall practice.

General

1. I believe there are many of life's lessons to be learned as a member of a basketball team. One of my responsibilities as a coach is to expose my players to these lessons as much as I possibly can. Through coaching, a player learns the value of hard work, sacrifice, personal and group discipline, cooperation, honesty and fair play, competitiveness, enthusiasm, determination, personal pride, integrity, punctuality, and other values that contribute to success in life.

2. Winning should be emphasized—not the "winning-at-all-costs" philosophy—but winning fairly under the rules of the game. Ideally we should strive to win in all aspects of our personal lives; the qualities we need for winning basketball are the same ones we need to be successful throughout life. I have heard some coaches say they avoid stressing winning to their players but instead emphasize "doing your best." However, I personally believe that it is very important for a player to strive to win and for a coach to emphasize the importance of winning. Again, I do believe strongly that winning should be done fairly and under the rules of the game. Winning any other way would be meaningless.

3. All successful teams are disciplined. In fact, *discipline may be the very cornerstone on which coaching success rests*. Without discipline, team cohesion breaks down, team spirit is destroyed, and physical condition suffers. Discipline is necessary both on and off the court. Discipline off the court involves training rules, punctuality, and appropriate dress and conduct, while discipline on the court involves practice, regulations, and game play. The coach should have as few rules as possible, but those important rules should be administered fairly, consistently, and as soon after the violation as possible.

   A player's self-discipline is an extremely important part of total team discipline, since it is virtually impossible for a coach to keep a player from breaking training if that player so desires. If a team member has a genuine desire to be a successful player, he or she will be self-disciplined off court as well as on court.

4. Motivation is important to team success. Clean locker rooms, attractive bulletin boards, good practice equipment, well-organized practice sessions, and classy uniforms set the proper stage for motivating a team. Using motivational materials including books, cassettes, and films and establishing team and individual goals are also good motivational tools that help develop the desire, pride, confidence, and determination necessary for winning play.

5. Successful teams win by playing together, not by playing as five separate individuals; therefore, the importance of *team play* cannot be over-emphasized. Good team play does not come easily, because basketball players really do enjoy shooting more than anything else. They love to look in the papers and see their names in the scoring column. After each game they want to know how many points they made. Without quality coaching and constant emphasis on team play, a basketball team tends to play individually. You must emphasize *we* instead of *I*. Slogans to emphasize teamwork, on-court actions (such as pointing at a player who makes an assist), playing as many players as possible to develop the feeling of contribution, and participating in outside activities together are ingredients that help build team unity.

6. Academics should come ahead of basketball. If a player does not go to class or does not display the right attitude toward academic endeavors, that player does not deserve to represent the school on an athletic team.

7. I believe in a warm coach-player relationship. The coach *cannot* be "one of the boys" but *can* make an effort to be a friend to each player. You must be consistent in dealing with players and must treat all players equally. No favorites should exist, and the star should receive the same praise, criticism, or punishment as the twelfth man. Telling players exactly how they stand on the team and making certain they understand their roles is necessary for a good coach-player relationship. If it is unlikely that some players will get in the game, it is better to tell them prior to the game instead of letting them become increasingly upset as the game progresses and they sit on the bench expecting to play.

8. Good school and community relations are part of a quality basketball program. The coach should involve the student body as much as possible. Involving students in statistics, pep clubs, and drill teams, and having special nights for them, all enhance the overall basketball program. Build your exposure in the community by speaking at various service clubs, holding membership in civic organizations, organizing support clubs such as "booster" clubs, and sponsoring events for fans such as "meet-the-player" nights. These all contribute to team success.

9. Peer pressure is a very important coaching tool. Players tend to put far more pressure on themselves than the coach does. Penalizing the entire team for a mistake or violation by an individual can have definite impact. When players know that their mistakes can cause the entire team to be penalized, peer pressure often motivates them to concentrate on avoiding similar mistakes in the future. As an example, I once had a player who had the bad habit of bouncing the basketball immediately after receiving a pass. This, of course, eliminated any driving threat he might have had. Consequently, I repeatedly corrected him, but to no avail. One of my assistant coaches suggested we run the entire team every time he made the mistake. We did this, and within a week we had broken the offending player of the habit. We accomplished something with peer pressure that we had failed for several months to do with coaching pressure.

10. You win with quality people. I would rather have a team with less-than-perfect talent but with real character than one with superior talent and no character.

Discussion Questions

1. Why is it important to write down your philosophy of coaching?
2. How often should your philosophy change?
3. Should your philosophy differ at various levels of play?
4. How much of your philosophy should be copied from another coach?
5. What do you believe is the general basketball philosophy of Bobby Knight? Dean Smith? Hubie Brown?

Projects

1. Write a paper detailing your basketball coaching philosophy. This paper will not be due until the last day of class after you have benefitted from the discussions and readings of the term.
2. Interview a local coach and write two collegiate coaches to ask them about their philosophies.
3. Develop a questionnaire that can be mailed to leading coaches to determine their philosophies.

Suggested Readings

Hankinson, Mel, *Progressions for Teaching Basketball,* pp. xiii–xix. 3d rev. ed. Tupelo, Miss.: Sparks Printing, 1980.

Kennedy, Barry. "Developing the High School Feeder System." *Scholastic Coach,* January 1980, pp. 82ff.

Simpson, Alice. "The Only Road to 'Greatness' in Basketball Coaching." *Scholastic Coach,* May–June 1978, pp.83ff.

Stewart, Norm, and Scholz, George. *Basketball: Building the Complete Program,* pp. 2–23. Marceline, Mo.: Walsworth Publishing Company, 1980.

Tarkanian, Jerry, and Warren, William E. *Winning Basketball Systems,* pp. 22–32. Boston: Allyn & Bacon, Inc., 1981.

Wooden, John R. *Practical Modern Basketball,* pp. 1–12. 2d rev. ed. New York: John Wiley & Sons, 1980.

chapter two

Shooting

Shooting is the most important fundamental in the game of basketball. A team may possess fine passers, superb dribblers, excellent rebounders, and other strong assets, but without good shooters, they may still find it difficult to win consistently. Many coaches feel that shooters are "born" and not "made," and the brilliant touch of the nation's great shooters today lends support to this argument. Surely some players naturally possess the "touch" that other players strive a lifetime to achieve. However, the vast majority of good shooters are *made* shooters; they have combined sound shooting fundamentals taught by good coaching with countless hours of practice to develop themselves into good percentage shooters.

Most coaches agree that it is extremely important to learn correct shooting fundamentals at an early age. After players have learned poor shooting habits through many hours of practice, it is very difficult to correct the poor techniques. Junior and senior high school coaches must be particularly observant in looking for shooting flaws. They must suggest changes in technique quickly and supervise the individual's shooting practice carefully so the player can develop proper shooting form.

Secret to Good Shooting

Is there a secret to good shooting? If such a secret exists, it is numerous hours of correct practice. The coach must guide the player into proper shooting form and must supervise shooting drills in practice so that the proper form becomes habitual. However, it is up to the player to spend a great amount of time shooting the basketball before and after practice hours and in the

Figure 2.1 Proper method for holding the basketball.

off season. Why do all coaches love to see goals nailed to the sides of garages in students' backyards? Because these goals afford those hours and hours of shooting practice that have probably made more shooters than ever have been made in gymnasiums.

Holding the Basketball

Before the ball can be shot properly, a player must know how to hold it. Holding it improperly will result in not only poor shooting mechanics but faulty execution of other ball-handling fundamentals.

The most important thing the player must be taught in holding the basketball is that the palms of the hands should never touch the ball. The ball must be held with the fingers spread comfortably but as widely as possible (fig. 2.1). Whether the player is shooting or passing, the ball is always held in this manner.

Basic Types of Shots

There are four major types of shots used in present-day basketball:

1. Lay-up shot
2. Jump shot
3. Hook shot
4. Free-throw shot

The Lay-up Shot

The lay-up shot is used close to the basket and is usually taken on the move, either as the player is driving toward the basket off a dribble or after receiving a pass after cutting to the basket. Since it is taken from close range, you should expect a high degree of accuracy. Consistently missing the lay-up usually means improper fundamental technique or lack of concentration.

In shooting the lay-up, the right-handed shooter receives the pass or picks up the dribble as the *right* foot touches the floor. The player then steps

Figure 2.3 Another view of the lay-up shot.

forward onto the *left* foot, using this foot to break the drive and to push upward toward the goal. The ball should be brought upward with both hands, on the side of the body away from any defensive player who may be challenging the shot. The ball is brought to a position with the arms extended in front and above the shooter's head. The left hand is under the ball for control and is released as the right hand pushes the ball *softly* toward the backboard. The ball should be aimed at a spot on the backboard approximately 12 inches above and slightly to one side of the goal. When shooting on the left side of the basket, the left hand should be used most often, with the shooter jumping off the right foot instead of the left.

Players must be able to make the lay-up shot while driving or cutting to the basket from different angles. Therefore, drills should allow practice of the lay-up from both the right and left sides of the basket, along either baseline, and down the middle of the court (diag. 2.1).

Common Errors in Shooting the Lay-up

1. *Broad jumping the lay-up.* This common error is caused by failure to spring upward as the shot is taken, a move needed to break the forward momentum caused by the drive or cut to the basket. Failure to jump upward decreases the accuracy of the shot because, first, the player is not as close to the basket as possible, and second, the forward momentum of the player's body causes the ball to be released with more force against the backboard.

2. *Jumping off the wrong foot.* If the player is shooting with the right hand, it is important to jump or "take off" from the left foot. The opposite is true when shooting with the left hand.

3. *Laying the ball too hard against the board.* The softer the player can lay the ball against the backboard, the better the chance of making the shot.

4. *Putting spin or "English" on the ball.* Any spin on the ball should be from the natural release of the ball, not from any conscious effort to cause spin.

5. *Shooting the ball too low on the board.* This is one of the more common errors even accomplished players make. They will shoot the ball at a spot no higher than 6 to 8 inches above the goal instead of the more desirable 12 to 15 inches above.

Figure 2.4 The lay-up shot after driving under the basket. The coach must make certain players practice lay-ups from all angles.

6. *Holding the ball too loosely on the takeoff.* Many players hold the ball so loosely on the takeoff they miss the chance to shoot should any contact from the defense occur. If the ball is held firmly, the shot can still be made even with contact from an opponent. This results in what is commonly called the three-point play—making the basket *and* the free throw awarded for the foul.

Figure 2.5 *The power lay-up shot.* The shooter springs into the air off both legs. Notice the intense eye concentration on the target.

7. *Failure to concentrate.* The lay-up is so basic that players have a tendency to take the shot for granted and risk losing their concentration. Concentration is essential in avoiding some of the common errors mentioned above. The alert coach demands concentration on the lay-up and is quick to penalize players for careless lay-up shooting.

The Jump Shot

Although the jump shot did not become popular until the early 1950s, it is now considered the most effective shot in basketball. Present-day jump shooters are very proficient from as far as 25 feet from the basket. Also, since the shot is taken when the shooter is in the air, it is very difficult to defense. The jump shot has resulted in a greater improvement in scoring than can be credited any other basketball innovation.

Basic Mechanics of the Jump Shot

Prior to the jump, the ball is held in both hands with the shoulders square to the goal and the knees slightly bent. The right-handed shooter has the right foot slightly forward of the left foot and both feet pointing toward the basket. The jump is made with an upward thrust by both legs. Height of the jump varies with the individual, but, as a general rule, the player does not leap as high as possible but rather takes a smooth, effortless jump into the air for the shot. As the jump is made, the ball is brought to a position slightly above and in front of the head. The left hand is under the ball for control, and the back of the right hand faces the shooter. The right elbow is under the ball on a line between the player and the basket. Sight at the goal is just under the ball. The shot is released by an upward movement of the right elbow and a simultaneous forward push of the forearm and wrist. The wrist should snap completely forward to provide a good follow-through. It is very important that the player take the shot at the height of the jump rather than as his or her body is moving upward or downward. Figures 2.6, 2.7, and 2.8 illustrate the basic shooting mechanics of the shot.

Balance is very important to the success of the shot. The shooter cannot fall forward, sideways, or backward when taking the jump shot; this decreases accuracy and often leads to offensive fouls. The shot should be initiated from a balanced position and the jump should be straight upward.

Practice drills must give the shooter jump-shooting practice in three specific situations: from a stationary position, after a dribble, and after cutting to receive a pass. Balance and the upward jump are more difficult in the latter two situations but can be achieved by sufficient practice.

Common Errors in Shooting the Jump Shot

1. *Shooting while off balance.*

2. *Improper elbow position.* Many poor jump shooters hold the elbow too far away from the body. Many shooters also hold the elbow too high, which forces the ball behind the head and results in a line-drive type of shot rather than a nice, arching shot.

3. *Poor target area.* It is important that the shooter concentrate on the specific area of the basket toward which to shoot. Some players aim at the front of the rim, others at the back, while others seem to sight the middle. Any can be correct as long as the player knows the shooting target exactly and consistently aims at it.

4. *Faulty foot position.* The jump shot shot actually begins with the feet. Setting the feet apart too widely or pointing the toes sideways results in poor body balance and low accuracy.

Figure 2.6 The *jump shot* just prior to releasing the ball. Notice that the elbow points to the basket.

5. *Forcing the shot.* Since the jump shot is taken from the height of the jump, many players feel they can shoot it even though they are closely guarded. This forcing of the shot results in a decreased accuracy that can be very bad for team morale.

The Hook Shot

The hook shot is used most often by post players near the basket, for it normally begins with the player's back to the basket. For a right-hand shot, the player steps onto the left foot and extends the right arm fully away from

Figure 2.7 Another view of the jump shot just prior to releasing the ball.

Figure 2.8 The jump shot after releasing the ball. Notice the follow-through of the wrist on the right hand.

Figure 2.9 *The hook shot.* This shot is extremely difficult to defend but is not easy to learn for the average player.

the body with the right hand under the ball for control (fig. 2.9). The left hand is kept on the ball as long as possible. The player steps and turns toward the basket and brings the right arm straight upward in a swinging motion to the basket. The player releases the ball at the height of the extended arm. As the wrist snaps in a complete follow-through the ball takes on backspin. Most hook shooters shoot against the backboard and let the ball carom into the goal. The target on the backboard is approximately the same area as for the lay-up shot, some 12 to 15 inches above the goal.

Figure 2.10 *The free-throw shot.* Most players use the same type of shot they use from the field.

The hook shot is difficult to master for the average player. However, since the shot is taken with the shooting arm fully extended, it is so difficult to guard that players who develop this shot—particularly the taller players who play near the basket—increase their scoring ability considerably. The range of the hook shot is limited, and the shot should not be attempted when the player is more than 10 feet from the basket.

The Free-throw Shot

The vast majority of shooters use a one-hand push shot when shooting a free throw. This is because they use a one-hand jump shot from the field and the mechanics of the jump shot and push shot are very similar.

To shoot a one-hand free throw, the right-handed player stands with the right foot approximately one inch behind the free-throw line and the left foot approximately 12 inches back. The feet are shoulder width apart and the knees are slightly bent. Although most of the weight will be forward, balance must be maintained throughout the shot. The ball is held by both hands, just in front of the face. As in the jump shot, the player's left hand is under the ball in order to control it, and the back of the right hand faces the body. The right elbow is close to the body. The shot is initiated by a simultaneous straightening of the knees and raising of the right elbow. As the elbow is raised, a forward push of the forearm and snap of the wrist pushes the ball toward the basket. The ball leaves from the index and forefinger of the right hand. A complete follow-through leaves the arm fully extended and the wrist broken completely over so that the palm faces downward.

Proper shooting mechanics are a necessity for good free-throw shooting; however, three additional factors determine just how successful a player will become at the free-throw line:

1. *Relaxation.* Tense players cannot shoot well. Therefore they must develop the ability to relax at the free-throw line. Most players develop a routine to help them relax prior to shooting, such as taking three or four deep breaths or bouncing the ball several times before shooting.

2. *Concentration.* Players must develop the ability to concentrate solely on the free-throw shot. They cannot be thinking of the distracting actions of opponents, the noise of the spectators, or the photographer who may be taking a picture.

3. *Practice.* All players can learn to shoot free throws well if they are willing to practice enough. Practice should be under competitive situations whenever possible. Free-throw shooting contests, penalties for misses, and team free-throw ladders are an important part of a coach's practice plans.

Free-throw Shooting Drills

A number of good free-throw shooting drills are available to help teach free-throw shooting. The more competitive the drill, the better it is for developing concentration and the ability to shoot under game pressure. The following are some general teaching methods for free-throw shooting:

1. *Free-throw ladder.* Post all players' names on the bulletin board in order of free-throw competence. Any player may challenge other players one or two rungs up the ladder. The object is to be at the top spot at the end of the season. An award should be presented the winner.

2. *Weekly record.* Players shoot a designated number of free throws daily and make a record of made and missed. Weekly totals indicate who needs extra work.

3. *Consecutive free throws.* Players compete to see who can make the most consecutive free throws. Also, a coach can establish a definite number to be made consecutively before a player can leave practice.

4. *Windsprint misses.* Players shoot a designated number of free throws and run a windsprint or conditioning drill for each miss.

5. *Ten-point game.* Two teams compete against each other. Each player shoots one shot and rotates. Starting score is ten. A miss adds a point to the total and a made free throw subtracts a point. Object is to get to zero first.

Shooting Drills

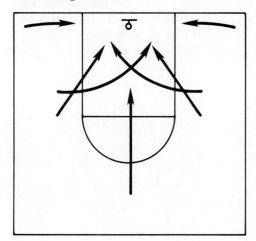

Diagram 2.1 *Angles from which players should practice the lay-up shot.*

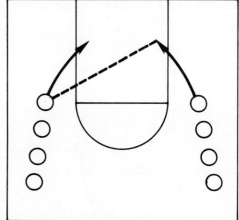

Diagram 2.2 *Simple two-line lay-up drill.* Ball begins in the left line. Pass is made to front player in right line who shoots driving lay-up. Front player in left line rebounds and passes to next player in right line. Players should cut hard and shoot from the left side after sufficient practice from the right. Two balls can be used, and shots can be taken from the angles shown in diagram 2.1.

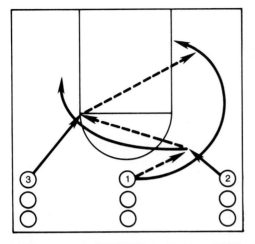

Diagram 2.3 *Figure 8 lay-up drill.* ① passes to ② and cuts outside. ② passes to ③ who passes to ① for the lay-up. ② cuts around ③ for the rebound.

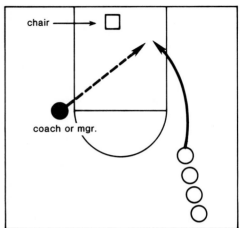

Diagram 2.4 *High-jump drill.* Designed to teach players to plant the take-off foot and jump upward for the lay-up shot. If players "broad jump" the lay-up shot, they make contact with the chair.

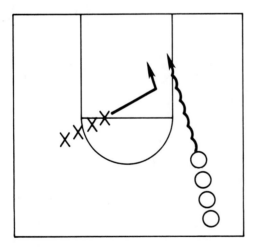

Diagram 2.5 This is a drill designed to put defensive pressure on the lay-up shooter. The defensive player is allowed to make contact with the shooter. This helps the shooter concentrate, grip the ball firmly when taking the ball into shooting position, and learn to make the three-point play.

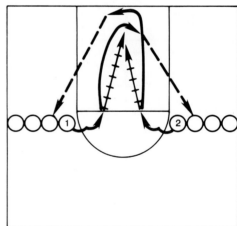

Diagram 2.6 ① and ② drive hard to free-throw line and shoot the jump shot. Each retrieves own shot, passes to the next player in the opposite line, and goes to the end of that line. Players can also drive toward the baseline for the shot.

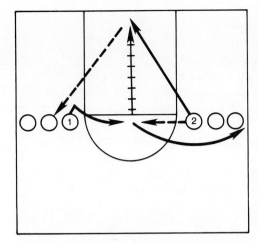

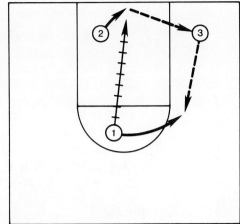

Diagram 2.7 ①cuts hard to free-throw line and takes pass from ②. ①shoots the jump shot and goes to end of the passing line. ② retrieves the ball and passes to next player in shooting line. Two balls can be used in the passing line to get more shooting.

Diagram 2.8 *Rapid-fire shooting drill.* ①is the shooter, ②the retriever, and ③the passer. Two balls are used. ①shoots the jump shot and cuts to take pass from ③as ②retrieves shot. ①shoots again and cuts again for another pass from ③who has received pass from ②. After ①has shot for 30 seconds, players rotate.

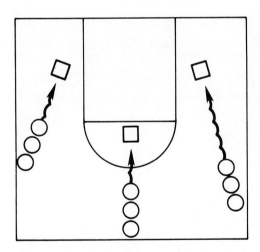

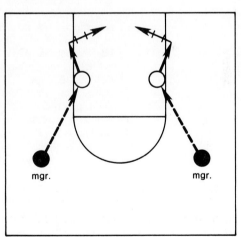

Diagram 2.9 Chairs are placed in front of each line. Players drive forward, stop at the chair, and shoot the jump shot. They retrieve the shot, pass ball back to next player, and rotate lines. This drill is very good for teaching players to go straight up for the shot rather than falling forward.

Diagram 2.10 *Hook shot drill.* A player is stationed on each side of the lane with a manager passing to each. After receiving the pass the player shoots a hook shot, retrieves the ball, and passes back to the manager. After several shots, players exchange sides.

Discussion Questions

1. If a shooter is making a high percentage of shots but has bad form, should that form be corrected?
2. How can a coach help a player gain confidence in shooting?
3. Discuss methods for developing shooting concentration.
4. Should all players shoot approximately the same number of shots in a game?
5. What is the best way to teach players the difference between a good and a bad shot?
6. Should there be a period of free shooting before practice or should this period be controlled by the coach?

Projects

1. Obtain a game film and write a criticism of shot techniques displayed in the film.
2. Using students in the class, teach a shooting drill.
3. Diagram and explain five shooting drills.

Suggested Readings

Baumgartner, Dick. *Techniques for Great Outside Shooting.* Dick Baumgartner, 549 Meadowbrook Lane, Richmond, Indiana, 47374.

Baumgartner, Dick. "Thrust, Release, and Follow Through in the Jump Shot." *Scholastic Coach,* October 1975, pp. 24ff.

Baumgartner, Dick. "Wrist Cock in Jump Shooting." *Scholastic Coach,* November 1977, pp. 28–29.

Ebert, Frances H., and Cheatum, Billye Ann. *Basketball,* pp. 82–96. 2d rev. ed. Philadelphia: W. B. Saunders, 1977.

Foster, Bill. "Free Throw Shooting the Duke Way." *Scholastic Coach,* October 1978, pp. 20–21.

Frederick, Lee. "High Percentage Stab Shot." *Scholastic Coach,* October 1976, p. 31.

Hankinson, *Progressions,* pp. 143–50.

Ostby, Marnold. "Start Your Shooters One-Handed." *Scholastic Coach,* December 1978, pp. 17ff.

Snyder, Jack. "Drill with a Purpose." *Scholastic Coach,* November 1978, pp. 10–12.

Stewart and Scholz, *Complete Program,* pp. 33–44.

Tarkanian and Warren, *Winning Basketball,* pp. 412–28.

West, Jerry. *Basketball My Way.* pp. 56–101. Englewood Cliffs, N.J.: Prentice-Hall, 1973.

Wooden, *Modern Basketball,* pp. 94–115.

chapter three

Passing

Although shooting may be the most important offensive fundamental in basketball, passing ranks very close in importance. In fact, many coaches contend that passing is more important than shooting. Suffice it to say that few teams not accomplished in both can be big winners—as many games probably are lost by sloppy passing as are lost by poor shooting.

Good passing teams are hard to defeat. The ability to move the ball quickly from one player to another with a minimum of bad passes sets up better shots and results in higher shooting percentages. However, like shooting, good passing does not come by accident. It requires the understanding of correct passing and receiving fundamentals, a clear knowledge of where and when to pass, concentration by both the passer and receiver, and a great deal of proper practice. It takes good coaching to give a team these important passing characteristics.

Holding the Ball for Passing

As in shooting, holding the ball is fundamental to correct passing. The ball is held with both hands on the sides of the ball with the fingers spread. *The ball should not touch the palms of the hands.* It should be held close to the chest in initiating most passes, and the grip should be firm enough so it cannot be easily knocked out of the hands by an opponent.

Receiving the Ball

Passing skills and receiving skills must be closely synchronized, for one is dependent on the other. A passer is only as good as his or her receiver, because all passes—regardless of how beautiful they may be—must be caught by a teammate to be successful.

A player must be able to receive the various types of passes from both a standing position and a moving position. Both hands are cupped to receive the ball with the heels of the hands about 5 inches apart, the fingers spread, and the arms extended. The ball does not touch the palms but is caught in the fingers. As the ball strikes the hands, the player "gives" with the pass—in other words, the elbows are flexed so that the hands move in toward the body as the ball is received. This is very important, because stiff arms and hands result in fumbled passes.

The most common error receivers make in catching a pass is to take their eyes off the ball too quickly. The fine hand-eye coordination needed for good receiving must be practiced and must receive coaching emphasis. I use the phrase "look the ball into your hands," when coaching my players, and I constantly emphasize this when working on passing drills.

Other causes of receiving fumbles are lack of concentration, lack of alertness, misjudgment of passes, stiff hands, poor body balance, poor physical condition, and lack of wrist and hand strength.

Types of Passes

The following are the types of passes most often used:

1. Two-handed chest pass
2. Two-handed bounce pass
3. One-handed push pass
4. Two-handed overhead pass
5. Baseball pass
6. Hook pass
7. Flip pass

Two-Handed Chest Pass

The ball is held close to the chest with the elbows close to the body. The pass is made with a forward thrust of both arms and a snap of the wrists. The passer should always follow through. A step forward onto one foot is helpful, especially to the beginning passer. Aimed at the chest of the receiver, the ball is passed with as little spin as possible. The pass is quick and snappy to prevent interceptions. The force of the pass depends on the distance between receiver and passer. A soft pass is necessary in close range to prevent fumbles.

Two-Handed Bounce Pass

The ball is held and the pass made in the same manner as the chest pass. The difference is that the ball strikes the floor a few feet away from the receiver and bounces up toward his waist for easy handling. The ball must not hit the floor too far away from the receiver. This error will result in the ball "floating" after the bounce and can be easily intercepted. (See fig. 3.2.)

Figure 3.1 Player in position to make the *two-handed chest pass*.

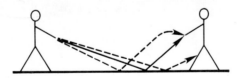

Figure 3.2 Dotted lines indicate incorrect path of *bounce pass*. Unbroken line indicates correct path.

One-Handed Push Pass

Both hands take the ball to the side of the body where the pass is made with a forward push by the passing hand. Complete arm extension and wrist follow-through of the passing hand is as important as in the other passes. This pass is more difficult than other passes and is recommended for accomplished players only.

Figure 3.3 Number 14 has just executed the *one-handed push pass*.

Two-Handed Overhead Pass

This pass is excellent for feeding the pivot player or for passing over the head of a defensive player. The ball is held with the hands on the side of the ball with the arms extended over the head. Thumbs point inward. The pass is made with a forward motion of the forearms and a snap of the wrists.

Figure 3.4 *The two-handed overhead pass.*

Baseball Pass

The baseball pass is good for making a long pass downcourt or for getting the pass out to begin the fast break. The technique is the same as the baseball throw. The right-handed passer brings the ball back behind the right ear. The right hand is behind the ball with fingers spread, and the weight is shifted to the right foot. As the pass is made with a forward motion of the arm and wrist, the weight shifts to the left foot. Any spin or "English" should not be imparted to the ball except the natural backspin caused by a good follow-through. However, few players can avoid a spin unless they are properly coached. As the right-handed passer makes the baseball pass, it is natural for the right hand to turn right on the follow-through, which causes the basketball to spin. To avoid this, the passer must consciously turn the right hand slightly to the left on the follow-through.

Hook Pass

The hook pass is similar to the hook shot. Used to pass over a defensive player, it is particularly good for making the outlet pass on the fast break. The right-handed passer steps onto the left foot and springs into the air. The right arm is extended to the side of the body with the left hand used to control the ball. As the pass is made over the head with a sweeping or "hooking" motion of the right arm, the left hand is released and brought high for protection.

Flip Pass

This pass is absolutely necessary for use in close quarters. The pivot player often uses the flip pass to feed cutters, and the dribbling screener uses it to pass to players cutting by the screen. The ball is held on the side of the body away from the defensive player. When passing right-handed, the passer holds the right hand under the ball. A slight flip of the wrist causes the ball to move softly into the air a few inches away from the passing hand. The receiver can easily handle a pass made like this.

Passing Suggestions

1. Don't telegraph the pass. Look one way and pass another.
2. Fake the chest pass and throw the bounce pass. Fake the bounce and throw the chest.
3. Follow through.
4. Keep the palms off the ball.
5. Throw the soft pass in close quarters.

Figure 3.5 Number 30 is beginning the *flip pass* to number 15. The ball will be flipped softly into the air for ease of receiving.

6. Pass to the receiver on the side away from the defensive player.
7. Pass to the receiver's chest area. Passes are more easily handled here, and the receiver is positioned to make another pass without adjusting the ball.
8. Avoid the long cross-court pass.
9. Concentration is essential.
10. The closer the defensive player, the easier it is to pass by him or her.

Teaching Suggestions

1. Use passing drills daily.
2. Constantly emphasize correct passing fundamentals.
3. Encourage players to make the simple, fundamental pass rather than the difficult pass.
4. Keep turnover charts both during practice and games so players can be aware of their passing mistakes.
5. Praise the good pass.
6. Penalize the careless pass.
7. Encourage deception in passing. Players should fake in one direction and pass another, never looking directly at the receiver. Work to develop peripheral or "split vision" in players. The two-ball passing drill described in diagram 3.2 is excellent for developing this ability.
8. Use weight exercises or heavy medicine balls to develop strength in the hands and arms. Strength adds to both passing and receiving ability.

Passing Drills

Diagram 3.1 *Four-corner passing drill.* ② takes dribble, passes to ③ and cuts for return pass from ③. ③ cuts downcourt and takes another lead pass from ②. ② goes to end of line vacated by ③. ③ dribbles down, passes to ④, and the procedure is repeated. As players learn this drill, balls can be added until four balls are in play.

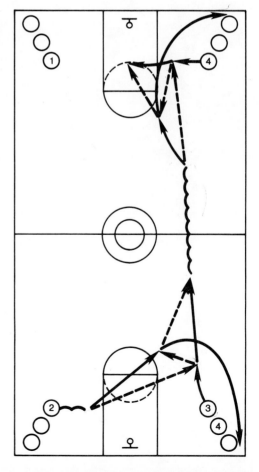

38

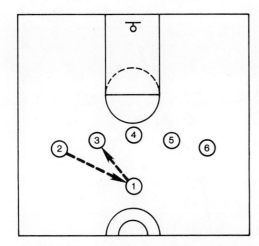

Diagram 3.2 *Two-ball passing drill.* Two balls are used. ① passes to ③ as ② passes to ①. ① will pass to ④ as ③ return passes to ①, and so on. Players rotate positions often. This drill is excellent for developing "split vision."

Diagram 3.3 *Post passing drill.* Two balls are used. ② passes to ① who passes to ④ as ③ passes to ①. Each ball is kept moving in its respective triangle. ① should use pivot footwork to slide back and forth to meet the passes coming from the guards. This is a very good drill for developing pass-off technique in the post player.

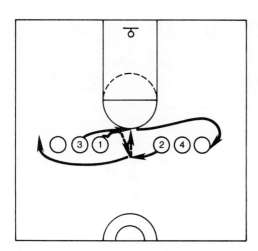

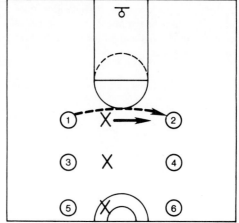

Diagram 3.4 *Flip pass drill.* ① dribbles out, passes to ②, and goes to end of line. ② flip passes to ③ and goes to end of line, and so on. All players keep moving. Use both the right- and left-hand flip pass.

Diagram 3.5 *Two-by-one passing drill.* Players are divided into groups of threes. One player is the defensive player. The offensive players must pass directly by the defensive player. Lob passes are not allowed. Players alternate defensive and offensive positions.

Diagram 3.6 *Baseball pass drill.* The coach or manager shoots the ball against the board. ①rebounds, takes quick dribble to side, and throws baseball pass to ④cutting downcourt.

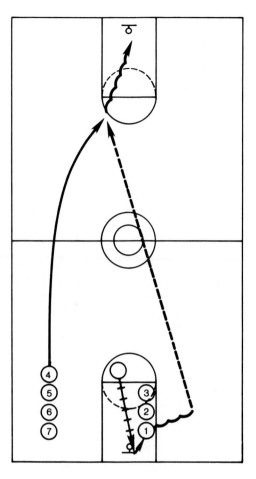

Diagram 3.7 *Bull in the Woods.* Players form a circle with one player designated as the defensive player. Offensive players attempt to pass to teammates without allowing the defensive player to touch the ball. Offensive players may not pass to the player directly to the left or right. The offensive player who allows the defensive player to touch the ball must become the defensive player.

Diagram 3.8 *Hook-pass drill.* Three lines are formed, two offensive and one defensive. A coach or manager shoots the ball against the backboard. ①takes the rebound and hook passes out to the guard at the outlet pass position. X_1 attempts to deflect the hook pass. This drill is excellent both for developing the hook pass and for teaching the fast-break outlet pass.

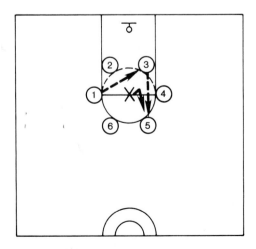

Diagram 3.7

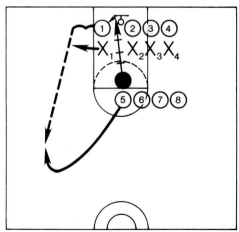

Diagram 3.8

Discussion Questions

1. Should a bad pass be severely criticized?
2. Are passing skills more important than shooting skills?
3. Discuss methods for developing concentration in passing.
4. Should players who pass well with one hand be corrected?
5. Where can bounce passes be used most effectively?
6. How important is strength in passing?

Projects

1. Diagram and explain five passing drills.
2. Using other students in the class, teach a passing drill.
3. Chart the number of bad passes in a game or scrimmage. Determine the value of each bad pass.

Suggested Readings

Byers, John R. III. "Try the One-Hand Chest Pass." *Scholastic Coach,* October 1978, p. 30.
Ebert and Cheatum, *Basketball,* pp. 58–69.
Hankinson, *Progressions,* pp. 138–41.
Stewart and Scholz, *Complete Program,* pp. 26–31.
Tarkanian and Warren, *Winning Basketball,* pp. 390–405.
West, *Basketball My Way,* pp. 34–54.
Wooden, *Modern Basketball,* pp. 85–93.

chapter four

Dribbling

Dribbling is an essential offensive skill. It has a variety of uses in making both individual and team play more effective. Good dribbling is necessary to initiate play patterns, attack pressing defenses, make successful fast breaks, penetrate zones, and execute various individual and team offensive maneuvers. Once considered only for guards or smaller team members, now players at all positions use the dribble successfully. Good dribblers are made, not born, for any player can master the dribble technique if he or she is willing to put in enough hours of practice.

Because the dribble has been misused often, many coaches take a negative approach to teaching it. However, the dribble's misuse is no more detrimental to a team than bad shots, careless passes, or sloppy defense. The coach is responsible for teaching the why and when of dribbling as well as correct dribbling technique. The goal is developing the dribbling skill of each player to its maximum, so this teaching should be done in a positive manner.

Basic Dribbling Technique

The dribble technique is relatively simple and can be mastered easily with proper practice. In fact, a player who is not a good dribbler simply has not been putting the necessary time into proper practice.

The dribble is executed by pushing the ball to the floor with a snap of the wrist and downward motion of the forearm. Fingers are spread comfortably in order to achieve maximum control. Body position varies with the type of dribble and the offensive situation. It is important that a player learn to dribble

(a) without looking at the ball and (b) with either hand. Dribbling without looking at the ball enables a player to see teammates who might break into the clear and openings for drives to the basket. The ability to dribble with either hand allows the player to drive in any direction, therefore making the task of the defensive player more difficult.

Foot Movement at Beginning and End of a Dribble

Observant coaching is necessary for players to learn the proper footwork for starting or stopping a dribble. To begin a dribble, the ball must leave the dribbler's hand before the pivot foot leaves the floor. Moving the pivot foot too quickly results in a traveling violation.

Terminating the dribble properly can be more difficult than starting it. After catching the ball at the end of a dribble, a player has only one step to make a legal stop. Because of body momentum, many young players take one step too many. Careful coaching will teach the player to keep the body under control and to bend the knees in order to stop properly.

Types of Dribbles

The good dribbler is able to control the ball while dribbling at full speed and to see the entire floor and make quick passes to players who may become open. The good dribbler is also able to dribble with either hand, switch hands, change direction, and use various types of dribble techniques.

The following are the most important dribble techniques to be learned:

1. *The control dribble.* This technique is used when a dribbler is closely guarded and the ball must be protected. In this situation, the knees are bent so the body is low and the ball is dribbled lower and closer to the body. The ball is dribbled on the side of the body away from the defensive player (fig. 4.1).

2. *The speed dribble.* This technique is used when the ball must be advanced quickly downcourt and no defensive players are harassing the dribbler. The body is more upright and the ball is pushed out in front. The ball is dribbled waist high since no defensive player is near—more speed can be attained by this higher dribble (fig. 4.2).

Figure 4.1 *The control dribble.* The ball is dribbled low, with the knees flexed and the head up.

Figure 4.2 *The speed dribble.* The ball can be dribbled higher, since this dribble is used when no defender is near.

3. *The switch dribble.* This technique involves simply changing the dribbling hand in order to change direction or afford better ball protection. The switch is made in front of the body and must be made as low as possible to prevent the defensive player from deflecting the dribble. Assuming the dribble is being made with the right hand, the ball is pushed sideways in front of the body so it bounces into position on the left side of the body where the dribble can be continued with the left hand. This skill is essential for a quick change of direction, but since it is done in front of the body, considerable practice is required to be able to protect the ball from the defensive player and to be able to execute the switch without looking at the ball.

Figure 4.3

Figure 4.4

Figure 4.5

4. *The reverse or spin dribble.* Throughout the reverse or spin dribble the body is kept between the ball and the defensive player; therefore more protection is given the ball than is possible with the switch dribble. The reverse dribble requires the body to turn 180 degrees in order to change direction. It is used usually when a defensive player is guarding the dribbler tightly and overplaying in the direction the player is dribbling.

If the player is dribbling to the right, the weight must be placed on the left foot and the right foot swung in almost an 180 degree rear turn (fig. 4.6). *The ball is pulled with the right hand.* After the complete turn of the body, the player is advancing toward the left and the dribble continues with the left hand. The whirl or spin move is made very quickly, and the player who develops proficiency in this move has a potent weapon to attack an opponent who is guarding closely and overplaying in the direction the dribbler is driving.

Figure 4.3 Beginning of the *switch dribble.*

Figure 4.4 The ball has been pushed from the right hand to the left.

Figure 4.5 Completion of the *switch dribble.*

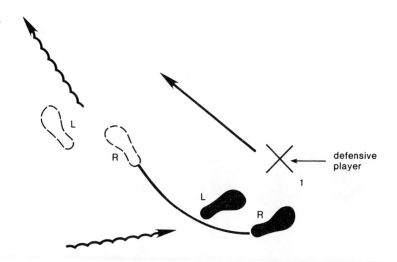

Figure 4.6 Footwork for the *reverse, or spin, dribble.*

5. *The change-of-pace dribble.* This technique is simply varying the dribbler's speed. By varying speed, the dribbler keeps the defensive player guessing and prevents moves to steal the ball. The change-of-pace is a very good scoring weapon. As the dribble is made toward the basket at full or near full speed, the dribbler slows down and comes to almost a complete stop. When the defensive player stops also, the dribbler then moves at full speed toward the basket. This stop-and-go dribble maneuver often results in a drive by the defensive player for an easy shot.

When to Dribble

Most players learn the fundamental techniques of dribbling easily, and, as in all basketball skills, some develop a greater degree of proficiency than others. However, many players fail to learn the most important part of the dribbling fundamental—when to dribble. The exceptional dribbler is a crowd pleaser but can also be a detriment to the team and adversely affect team morale if he or she misuses the dribble.

The dribble may be used in the following situations:

1. To advance the ball downcourt into offensive position.
2. To advance the ball against a full-court pressing defense.
3. To drive for the basket.
4. To move away from the congested area under the defensive basket after taking a defensive rebound.
5. To advance the ball in the middle lane of the frontcourt phase of the fast break.
6. To freeze the ball.
7. To set up offensive plays.

Figure 4.7 It is extremely important for the dribbler to be able to dribble with either hand without looking at the ball.

There may be a few other situations in which the dribble can be used satisfactorily. Though no ironclad rule can be made indicating when to dribble, a general rule is to *avoid dribbling when it is more advantageous to pass*. The ball can be moved much more quickly by passing than by dribbling and quick movement of the ball makes a team very difficult to defend.

Dribbling Hints

1. If a pass is more advantageous to the team, do not dribble.
2. Avoid looking at the ball when dribbling. (The drills shown in diagrams 4.2 and 4.3 are excellent for developing this ability.)
3. Learn to dribble equally well with either hand.
4. Avoid taking a dribble immediately upon receiving a pass. Save the dribble as a threat to the opponent.
5. Do not "bat" the ball. Push it to the floor.
6. Never attempt to dribble between two defensive players.
7. Avoid dribbling into the corners at either midcourt or on the baseline.
8. The dribble should be made with a purpose.
9. Over-dribbling hurts team morale.
10. It is as important to know *when* to dribble as *how* to dribble.

Drills for Teaching Dribbling

Diagram 4.1 *Dribble relay.* Chairs are placed at intervals along the court. Players are divided into two teams. Each member of each team must dribble in and out the chairs, change hands, make a lay-up, and return. Team finishing first wins.

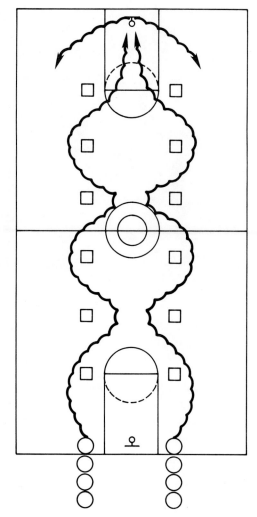

Diagram 4.2 *Dribble tag.* Each player has a ball with one player designated as "it." Players cannot go out of the boundary of the half-court. "It" must attempt to dribble and "tag" another player. Any player tagged or one who loses control of the dribble and goes out-of-bounds becomes "it." Players dribble for a prescribed time with the right hand and then the left.

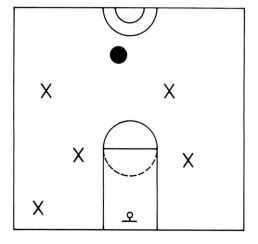

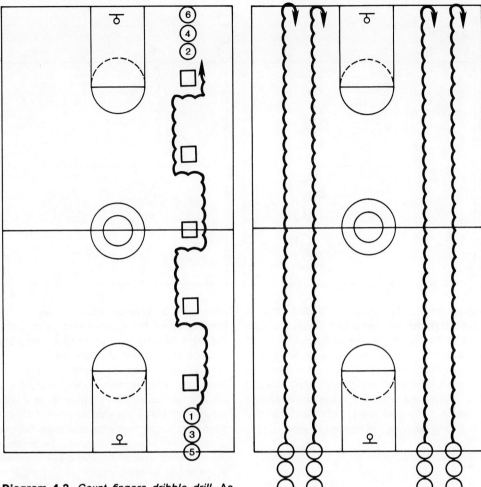

Diagram 4.3 *Count fingers dribble drill.* As ①dribbles in and out of chairs, ②varies the number of fingers held up. ①calls out the number of fingers showing. ②changes the number of fingers as ①passes each chair. When ①gets to ②, ②dribbles in the opposite direction with ③holding up fingers. This is an excellent dribble drill for teaching players to look downcourt.

Diagram 4.4 *Dribbling wind-sprints.* Players dribble to opposite baseline and back as fast as possible. They dribble down with the right hand and back with the left. Emphasis must be placed on looking downcourt instead of at the ball.

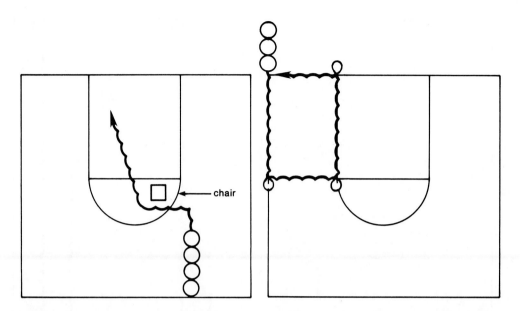

Diagram 4.5 *Switch-dribble drill.* A chair is placed at the free-throw line. Using the right hand, the player dribbles to the chair, switch dribbles to the left hand, and drives in for a lay-up shot. After each player has had several opportunities from the right side, the chair and line are moved to the left so the switch dribble can be made from left to right hand and the lay-up taken from the opposite angle.

Diagram 4.6 *Reverse-dribble "square" drill.* Players start in the corner of the court. Using the right hand only, they dribble along the sideline to a point even with the free-throw line, reverse dribble, and dribble to the free-throw line. Players then reverse dribble and drive to the baseline where they reverse dribble and dribble to the starting point. Only the right hand should touch the ball when the drill is run in the illustrated direction. To practice the left hand reverse dribble, players dribble in the opposite direction.

Discussion Questions

1. Should all players practice dribbling skills regardless of position?
2. What coaching methods should be used to discourage over-dribbling?
3. When a player over-dribbles, what are other players normally doing?
4. What coaching methods can be used to teach players to dribble without looking at the basketball?

Projects

1. Diagram and explain three dribbling drills.
2. Using other students in the class, teach a dribbling drill.
3. Make a set of "dribble blinders" by using old glass frames and cardboard.

Suggested Readings

Ebert and Cheatum, *Basketball*, pp. 74–78.
Hankinson, *Progressions*, pp. 141–43.
Stewart and Scholz, *Complete Program*, pp. 32–33.
Tarkanian and Warren, *Winning Basketball*, pp. 405–12.
West, Jerry, *Basketball My Way*, pp. 19–33.
Wooden, *Modern Basketball*, pp. 130–35.

chapter five

Individual Offense

Basketball has a number of great offensive patterns. However, the success of the best offensive patterns depends a great deal on the individual offensive abilities of each player. The offensive pattern may set up numerous opportunities for shots and drive situations, but unless players develop the basic offensive fundamentals required for these situations, the offensive pattern is useless.

Body Position and Balance

Individual offense begins with good body position and balance. The offensive player's best body position is weight evenly distributed on both feet toward the balls of the feet, with a slight forward body lean. The head is up and directly over the feet, the knees flexed so that the player is in a semi-crouch, and the feet comfortably spread. This position gives the individual perfect balance and allows quick cuts to meet passes or to cut for the basket. Good body balance is absolutely essential for successful execution of the fundamentals.

Body Control

Body control is important both offensively and defensively. Offensively, the player must have total body control in order to be able to make quick starts or stops, elude a defensive player, make quick cuts to the basket, move around an opponent, get to an offensive rebound, prevent charging into a defensive player, and execute various offensive maneuvers.

For total body control, a player must always maintain correct body position and balance. *The most common reason for lack of balance and body control is failure to flex the knees properly.* When a player stands too erect, it is virtually impossible to start or stop quickly, and body balance and control are easily lost.

Offensive Movement Without the Ball

Many players do a very fine job offensively when they have possession of the basketball but cannot perform well without the ball. The ability to move without the basketball is an important basketball fundamental that requires considerable coaching. Perhaps one of the reasons players find it more difficult to learn to move without the basketball is the abundance of zone defenses played, particularly in high school basketball. Offenses against zone defenses use less player movement than do offenses designed for attacking man-for-man defense. Many young players, therefore, do not get the proper grounding in movement-without-the-ball fundamentals.

There are several key movements a player should be able to use when he does not have the ball:

1. Change of direction
2. Change of pace
3. Cutting
4. The reverse
5. The screen-away
6. The rear screen
7. Spot-up

Change of Direction

A player running to the right who wants to change direction to the left plants the right foot, shifts the majority of weight onto it, then pushes off it to the left. The step with the left foot should be long, with the toe of the left foot pointed clearly toward the left. Again, the knee is flexed to enable total body control.

Change of Pace

The change of pace is simply a change of speed designed to elude the defensive opponent. The player is running at normal speed, then slows down for two or three steps, then cuts forward at maximum running speed. Despite the emphasis on modern-day defense, a quick cut to the basket is still a very good maneuver and often frees a player for a lay-up shot. Many basketball

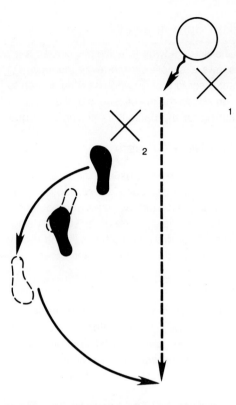

Figure 5.1 *The reverse.* This move helps shake an aggressive defensive player. Shaded area indicates position of the feet after cutting to meet the pass, while dotted line area indicates position of the feet after the pivot has been made.

offenses have plays designed for a quick cut directly to the basket or a play off a screen set by a teammate. A cut is usually preceeded by a fake in an opposite direction, and the cut is usually made at full speed. However, the body still must be under control should a defensive player jump in front of the cut.

The Reverse

The reverse move is very good for shaking an aggressive defensive player. It combines a step toward the ball as if the player is to receive a pass, then a pivot to the outside and a quick cut to the basket. As figure 5.1 shows, the tightly guarded player pivots to the outside of the rear foot and then makes a quick cut to the basket. With practice, the move can be quick, resulting in many scoring opportunities. Coordination between the passer and the player executing the reverse is essential. The reverse move is preceded by a fake cut to meet the pass. The passer fakes the pass to the receiver to draw the defensive player tighter and then makes the good pass to the reversing player.

The Screen-away

The screen-away is a simple screen set away from the ball. Diagram 5.1 shows a simple screen-away maneuver. ① has passed the ball to ② and set a screen for ③ who uses the screen to cut for the basket. The screener can add to the effectiveness of the move by faking the screen-away and then cutting for the basket, as shown in diagram 5.2.

The Rear Screen

The rear screen is usually made by a player without the basketball moving up from the baseline. The screen is set to the rear of the defensive player, and, unless the defense uses good defensive talking techniques, the defensive player may be unaware of the screen being set. The screen is doubly effective since it can free the cutter or, if the defensive player guarding the screener sloughs off, it can open up the screener, as shown by diagram 5.3.

Spot-up

The spot-up move is a simple move to a spot opened by a defensive player leaving to help a teammate. The player "spotting up" moves to a spot (a) in shooting range and (b) far enough from the defensive opponent to make it difficult for the opponent to recover. The spot-up player should give a target and face the basket in position to shoot.

Individual Offense with the Basketball

Pivoting

Pivoting technique is necessary for the player with the ball to be able to position the body to protect the ball. Once the pivot foot has been established, basketball rules allow a player to pivot on the foot at complete 180-degree turns to protect the ball from an aggressive defensive player. The pivot is always made on the ball of the foot. A walking or traveling violation results if the pivot foot is moved, unless moved into the air for a pass or a shot attempt.

In executing the *simple pivot,* the dribbler advances to the defensive player and comes to a stop with one foot in front of the other (fig. 5.3). As the stop is made, the rear of the body is brought low to maintain balance. The rear foot here is the pivot foot. If the player has the right foot to the rear, the pivot can be made by picking up the left foot and moving left or right. However, the player gains maximum protection for the ball by moving the left foot to the right. There are a few situations when the ball may be caught when both feet hit the floor simultaneously. In these cases, either foot may become the pivot foot.

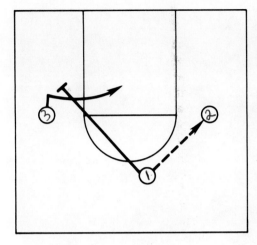

Diagram 5.1 *A screen-away.*

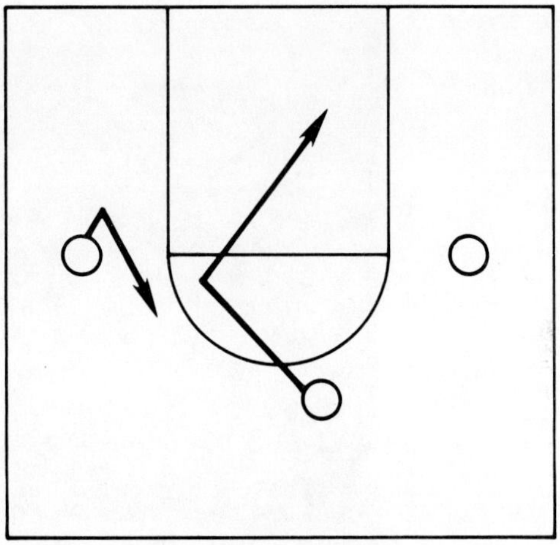

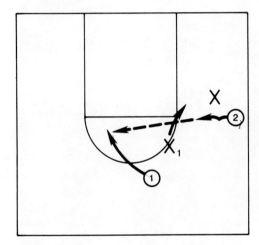

Diagram 5.2 *Fake screen-away.*

Diagram 5.3 *Spot-up technique.* As X₁ helps
on ②, ① spots up in shooting range far
enough away from the ball to make it very
difficult for X₁ to recover.

Figure 5.2 *The rear screen.* Number 40 has set a rear screen for number 24 who drives for basket.

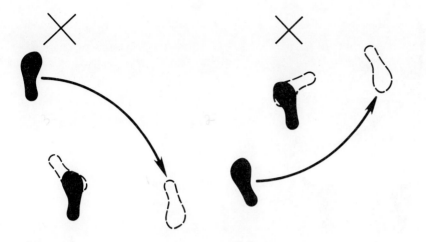

Figure 5.3   **Figure 5.4**

Figure 5.3 *The simple pivot.* Dark area indicates position of feet as the stop is made. Dotted lines indicate position of feet after the pivot. The pivot should be made on the balls of the feet.

Figure 5.4 *The reverse, or trailer, pivot.* The dribbler picks up the dribble after the front foot strikes the floor and establishes this foot as the pivot foot. This pivot is more difficult to master than the simple pivot and is used most often by more highly skilled players.

The *reverse,* or *trailer pivot,* may be used by the dribbler to pass off to a cutting teammate. As shown by figure 5.4, the dribbler has the right foot on the floor, advanced slightly to the front, when catching the ball. Instead of bringing the left foot forward, the player swings the foot to the rear and pivots so his or her back is to the player. The player is now in a low crouch and may pass off easily to a cutting teammate. This pivot is more difficult to master than the simple pivot and is used most often by more highly skilled players.

One-on-One Offensive Moves

The success of most offensive moves is dependent on scoring from the many one-on-one situations that arise during the game. Many teams build their entire patterns around these situations. When receiving the ball in a one-on-one situation away from the basket, an offensive player should pivot to face the defensive opponent and make one of several one-on-one moves. These moves include:

1. Fake right, shoot
2. Fake left, shoot
3. Fake right, fake shot, drive right
4. Fake right, fake shot, drive left
5. Fake left, fake shot, drive left
6. Fake left, fake shot, drive right
7. Fake right, drive left
8. Fake left, drive right
9. Fake right, fake left, drive
10. Fake left, fake right, drive left

Figure 5.5 *The cross-over step.* With the left foot as the pivot foot, the offensive player fakes a drive to the right by either stepping to the right or faking the head and shoulders to the right. He or she quickly pivots on the left foot and simultaneously brings the right foot across so that the initial step on the drive left will be with the right foot.

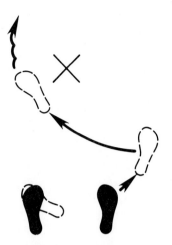

In order to be a good one-on-one player, a player must master the *cross-over step.* If a player desires to fake right and shoot, or fake right, fake the shot, and drive right, he or she will not need the cross-over step. However, if the player should fake right and drive left, he or she will need the cross-over step, shown in figure 5.5. With the pivot foot to the left, the offensive player fakes a drive to the right by either stepping to the right or faking the head and shoulders to the right. He or she pivots on the left foot and simultaneously crosses the right foot over so the initial step on the drive left is with the right foot. *This first step should be a long one—as is the initial step in any drive situation.*

Improper use of the cross-over step in the driving situation is a common error for many basketball players and should be carefully watched by the coach. Many players fake right with the right foot and then make their initial move to the left with the left foot. This results in a traveling violation. A coach must be careful to discover this in practice situations in order to correct it prior to game time. As coaches, it is easy to get involved in offensive patterns or direct our attention to the location of our offensive players and not see if they are making the correct cuts or how the defense is playing. And it's easy this way to overlook the basic fundamentals such as the correct cross-over step. Remember, the best play known in basketball is worthless if a traveling violation goes with it.

Each day's practice should be organized to include time for practicing various one-on-one situations. Hours of practice are necessary before the individual moves can be perfected. Players must learn when to fake with the

Figure 5.6 The player with the ball is getting ready to use a one-on-one offensive move against the defensive player.

feet, head, or eyes. The cross-over step and other techniques of one-on-one play must be mastered; therefore, the coach must direct individual attention to each player if effective one-on-one moves are to be learned.

Head Fake

The opportunity for a very important one-on-one maneuver occurs when the player receives the ball near the basket. Most defensive players jump into the air with a shooter near the basket in an effort to block the shot. A simple fake of the head and ball towards the basket many times results in the defensive player jumping too soon. Then the offensive player can power the ball to the basket, score an easy lay-up, and often get fouled in the attempt.

Head faking does not come automatically. It must be practiced and practiced regularly. I try to have some form of head faking drill in my practice plan every day. At one time in my coaching career I practiced this skill only once weekly. Rarely did my players head fake in a game. Since I began almost daily head-faking drills, we now score quite a number of points each game by use of this technique, and it has been a very important part of many of our players' one-on-one moves near the basket.

Figure 5.7 Good players learn to play one-on-one with their back to the basket as well as when facing the basket. Here, number 5 has received the ball with his back to the basket and is getting ready for his scoring move.

Discussion Questions

1. How is individual offensive ability important to the success of play patterns?
2. Discuss methods for developing individual offensive skills.
3. Why does one player have better body control than another?
4. Should starting and stopping receive practice attention?

Projects

1. Diagram and explain three drills for developing individual offensive ability.
2. Study a game film to determine the type of individual offensive moves used.
3. Using other students in the class, teach an individual offensive drill.

Suggested Readings

Baumgarten, Carole. "Offensive Moves." *Athletic Journal,* October 1979, p. 56.

Ebert and Cheatum. *Basketball,* pp. 39–46.

Edwards, Mark. "Situation Moves from the Low Post." *Scholastic Coach,* November 1979, pp. 21ff.

Gomulinski, Paul J. "Agility Drills for the Green Big Man." *Scholastic Coach,* December 1977, pp. 80ff.

Hankinson. *Progressions,* pp. 132–35, 153–63.

Holzman, Red, and Lewin, Leonard. *Holzman's Basketball,* pp. 58–69. New York: Macmillan, 1973.

Landa, Howie. "Individual Offensive Moves for Women Basketball Players," *Pro-Keds Coaches' Digest,* 1980, pp. 12–15.

Tarkanian and Warren. *Winning Basketball,* pp. 344–59.

Winter, Tex. "Developing the Big Man." *Pro-Keds Coaches Digest,* 1980, pp. 12–15.

Wooden, *Modern Basketball,* pp. 79–82.

———. "Inside Moves for the Big Guard or Forward." *Scholastic Coach,* December 1977, pp. 26–29.

———. "Big Man Drills in the University of Tennessee Program." *Scholastic Coach,* November 1977, pp. 26–27.

chapter six

Individual Defense

The foundation of sound team defense lies in the defensive ability of each player. Players who have not developed the ability to play defense are incomplete basketball players. Many potential stars have spent most of their careers on the sidelines because of lack of defensive skill. Players love to play offense—no coach is needed to instill this love. But this is not the case for defensive play. The successful coach must work hard on individual defense to help the players develop a genuine desire to learn proper techniques. The time spent will be well rewarded.

Qualities Necessary for Individual Defensive Play

Sound individual defense is dependent on the following factors:

1. Desire
2. Stance
3. Position
4. Footwork
5. Vision
6. Talk

Desire

The basketball player must *want* to play defense. He or she must be willing to spend hours and hours of hard work on individual defensive fundamentals. The player must develop aggressiveness and hustle, creating a personal desire to defeat the assigned opponent. This frame of mind can never be overemphasized. The player who enters the game thinking primarily of reading

Figure 6.1 *Individual defensive stance.*

his or her name in the morning paper after scoring twenty points rarely does a good defensive job. With constant stress on the importance of defensive play, sufficient practice time devoted to techniques, and equal praise for players who do outstanding defensive jobs as well as those who score, the coach can develop individual desire and pride in defensive play.

Stance

The player with the correct defensive stance has the body crouched, knees bent, and weight evenly distributed on both feet. The rear of the body is low. The head is erect, and the back is almost straight. One foot is advanced, with the toes of both feet at a 45-degree angle to the opponent (fig. 6.1).

Position

As a general rule, the defensive player should maintain a position between the opponent and the basket. Exceptions to this rule depend on the location of the ball and of the opponent.

Guarding Opponent with Ball

When guarding an opponent with the ball, the defensive player should maintain a position between the opponent and the basket, usually on an imaginary straight line from the opponent to the basket (diag. 6.1). However, it may sometimes be necessary for the defensive player to play slightly to one side of the imaginary line to protect the side to which the opponent prefers to drive (diag. 6.2). Also, some coaches prefer their team defense to force opponents to the middle of the floor, while other coaches force opponents to the baseline. If the offensive player is within shooting distance, the defensive player maintains a position with the advanced foot approximately three feet from the offensive player. The eyes should be focused on the belt of the opponent, because the mid-region is the only body part that cannot be used in faking.

Figure 6.2 *Defensive stance* in game action. Player should be approximately an arm's length from offensive player and should watch the opponent's midsection.

Figure 6.3 *Defensing the jump shooter.* Defender should reach one hand into the air as high as possible but should control the body to avoid jumping into the shooter.

Figure 6.4 *Defending the dribbler.* Emphasis should be on moving the feet and avoiding reaching in with the hands.

Guarding Opponent Without Ball

As long as the opponent is outside the dangerous area near the basket, the defensive player again maintains a position between the opponent and the basket. The distance of the defensive player from his or her particular opponent depends on the location of the ball, the offensive ability of the opponent, and the type of team defense being played. A player guarding an opponent near the ball should play very close, as shown in diagram 6.3, while a player guarding an offensive player a considerable distance from the ball should sag away from the opponent in order to congest the lane area and be able to help teammates defensively (diag. 6.4). Again, the opponent is playing in the dangerous area near the basket, and the defensive player must play between that player and the ball (diag. 6.5).

Footwork

Three major steps must be mastered:

1. The approach step
2. The slide step
3. The retreat step

The approach step is used when moving into proper defensive position as the opponent receives the ball.

The slide step is used when guarding an opponent moving laterally, vertically, or obliquely across the court.

The retreat step is used to defense an opponent on a drive attempt for the basket.

The Approach Step

As the opponent receives the ball in scoring range, the defensive player must advance quickly into defensive position. The body must be low and the weight distributed on both feet. The advance is made by a quick and almost simultaneous slide of both feet forward. The rear foot never advances in front of the right (fig. 6.5). The number of approach steps needed depends on the distance of the defensive player from the opponent.

The Slide Step

As the opponent moves across the court, the defensive player brings both feet on a line parallel to the opponent. Neither foot is in advance of the other. The body is again crouched with the weight equally distributed on both feet.

If the defensive player moves to the right, the first movement is a move of the left foot to a position close to the right. As the left foot touches the floor, the right foot is moved about a foot and a half to the right. The movement of the right foot follows the movement of the left foot so quickly that it is almost simultaneous. Successive movements of the left and right feet follow,

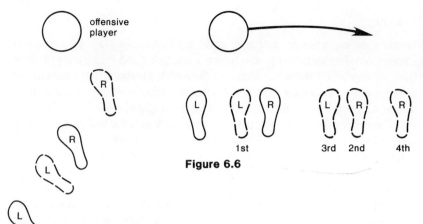

offensive player

Figure 6.6

1st   3rd 2nd   4th

Figure 6.5 *The approach step.* Dotted lines indicate position of feet after sliding both feet forward. The rear foot never advances in front of the forward foot.

Figure 6.6 *The slide step.*

Figure 6.5

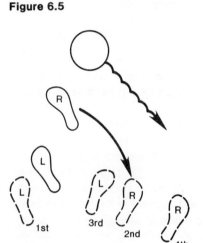

R

L

L
1st

L
3rd

L
R
2nd

R
4th

Figure 6.7

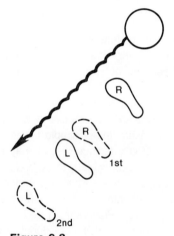

R

R

L
1st

L

L
2nd

Figure 6.8

Figure 6.7 The *retreat step* on a drive to the defensive player's right when the right foot is forward. After the step back with the left foot and the swing of the right foot, the *right oblique slide step* is used. This footwork maneuver is often called the *drop step.*

Figure 6.8 If the defensive player's right foot is forward, the *retreat step* for a drive to the left is the *left oblique slide step.*

allowing the defensive player to remain in position with the movement of the offensive player (fig. 6.6). Of course, if the movement of the defensive player is to the left, the initial step will be made with the right foot.

The Retreat Step

If the opponent makes a drive or cut for the basket, the retreat step must be used. If the defensive player has the right foot advanced and the offensive drive is to the defensive player's left, the oblique slide step is all that is necessary. However, if the drive is to the defensive player's right, the defensive player must swing the right foot back so that the body turns approximately 90 degrees (fig. 6.7). This move is often referred to as a defensive *drop* step. After the body shift has been made, the *oblique slide step* will be used (fig. 6.8).

Vision

Vision is as important to defensive play as to offensive play. Proper vision allows the defensive player to see both the opponent and the ball at the same time, as well as offensive screens and defensive situations that may call for help. Peripheral vision is important. Players with good eyesight should be able to see action within an almost 180-degree area (diag. 6.6).

The defensive player guarding an opponent with the ball should focus on the offensive player's belt or mid-section, because, as stated earlier, this is the only part of the body the offensive player cannot use in faking. With peripheral vision the defensive player should be able to see action both to the left and right.

The defensive player guarding an opponent without the ball should focus on a spot approximately midway between the opponent and the ball (diag. 6.7). This way, peripheral vision allows sight of both opponent and the ball, an important requirement for man-for-man defensive play.

Talk

A good defensive team is a *talking* defensive team. The various defensive maneuvers that must be used to properly defend the numerous offensive screens, cuts, and plays demand communication among the defensive players.

Simple verbal calls that can be made and understood quickly are a must. Terms such as *switch, help, screen left, screen right, ball, board,* and *slide* are examples of simple terms that players can understand easily.

Plain as these terms may be, it is not easy to get players to call them out and particularly to do so loud enough for a teammate to hear over crowd noise. Defensive talk is a fundamental skill as important as the other defensive fundamentals, and properly supervised practice is the only way it can be achieved. Players must be required to yell these terms in practice if they are expected to yell them during a game.

Defensive Hints

1. Defense begins with a *desire* to play defense.
2. Proper stance requires the knees to be bent, the rear low, and the back straight. The head remains erect.
3. The eyes should be kept on both the ball and the opponent.
4. As a general rule, the defensive player should remain between the opponent and the basket.
5. The feet should be slightly more than shoulder width apart, with the weight spread evenly on the soles of the feet. The heels should be on the floor, but the weight should be forward.
6. When guarding an opponent with the ball, watch his or her belt or mid-section—it cannot be used to fake.
7. Avoid crossing the legs. Slide step quickly.
8. When guarding a shooter, do not jump into the air until the *shooter* has jumped.
9. Never turn the head to look for the ball, because this gives the opponent a chance to cut to the basket for an open shot.
10. Prevent offensive players from receiving the ball near the basket.
11. Block the opponent off the board when a shot goes up.
12. *Talk* on defense.
13. Change quickly from offense to defense. *Sprint* downcourt into defensive position.
14. Study the opponent. Learn his or her strengths and weaknesses and play accordingly.
15. Defensive *pride* builds great teams.

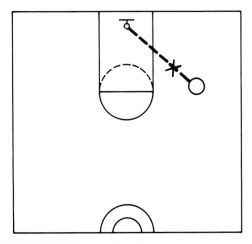

Diagram 6.1 *Correct defensive positioning on an imaginary line between the opponent and the basket.*

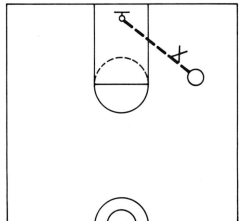

Diagram 6.2 *Shifting the defensive position slightly off the imaginary line to better protect the baseline or a preferred driving side.*

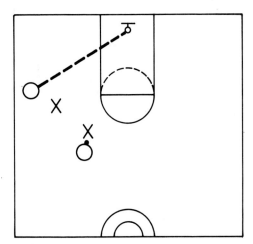

Diagram 6.3 *Defensive position when guarding an opponent near the ball in an aggressive or overplay man-for-man defense.*

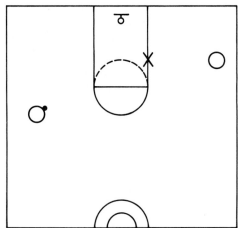

Diagram 6.4 *Defensive position when guarding a player on the side of the court away from the ball.*

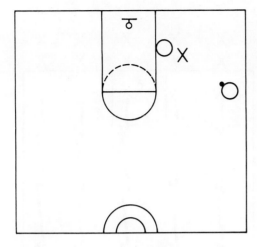

Diagram 6.5 *Defensive position when guarding an opponent near the basket.*

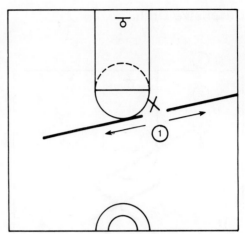

Diagram 6.6 By use of peripheral vision, the defensive player is able to see action within nearly 180 degrees.

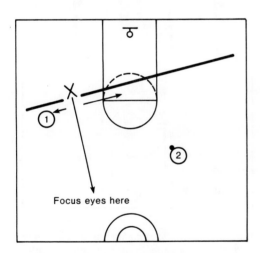

Focus eyes here

Diagram 6.7 When guarding an opponent without the ball, the defensive player should focus on a point between the ball and the opponent. This enables the defensive player to see both opponent and ball at the same time.

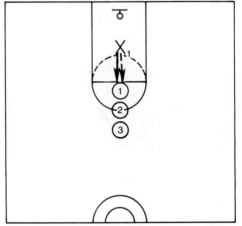

Diagram 6.8 *One-on-one defensive drill.* X_1 passes to ① and uses approach step to get into proper defensive position quickly. ① makes move to score as X_1 defends. After ① either scores or X_1 gets the ball, X_1 goes to the end of the line and ① assumes defensive position.

Defensive Drills

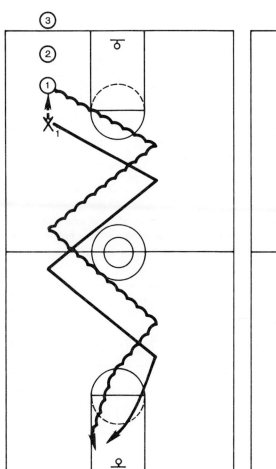

Diagram 6.9 *One-on-one full-court defensive drill.* X_1 passes ball to ① and assumes defensive position. ① dribbles downcourt, with X_1 turning ① as often as possible. After ① scores or X_1 gets ball possession, ① assumes defensive position on ② as X_1 goes to the end of the line.

Diagram 6.10 *"Man-maker" mass defensive drill.* A coach stands downcourt with a whistle. The first row of defensive players assumes defensive stance. When whistle blows, players advance using proper defensive footwork. Players retreat when whistle blows again. Each succeeding time the whistle blows, players change direction. After reaching the coach, players return to the end of the lines. This is a good conditioning drill as well as a defensive footwork drill.

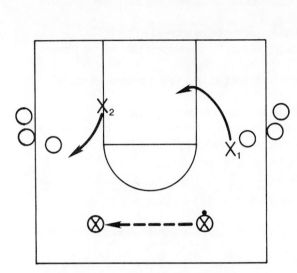

Diagram 6.11 *Two-on-two deny drill.* X_1 and X_2 work to deny their opponent the ball when the ball is near. They drop to a defensive help position when the ball is on the side of the court away from them.

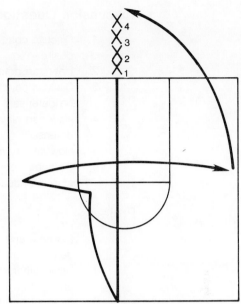

Diagram 6.12 *Defensive footwork and communication drill.* Defensive players slide to midcourt, back to the free-throw line, to the sideline, and back to starting point. All proceed together, and defensive talk must be used to avoid colliding at free-throw line.

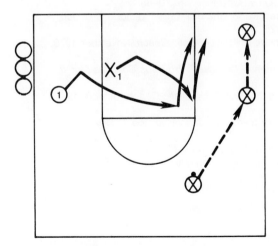

Diagram 6.13 *Defense-the-flash drill.* As ball is moved by coaches or managers, ① attempts to flash into pivot area, and X_1 attempts to prevent ① from receiving pass.

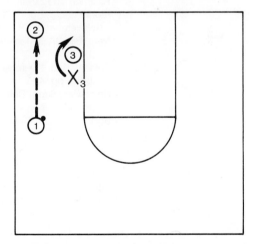

Diagram 6.14 *Post-defensive drill.* As ① and ② pass the ball back and forth, X_3 works on proper footwork for defensing ③.

Individual Defense   79

Discussion Questions

1. Discuss coaching methods for developing individual defensive desire.
2. How can defensive quickness be increased?
3. Discuss coaching methods for developing talk among players on defense.
4. How can players be taught to stay in the proper stance on defense?
5. How important are the hands in defensive play?
6. Do zone defensive players need competence in basic man-for-man individual defensive skills? Why?

Projects

1. Diagram and explain three drills for developing individual defensive ability.
2. Using other students in the class, teach an individual defensive drill.
3. Pick out one individual in a game film and write a critique of his or her defensive footwork.

Suggested Readings

Capano, Vincent L. "Do-it-all Defensive Drill." *Scholastic Coach,* January 1979, p. 88.

Ebert and Cheatum, *Basketball,* pp. 148–57.

Hankinson, *Progressions,* pp. 15, 64–65.

Holzman and Lewin, *Holzman's Basketball,* pp. 70–88.

Kloppenburg, Bob. "Progressive 'on the ball' Drills." *Scholastic Coach,* November 1978, pp. 22ff.

Neal, Bill. "A 7-Man Defensive Drill." *Scholastic Coach,* November 1979, p. 78.

Presley, Bud. "Defense! Defense! Defense!" *Pro-Keds Coaches Digest,* 1980, pp. 4–5.

Rojcewicz, Sue. "Defensing the Post." *Scholastic Coach,* October 1977, pp. 56ff.

Schuyler, Paul. "Defensive Corner Drill." *Scholastic Coach,* November 1977, pp. 73–75.

Stewart and Scholz, *Complete Program,* pp. 131–59.

Stockard, Bessie A. "Alert, Aggressive Individual Defense." *Scholastic Coach,* October 1976, pp. 79–81.

Tarkanian and Warren, *Winning Basketball,* pp. 368–90.

Wooden, *Modern Basketball,* pp. 245–67.

chapter seven

Rebounding

The team that controls the boards wins the majority of their games. Control of the boards reduces the number of shots taken by the opponents and increases the number of shot attempts by the good rebounding team. Though a great deal of rebounding is dependent on the size of a team, size alone does not result in backboard control. Through diligent work in practice, techniques must be developed that lead to successful rebounding on both the offensive and defensive boards.

Defensive Rebounding

The defensive rebounder must maintain a position between the opponent and the basket. This position is commonly called "blocking out" or "screening off" the boards.

As a shot is taken, the defensive player steps forward and pivots so that his or her rear and back make immediate contact with the assigned opponent. Since the rebounder has only one or two seconds before having to find the ball, it is important to quickly establish a position to enable "feel" of the opponent with the body and to be able to use a slide step to keep the body between the opponent and the basket. The elbows in this position are wide and almost parallel with the shoulders, and the feet are slightly wider than shoulder width, presenting as big an obstacle as possible to the offensive player. The defensive player's body should be crouched with the knees bent, ready to spring upward for the ball. The head is erect and the eyes are focused on the ball.

Figure 7.1 Footwork for the *front pivot* used in the defensive block-out technique.

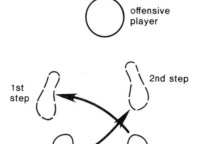

Figure 7.2 The beginning of the *front pivot* for defensive blocking out. Number 00 has moved his right foot into position near the offensive rebounder and has his right arm high to help "feel." The amount of body contact varies with the level of play and with the style of officiating, and a coach must adjust teaching methods accordingly.

Figure 7.3 Completion of the *front pivot* for defensive blocking out. Defender has pivoted on his right foot and has brought his left foot into parallel position.

As the rebound comes off the board, the defensive player leaps into the air with elbows wide and body in the slight jack-knife position commonly called the eagle spread. The jack-knife movement of the body throws the rear of the body backward and keeps the opponent off the defensive player's back. The defensive rebounder grabs the ball firmly with both hands and keeps it moving to prevent the opponent from gaining possession or a jump ball. Care must be taken not to move the elbows back and forth, since this is a violation and results in loss of the ball.

Figure 7.4 Rebounding in game action.

Offensive Rebounding

The offensive rebounder faces the defensive player's efforts to screen him or her off the boards. Realizing that the defensive player will turn into his or her path, the offensive player must attempt to get through to the basket by using quick fakes. The offensive player fakes left, goes right; fakes right, goes left; fakes right, left, goes right, and so on, in an effort to avoid defensive blockout. However, fakes must be done quickly, for only seconds exist between the shot attempt and the rebound. The offensive rebounder who hustles toward the boards using clever fakes is difficult to block out.

The offensive player must not allow the defensive player to "feel" him or her with the back or elbows, or the defensive player will be able to slide with any change of direction that is made. If the offensive player senses the slight contact with the opponent's back that allows the opponent to "feel" him or her, he or she steps backwards, then fakes and cuts around the blockout.

If the offensive player succeeds in getting by the blockout, he or she crouches with knees bent, enabling a quick spring into the air for the rebound. If the rebound is close to the goal, he or she may use a one-hand tip to attempt a quick score. The tip is executed with widely spread fingers and a forward movement of the wrists. The ball is controlled and guided toward the basket, not batted. If the rebound is not close enough to the basket for a tip, the ball should be caught with two hands. The rebounder returns to the floor and goes immediately back up for a shot attempt.

Some offensive players want to dribble the ball out from under the basket after grabbing the offensive rebound, but this should seldom be done. The ball is in the dangerous area near the basket, an objective of the team's offensive pattern. Why take it out from this area? The rebounder can thrust upward for the second shot and score. In addition, he or she is often fouled in the process and can turn the rebound into the devastating three-point play.

Mental Qualities of Offensive Rebounding

The most important qualities of offensive rebounding are mental. They include:

1. *Anticipation.* The good offensive rebounder learns to anticipate teammates' shots and moves into rebounding position before the defender attempts to block out.

2. *Hustle.* It takes tremendous effort to constantly go for the offensive board. A player may go to the board five consecutive times only to see the ball come through the net or rebound away. The sixth time, however, the ball may come directly to

him or her. It takes considerable determination for a player to continually go to the board, particularly as the game progresses and fatigue begins. However, players who hustle to the boards every time a shot is attempted are rewarded with a considerable number of offensive rebounds and the subsequent shot attempts.

Defensive Rebounding Suggestions

1. Each defensive player must screen the respective opponent off the board.
2. Use the front pivot to move the body into contact with the offensive player.
3. The body should be crouched with arms held wide to present an obstacle to the offensive player and to be ready to go up for the rebound.
4. Grab the ball firmly with both hands to prevent an opponent from slapping it out.
5. Use the eagle-spread body position to protect the ball as it is rebounded.
6. Keep the ball moving to prevent tie-ups.
7. Get the ball away from the basket as soon as possible. If a teammate is open for a pass-out, make the pass quickly.
8. Do not get pushed too far under the basket. Rebounds are no good coming out of the opponents' basket.

Offensive Rebounding Suggestions

1. Use fakes and quick changes of direction to get around a defensive blockout.
2. Be aggressive. The hustling offensive player is difficult to screen off the boards.
3. Anticipate a shot by a teammate.
4. Attempt to tip in if the rebound is near the basket.
5. Catch the ball with two hands if it rebounds away from the basket. If the rebound is taken in the area inside the free-throw line, go back up immediately for a second shot attempt.
6. Know offensive and defensive responsibilities. Don't crash the board if no one is back for defensive balance.
7. Don't foul the defensive rebounder as he or she comes down with the ball. His or her basket is 90 feet away—such a foul here is foolish.
8. If you are the nearest player, press the rebounder to prevent him or her from making an easy pass-out to a teammate for a fast break.

Rebounding Drills

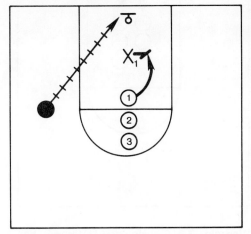

Diagram 7.1 *One-on-one block-out drill.* Coach or manager shoots the ball. X_1 attempts to block out ①. After rebound, X_1 goes to end of line, and ① becomes defensive player.

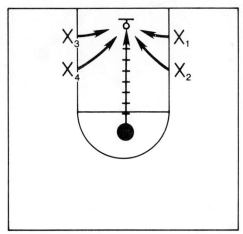

Diagram 7.2 *Three-on-three block-out drill.* Coach or manager shoots the ball and defensive players attempt to block out offensive players. After several shots, defensive players go to end of line. Drill is more effective if offensive players are required to move prior to the shot.

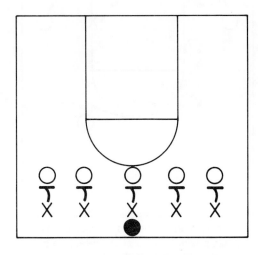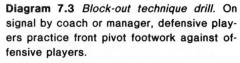

Diagram 7.3 *Block-out technique drill.* On signal by coach or manager, defensive players practice front pivot footwork against offensive players.

Diagram 7.4 *Rebounding drill designed to develop aggressiveness.* Coach shoots and all players go for rebound. Player who gets ball attempts to score. Rebounding continues until a score. Drill is more effective if a rim is placed on the basket.

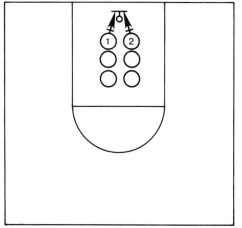 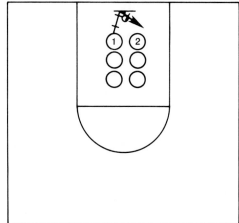

Diagram 7.5 *Tipping drill.* ①and ② each have a ball. They tip against the board 20 times, then give the ball to the next player in line and go to the end of the line.

Diagram 7.6 *Tipping drill.* ① throws ball over goal and against backboard. ② attempts tip-in. ② then throws ball over board, and ① attempts tip-in. After several tries ① and ② go to end of line.

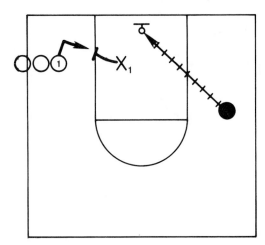 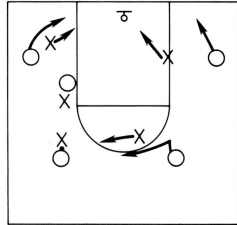

Diagram 7.7 *Offside or weakside rebounding drill.* Coach or manager shoots ball. X_1 attempts to block out offensive player coming from the weakside.

Diagram 7.8 *Five-on-five rebounding drill.* Offensive players move and defensive players maintain position until a shot. Defensive players then all attempt block out.

Discussion Questions

1. Is size the most important factor in rebounding?
2. What part does strength play in rebounding ability?
3. Some outstanding jumpers do not rebound well when they try to block out. Should such a player be required to block out the opponent or just be told to rebound the ball?
4. When should the shooter follow his or her own shot?
5. Fast breaks are difficult to get off a good offensive rebounding team. Should four players be sent to the boards when opposing a good fast-breaking team?

Projects

1. Diagram and explain three drills for developing rebounding ability.
2. Using other students in the class, teach a rebounding drill.
3. Pick out one player in a game film and write a critique of his or her defensive rebounding, and of his or her offensive rebounding.
4. Devise a method for measuring jumping ability.

Suggested Readings

Crawford, Charles L. "Five Keys to Defensive Rebounding." *Scholastic Coach,* October 1976, pp. 42ff.

Layton, Terry. "A New Angle on Rebounding." *Scholastic Coach,* October 1978, pp. 26ff.

Raveling, George. *A Rebounder's Workshop.* Pullman, Wash.: Cougar Book World, 1977.

Stewart and Scholz, *Complete Program,* pp. 278–313.

Wooden, *Modern Basketball,* pp. 227–28, 272–74.

chapter eight

Conditioning

Physical and mental condition is important in all sports. In basketball, conditioning should be considered the foundation for basketball coaching success. Basketball is both a fast-paced and a team-oriented game. Sprints up and down the court and constant player movement with few time outs and breaks in the action require players to be in top physical condition if they are to perform at their best. Also, the game's team requirements demand that players play together for a common goal, making proper mental condition or "team morale" an absolute essential.

Both physical and mental conditioning are the full responsibility of the coach. There is simply no excuse for losing a game because your team is in inferior condition. One team may have superior talent, but both teams possess the same opportunities for getting into shape. However, few players reach peak physical condition unless expertly guided. Plans for an upcoming basketball season must include proper drills and procedures for maximum squad conditioning.

Physical Condition

A carefully organized physical conditioning program is required to prepare players to exert maximum effort throughout a basketball game. This program should include an extensive amount of running to develop leg strength and cardiovascular endurance, a weight training program for overall body strength, and training regulations designed to guide players in proper living habits that affect performance. Such a properly organized conditioning program pays dividends in the form of increased team performance. Not only are players able to move at full speed throughout a game, their execution of individual and team fundamentals improves, and their susceptibility to injury decreases.

The physical conditioning program can be organized into four areas:

1. Pre-practice
2. Pre-season
3. In-season
4. Post-season or off-season

Pre-Practice

A program of conditioning prior to the opening of practice sessions is very beneficial and a part of most quality basketball programs in high school and college. Most activities used in pre-practice conditioning programs are conducted outside the gymnasium and ready the body gradually for the rigorous work inside. The feet are gradually toughened on a surface less hard than the gymnasium floor, thereby reducing the possibility of blisters. The outdoor surface aids in conditioning the legs for work on the hardwood, reducing the possibility of shin splints.

Activities most often used in pre-practice conditioning programs are:

1. Calisthenics and flexibility exercises
2. Cross-country running
3. Sprints
4. Strength training

The pre-practice conditioning program encompasses the time from the beginning of the school year in September until the opening of official practice, usually in mid-October. Most teams spend this period in some type of cross-country running and sprinting. There is no better way for a basketball player to develop the legs and lungs than to run—both long distance and sprints. Long distance running can help leg condition and lung capacity, while short distance sprints are great for the lungs and for increasing speed, both so vital in basketball.

I prefer a pre-practice conditioning program of flexibility exercises, outside running, and strength training on Monday, Wednesday, and Friday, with players having the opportunity to play basketball on Tuesday and Thursday. Outside running should be done after flexibility exercises and prior to strength training. A suggested running program is as follows:

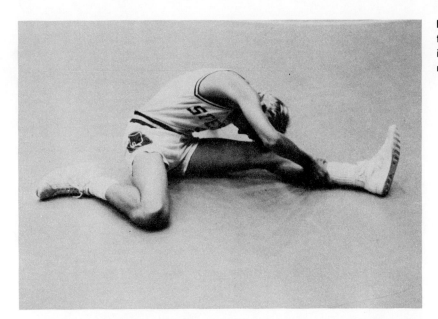

Figure 8.1 Stretching and flexibility exercises are important prior to any type of running or practice session.

Figure 8.2 Another example of a flexibility exercise.

First Week:

Monday:	Jog 1½ miles
Wednesday:	Jog 1½ miles
Friday:	Jog 1 mile, run 1 mile, walk ¼ mile

Second Week:

Monday:	Jog ¼ mile
	Sprint 50 yards, walk 50 yards, sprint 50 yards
	run 1 mile, walk ¼ mile
Wednesday:	Jog ¼ mile, sprint 50 yards 4 times
	Run 1 mile, walk ¼ mile
Friday:	Jog ¼ mile, sprint 100 yards twice
	run 1½ miles, walk ¼ mile

Third Week:

Monday:	Jog ¼ mile, sprint 50 yards 6 times
	run 1 mile, walk ¼ mile
Wednesday:	Jog ¼ mile, sprint 100 yards 3 times
	run 1½ miles, walk ¼ mile
Friday:	Jog ¼ mile, run 2 miles under 12 minutes

Fourth Week:

Monday:	Jog ¼ mile, sprint 50 yards 6 times
	run 1½ miles, walk ¼ mile
Wednesday:	Jog ¼ mile, sprint 220 yards twice
	run 1 mile in under 6 minutes
Friday:	Jog ¼ mile, sprint 100 yards twice
	run 2 miles in under 12 minutes

Fifth Week:

Monday:	Jog ¼ mile, sprint 100 yards 4 times,
	sprint 220 yards twice
Wednesday:	Jog ¼ mile, sprint 50 yards 4 times,
	run 1 mile in under 6 minutes
Friday:	Jog ¼ mile, run 2 miles in under 12 minutes

Pre-Season

Most teams practice six weeks before their opening game. During this practice period, physically challenging drills must be used to allow players to attain a prime conditioning level. Full-court running drills, pressing defensive drills, and drills incorporating quick starts, stops, and changes of direction are excellent conditioners. Whenever possible, conditioning drills should include work on individual and team fundamentals, since more team objectives are accomplished while conditioning is being achieved.

It is usually better to start out with relatively light practice during the first few sessions and progress toward harder practice sessions as the legs and feet become conditioned to the hardwood. Many coaches like to think of themselves as tough conditioners and try to "pour it on" the players during the first few days of practice. If the coach is making the mistake of inflating his or her own ego by trying to attain the "tough" label, he or she may be doing the players more harm than good. Too strenuous a workout before the body has become conditioned to it can lead to injuries, shin splints, and foot problems. It is far better to postpone the hard practices until players are physically ready to participate in them. This is not to say that practices should not be very challenging—to develop endurance, players must be pushed beyond normal effort. But the harder practices should come *after* the feet and legs have become accustomed to the hard basketball floor. Once this happens, players must be put through practice sessions that are harder than the workout of an actual game. I agree wholeheartedly with the statement many coaches have made: *you must train in pain or you train in vain.* Improvement comes when a player keeps working out after pain is felt in the legs and lungs.

In-Season

Since your players will be thoroughly conditioned before the opening game, it is seldom necessary to plan practice drills designed solely for physical conditioning after the season begins. Playing two or three games weekly usually maintains conditioning, and practice sessions then are devoted to improving fundamentals and team defensive and offensive play.

One of a coach's problems during inseason play is keeping the reserves in condition. Many games will go by in which the reserves play little, if any. A few minutes of play is insufficient for maintaining condition. Light practice the day before a game, no practice on a game day, and sitting on the bench throughout a game can only result in regression of conditioning unless the coach plans special measures to combat this. Probably the best answer is to work the reserves extremely hard on days immediately following games. The starters may be allowed to leave practice early, and the reserves who saw little action the preceding night may be put through full-court scrimmage.

Figure 8.3 Jumping rope is very good for conditioning the legs and for footwork.

Figure 8.4 A well-supervised program of strength training is very important to total conditioning.

Figure 8.5 Most coaches use windsprints at the conclusion of practice. Any time windsprints are used they should be timed. If they are not, some players tend to ease up.

Post-Season

For a team to be thoroughly conditioned, it should never get out of condition. Conditioning is a year-round thing. It is essential that coaches stress this to their teams and guide them into off-season conditioning programs that maintain the level of conditioning achieved during the season. If a player gets out of shape during the summer, he or she cannot expect to gain the type of physical condition in the winter that would be possible if he or she had stayed in condition the year around.

The objectives of a post-season conditioning program are as follows:

1. Increased strength
2. Improved jumping ability
3. Improved fundamental skills
4. Maintenance of cardiovascular endurance or stamina
5. Injury prevention

The off-season conditioning program encompasses the time from the end of the season in early March until the beginning of the school year in September. The program includes outside running to maintain endurance levels. It also includes an assigned strength training program, as well as fundamental work on the court. A properly motivated player can use this time to improve playing ability. Most young players are in a period of growth, and their improvement in fundamentals and strength coupled with this growth can make a marked difference from one season to the next.

The more supervision you can give to the off-season program, the better the program will be. In many high school situations, the coach has the opportunity to have spring practice and to work with the players in the summer months, and off-season conditioning and fundamental improvement are achieved easily. However, in the situations where rules forbid a coach to work with players in the off-season, other methods of obtaining off-season conditioning and fundamental work must be used. Some type of written program usually is best. A written program provides exact guidelines for *individual* players. What is needed for a short, fast guard is quite different than what is needed for the tall center. An off-season program for an individual might be as follows:

1. Run 2 miles in 12 minutes twice weekly
2. Run 4 220-yard sprints twice weekly
3. Lift weights 3 times weekly
4. Practice a 1-hour basketball fundamental workout 5 times weekly
5. Scrimmage either 5-on-5 or 3-on-3 twice weekly

Mental Condition

Much of the basketball team's success certainly depends on the overall mental condition of the team. An overwhelming desire to win, a willingness to sacrifice self for the good of the team, a sense of pride in conditioning, and a burning love for the game can inspire players to efforts far greater than their bodies would be able to produce otherwise. Though physical condition must go jointly with mental condition, the importance of the proper frame of mind to overall team conditioning cannot be minimized. The body can do more physically when the player *believes* it can and wants it to do more. Breaking the 4-minute mile barrier is a superb example of what can be done when athletes realize mentally that the body is capable of greater things. When Roger Bannister ran the first mile in under 4 minutes, he did something hundreds had attempted for years. Since that great feat, the mile has been run in under 4 minutes on numerous occasions. This is a great example of the importance confidence plays in the attainment of a physical goal. Players must believe in themselves and their teams if they are to reach their full potential.

Yet mental conditioning requires more than confidence. It requires an attitude from each player that contributes to the success of the team. Team play is never enhanced by petty jealousies and bickering among players. Nor does team or individual play improve when attitudes toward the coach are faulty. The team with high morale, genuine friendship between the players and the coach, and a confidence in their ability to succeed is destined for championship play.

Techniques that contribute to high team morale and mental condition include the following:

1. Positive coaching techniques
2. Well-organized practice sessions
3. Firm but equitable team discipline
4. Realistic but challenging team goals
5. Awareness by each player of individual roles
6. Each player having a feeling of importance to the team
7. The coach giving individual attention to each player
8. A clean, well-painted gymnasium
9. Clean and attractive dressing rooms
10. Quality uniforms
11. Interesting and motivating bulletin boards
12. Motivational signs in locker room and gymnasium
13. Development of senior leadership
14. Recognition to individuals who excel in areas other than scoring
15. Avoidance of player criticizing player
16. Awards for intangible qualities such as "most dedicated"
17. Social activities to develop team spirit

Figure 8.6 Clean, attractive dressing rooms can contribute a great deal to the mental attitude of a team.

Figure 8.7 Even the attractiveness of the dressing room door can contribute to the development of good team morale.

Staleness

Staleness is chiefly a mental condition characterized by sloppy sub-par play and a decline in enthusiasm. It may affect individuals or the entire team. Chief causes of staleness are overwork in practice, fatigue, and lack of sleep. As the coach, insist on plenty of rest and sleep. Ease up and use fewer competitive-type drills in practice to help correct the condition. If the schedule permits, give players one or two days off from practice. Often they return to practice with early season vigor and hustle.

Care of the Feet and Legs

Because a basketball player must be prepared for the numerous starts and stops necessary to perform well, the care of the feet and legs becomes one of the most important parts of the conditioning program. A player cannot be expected to perform at best if hampered by the pain of blisters or shin splints.

It is far easier to *prevent* blisters than to heal them. Prevention begins with a proper fit in shoes and socks. As stated earlier, the outside pre-season conditioning program is a valuable aid in gradually toughening the feet. Practice workouts progress from the moderate to the more difficult as the feet gradually toughen. Players can paint the bottoms of their feet daily with tincture of benzoine to help prevent blisters, or they can use a lubricant on the more tender parts of the foot. Another good blister prevention technique is to turn the sock inside out and to rub the part of the sock that touches the foot with Ivory soap. Then turn the sock right side out and put it on. In play, the soap cushions the foot, thereby eliminating the friction that causes blisters. Also, any calluses should be kept filed, since blisters can form under them.

When a blister occurs, proper treatment means keeping it clean to prevent infection, covering it with gauze, and padding it with a foam rubber "doughnut." When the blister breaks, apply antibiotic ointment and cover it with gauze.

Care of the Ankles

A sprained ankle is one of the most common injuries in basketball. Daily ankle taping is the best method of prevention. However, few budgets and training facilities allow for daily taping for all players. Ankle wraps can be a reliable substitute. The wraps are relatively inexpensive, and players can wrap their own ankles after a little instruction.

If an ankle sprain occurs, wrap it in an elastic bandage and apply an ice pack immediately to reduce swelling. After application of the ice pack for thirty minutes, the ankle should be x-rayed to detect a possible break. The opinion of the coach or trainer alone is never satisfactory here, for it is impossible to judge on sight whether the ankle is broken. After an x-ray determines that the ankle is not broken, ice packs should be continued 24 to 48 hours, at which time heat should be applied.

Rehabilitation exercises designed to strengthen the ankle should begin as soon as possible. The following recommended series of ankle exercises should be done several times daily:

1. Toe raises from a standing position.
2. Toe raises after a half knee bend.
3. From a sitting position on the floor, isometric exercises as follows:
   a. Place the big toe against an immovable object and push hard against it for 6 seconds. Relax. Repeat several times.
   b. Place the little toe against an immovable object and push hard in the opposite direction for 6 seconds. Relax. Repeat several times.
   c. Place the foot under an immovable object and pull toes toward you for 6 seconds. Relax. Repeat several times.[1]

When the player is able to return to play, the ankle should be taped at every practice session and game for the rest of the season.

Shin Splints

Shin splints can be very painful and greatly hinder performance. They are usually caused by improper warm-up and too much running and jumping on a hard surface. Again, prevention is better than any cure, and adequate warm-up is essential. As mentioned previously, pre-practice outdoor work can ready the legs for work on the hard indoor surface.

Rest is the best cure for shin splints. The whirlpool and analgesic packs are invaluable. A hot whirlpool prior to practice and a cold whirlpool after practice are recommended. A small, thin layer of sponge rubber can be placed in the heel of the shoe to help absorb shock when landing on the floor after jumping. Particularly troublesome cases can be taped.

1. Spackman, Robert R. Jr. *Conditioning for Basketball*. Carbondale, Ill.: Hillcrest House, 1973.

Training Rules

Training rules vary a great deal from coach to coach—some coaches have many, while others have only a few. Since any training rule must be strictly enforced by the coach if it is to be effective, as few training rules as possible are recommended.

Here is a suggested list of training rules:

1. Avoid the use of alcohol, tobacco, or drugs at all times.
2. Get plenty of sleep. Be in bed by 10:00 PM on weekdays and 11:30 PM on weekends.
3. Conduct yourself as a representative of your school at all times.

Conditioning Reminders

1. Each member of the team must be convinced of the importance of mental and physical conditioning to the success of the team.
2. Warm-up and flexibility exercises should precede every practice session.
3. An outdoor conditioning program before practice begins is valuable in readying the body for the strenuous exertion of actual indoor practice.
4. Early practice sessions should be relatively moderate until the players' feet and legs have become conditioned to the hardwood.
5. Two full-court scrimmages weekly are sufficient in the pre-season practice programs. After the season begins, and when two or three games are played weekly, little scrimmage is necessary except for the reserve players.
6. Plan to give players a day off occasionally to combat staleness.
7. Make certain that each player wears correctly fitting shoes and socks.
8. Blisters can be prevented more easily than they can be healed.
9. The importance of adequate sleep and the avoidance of tobacco, alcohol, and drugs can never be overstressed.
10. Ankle wraps can be used inexpensively and will reduce ankle injuries.
11. All ankle sprains should be x-rayed to detect breaks.
12. When a sprain occurs, wrap the ankle with an elastic bandage and apply an ice pack. After 24 to 48 hours, apply heat.

Conditioning Drills

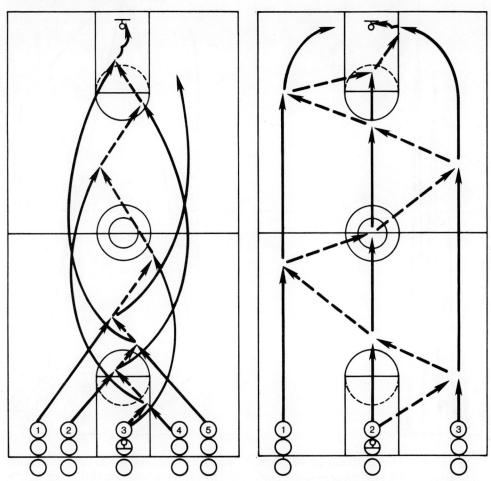

Diagram 8.1 *Five-player full-court weave conditioning drill.* After a pass, the passer goes behind two players. ③ passes to ④ and cuts around ④ and ⑤. ④ passes to ② and cuts behind ② and ①. ② passes to ⑤ and cuts around ⑤ and ③. This continues for the length of the court with the last pass receiver shooting a lay-up.

Diagram 8.2 *Three-line full-court passing and conditioning drill.* Players pass and cut downcourt with no weave involved. ② passes to ③ who return passes to ②. ② passes to ① who passes back to ②. Players run at full speed with the last pass receiver shooting a lay-up. Use more than one ball and begin the next wave as soon as the first group has passed midcourt.

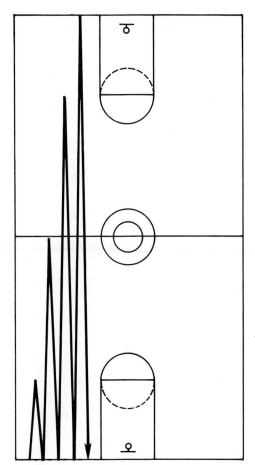 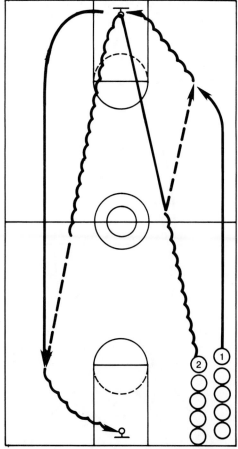

Diagram 8.3 *"Suicide" conditioning drill.* Each player runs in the path shown. Beginning on the baseline, the player sprints to the first free-throw line, returns to the baseline, sprints to midcourt, back to the baseline, sprints to the opposite free-throw line, back to the baseline, sprints to the opposite baseline and back to the starting point. Several players can run simultaneously, and a time goal of approximately 30 seconds should be set.

Diagram 8.4 *Driving lay-up conditioning drill.* ① sprints hard down the sideline as ② dribbles toward midcourt. ② passes to ① who shoots a driving lay-up and continues on down opposite sideline. ② gets ball out of net and again dribbles hard to midcourt for another pass to ①. Three balls should be used so that other waves of players may start downcourt as ① and ② come back up the opposite side.

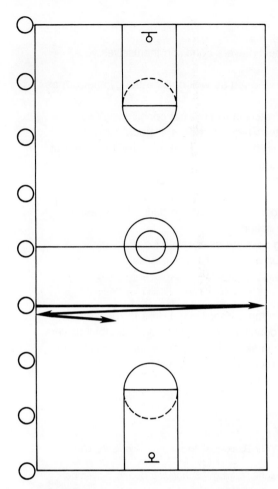

Diagram 8.5 *"Big 17" conditioning drill.* Squad members line up down sideline and on the whistle run the path shown. Each time a player touches either sideline counts one point. Each player must total 17 points in one minute.

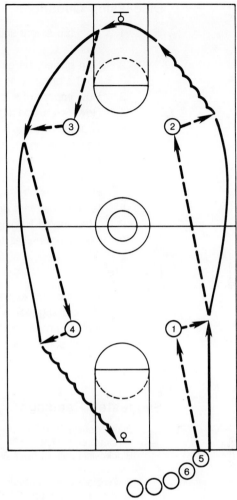

Diagram 8.6 *Full-court passing, receiving, and lay-up conditioning drill.* ①, ②, ③, and ④ are stationary posts. ⑤ passes to ①, takes a return pass, passes to ②, takes a return pass, and shoots a lay-up. ⑤ quickly gets ball out of net, passes to ③, receives a return pass, passes to ④, receives a return pass, and shoots a lay-up. ⑥ begins as soon as ⑤ gets to midcourt. Players continue this drill for several minutes at full speed.

Discussion Questions

1. To what extent should players condition themselves year round?
2. Can players be conditioned as well outside the gymnasium as on the practice floor?
3. How important is stretching to physical conditioning?
4. How can a coach tell when a player is in good condition?
5. A player who gets tired during a game may ask to come out. Should he or she be penalized?
6. Can a team be in good physical condition but in bad mental condition?
7. How can reserves be kept in condition during the season?
8. Is staleness fact or fiction?
9. How should training rules be established?
10. Discuss penalties for violation of training rules.

Projects

1. Diagram and explain three conditioning drills for basketball.
2. Write a suggested conditioning program for basketball players. Include pre-season, in-season, and post-season conditioning.
3. Solicit conditioning information from three coaches.
4. Write a paper on mental conditioning for basketball.
5. Develop a suggested weight program for basketball.

Suggested Readings

Blatt, Michele. " 'P.E.P' Up Your Basketball Program." *Scholastic Coach,* October 1977, pp. 53ff.

Blockovich, Joe. "Power Weight Training." *Scholastic Coach,* November 1977, pp. 54–58.

DeVenzio, Dave. "Motivating Your Bench Warmers." *Scholastic Coach,* January 1980, pp. 78ff.

Dunn, Ron. "Taking the Guesswork Out of Knee Rehabilitation." *Scholastic Coach,* November 1979, pp. 58ff.

Ebert and Cheatum, *Basketball,* pp. 14–38.

Hall, Joe B., and Casey, Swane. *Kentucky's Conditioning Program for Basketball.* Lexington, Ky.: University of Kentucky Press.

Hankinson, *Progressions,* pp. 303–4

Jensen, Dr. Clayne R., and Jensen, Craig. "Update on the Value of Warm-up," *Scholastic Coach,* October 1978, pp. 51ff.

———. "Update on Strength Training." *Scholastic Coach,* August 1978, p. 90.

Leyshon, Glynn A. "Alcohol and the Athlete." *Scholastic Coach,* April 1976, pp. 84–86.

Muehling, Jim. "Pre-practice Flexibility Routine." *Scholastic Coach,* December 1977, pp. 24ff.

Riley, Dan. "Accountability in the Weight Room." *Scholastic Coach,* January 1979, pp. 48ff.

————. "Administering the Strength Training Program." *Scholastic Coach,* November 1978, pp. 42–44.

————. "Prevention and Rehabilitation of Injuries," *Scholastic Coach,* March 1980, pp. 44ff.

Ronan, Donald M. "Introduction to Mental Training for the Competitive Athlete." *Scholastic Coach,* September 1978," pp. 116–20.

Schakel, Doug. "Basketball, From March to November," *Scholastic Coach,* December 1977, pp. 12ff.

Sheeran, Thomas J. "Contemporary Strength Training Modalities." *Scholastic Coach,* August 1977, pp. 50–53.

Stewart and Sholz, *Complete Program*, pp. 336–38.

Titley, Dr. Robert W. "Beware the Locker-Room Post-Mortem." *Scholastic Coach,* December 1977, pp. 74–76.

Wooden, *Modern Basketball*, pp. 35–40.

part two

Team Offensive Formations and Plays

chapter nine

Selecting and Teaching Team Offense

Selecting the team offense and a good teaching method for offense are important factors in building a championship basketball team. Selecting a suitable offense for the available personnel and careful, enthusiastic teaching of your selection certainly increases your chance for success.

Selection of the Offense

Prior to beginning practice for the season is the time to select an offense for attacking a man-for-man defense and an offense for attacking the various zone defenses. The major factor to be considered in selecting these patterns is the *type of player personnel available.* Offensive plays must take advantage of the strengths of individual team members. A team composed of three or four tall players may find a shuffle-type offense ineffective. A team without a good post player probably would find a pivot offense involving a great deal of feeding the post unsuitable. If two good post players are among the probable starters, a double-post offense could be used to advantage. The coach must analyze the players early, determine the strengths of each, and select team offenses accordingly. A correct initial selection is extremely important, for it is very difficult to change offenses in mid-season.

Consider the type of defense to be faced the *majority of time* when selecting your team offense. If the team will be facing a zone defense most of the time, as is often the case in high school basketball, an intricate continuity offense for attacking man-for-man defenses is impractical. True, the team must be prepared to face the man-for-man defense, but a simpler pattern is better.

It is important that the coach select an offense with which he or she is *thoroughly familiar*. Some high school coaches observe a college team running a particular offense well and try to teach it to their own teams before learning it and the drills needed to teach it thoroughly. Having a complete knowledge of the offense allows the coach to teach it confidently, properly answering questions and correctly analyzing mistakes.

Essentials for a Sound Team Offense

The following are the major essentials for a sound team offense:

1. Movement of the ball
2. Movement of players
3. Obtaining the high percentage shot
4. Obtaining the second shot
5. Maintaining floor balance
6. Simplicity
7. The one-on-one situation

Movement of the Ball

All offenses must move the ball if the defense is to be penetrated, whether the defense is man-for-man, zone, or a combination of both. The team that passes the ball slowly from one player to another is simply playing into the hands of the defense, providing an opportunity for the defense to shift, sag, fight through or around screens, or make some other move to counteract an offensive screen or maneuver. On the other hand, the team that keeps the ball moving from player to player keeps the defense constantly on the move. It is far easier to attack the defense when it is moving than when it is allowed to stand virtually motionless and concentrated around the basket.

Movement of Players

One quality that often distinguishes great players from good ones is the ability to be dangerous when not in possession of the ball. Most players can make an offensive move if they posses the basketball, but far fewer players remain dangerous after giving up the ball.

The sound offensive pattern allows players to move with the ball. Constant movement, fakes, and cuts are necessary. When players remain in one position and pose no offensive threat, most defenses quickly take advantage and use sinking or double-teaming tactics to congest a more dangerous area. This is far more difficult when all offensive players are kept on the move and each constantly poses a threat to the defense.

Obtaining the High Percentage Shot

The sound offense works for the good percentage shot. A team has to keep this principle in mind to win consistently. The team that is overly anxious to shoot and has poor play patterns that result in sub-par team play finds its members taking bad shots—and often finds itself on the short end of the score at game's end.

The sound offensive pattern is designed to get the high percentage, or "good" shot, as a primary objective. What exactly is a "good" shot? When can a player know the shot is a good one? First, the player must have the *ability* to make the shot. What may be a good shot for one player may be a bad one for another. The 20-foot jump shot by a guard could be a percentage shot, whereas the same shot taken by a big center could very well be a bad shot. Second, the player must *not be closely guarded.* Regardless of how good a shooter he or she may be, if closely guarded he or she should pass to a teammate. The exception to this rule, of course, is when the player is close to the basket and can make a power move that might result in both a score and a foul on the opposition. Third, rebounders must be *in position* for the shot to be a good one. Few things are more irritating in basketball than the player "gunning the ball up" from 20 feet out with no one even near the rebounding area.

The principle of the high percentage shot demands that the offense attempt to get the ball inside. Inside shooting not only increases a team's shooting percentage but results in more three-point plays and more fouls on the opposition.

Obtaining the Second Shot

Many coaches maintain that obtaining the second shot is the chief essential of offensive play. Statistics show that the team that consistently gets the offensive rebound and the resulting second shot attempt usually is successful. Therefore, plan the offensive pattern so at least three players are in position to rebound a shot attempt. Three rebounders in position, provided these players are grounded soundly in offensive rebounding fundamentals, usually results in an adequate number of second-shot attempts. Design the play patterns to get the better rebounders into the rebounding area.

Maintaining Floor Balance

All good offensive patterns eliminate congestion as much as possible. To do this, you have to keep the floor balanced. The type of offense being played determines just where players must be to maintain floor balance. In general, when two or three players are standing close together (unless part of a play pattern as on a single or double screen), they are easily defensed. One player can defense two players standing close together and allow another defensive player to sag and congest the scoring area. Proper floor spacing or balance helps prevent this.

Proper floor balance not only includes offensive balance but defensive balance as well. Be sure every play pattern provides for players to remain out to prevent fast-breaks by the opponents. Of course, the number of players needed for defensive balance responsibilities depends on the particular opponent. A fast-breaking opponent requires two players back for maintenance of defensive balance, whereas the slow-breaking or ball-control opponent requires only one player back for proper defensive balance.

Simplicity

A too complicated offense should be avoided. If players spend too much time thinking where they must go on the offense, they fail to react properly to defensive breakdowns and rebound opportunities, or they have problems with basic offensive fundamentals. Former UCLA Coach John Wooden once said that the secret to his offensive success was the simplicity of his offensive pattern. There are literally hundreds of sound basketball plays, and a coach must resist the temptation to select too many for offense or to add new plays before existing ones are thoroughly learned. The successful coach concentrates on executing a few plays rather than attempting to teach a larger number of plays.

The One-on-One Situation

The sound offense includes opportunities for the one-on-one situation that takes advantage of scoring abilities of the better offensive players and capitalizes on weak defensive players. The offensive guard who fakes a drive and shoots the jumper, the forward who drives the baseline for a lay-up, and the center who rolls for a score are all executing one-on-one scoring maneuvers. The stereotyped offense that does not allow such individual scoring moves is greatly reducing its effectiveness and can be more easily scouted and defensed.

Total Team Offense

In addition to a team's basic half-court offenses against man-for-man and zone defenses, prepare a total team offense with other offensive plays and techniques. Practice the fast break, a press offense for meeting both the zone and man-for-man pressing defenses, out-of-bounds plays, jump-ball situations, freeze or delay patterns, and special plays.

Teaching the Offense

The words "coach" and "teacher" are synonymous. All good coaches are good teachers; they must use proven teaching methods in coaching all phases of the game. When one coach is consistently more successful than another, it is usually due to superior teaching ability rather than a "pet" offense or knowledge of the game. And since teaching abilities can be improved, each coach should constantly strive to improve his or her teaching techniques.

When teaching a particular play or pattern, the coach should use a method similar to the following:

1. Explain the play clearly by diagramming it on a chalkboard. Discuss the play completely and answer all questions.

2. If returning players who already know the play are available, use them to demonstrate.

3. Allow each player on the squad to run through the play without defense until it is well learned.

4. After all players have learned the play, use a "dummy" defense against it. This means the defense follows the offensive players but makes no effort to intercept passes or block shots. A dummy defense allows offensive players to see scoring options clearly.

5. Add live defense. Allow defensive players to contest for passes and block shots. Simulate actual game conditions as nearly as possible. Always begin the offense beyond mid-court so guards are prepared to initiate plays when tightly guarded at mid-court.

6. Point out any mistakes and make proper corrections.

7. As players learn the offense, work on more than one phase of the game while practicing it. For example, the team may be working on the offense, their full-court man-for-man press, and their defense for the fast-break at the same time. If they score, the defensive team takes the ball out-of-bounds and attacks the press. This teaches the offensive team to react and set up their press immediately. A quick reaction from offense to defense is essential to the success of the press. If the team working on offense fails to score, the defensive team rebounds and attempts a fast-break. Again, this teaches the offensive team reaction from offense to defense but uses different team defensive fundamentals—delaying the outlet pass, sprinting to the defensive basket and picking up the opponents before they obtain a good shot.

8. Use breakdown drills for mastering parts of the play. A breakdown drill takes a 5-man play and breaks it down into parts—usually 2- and 3-man plays. For example, diagram 9.1 illustrates a basic single post play commonly called a second guard play. Diagram 9.2 illustrates how this play can be broken down for quick practice of the essential parts. Since ③ and ⑤ rebound only, lines are formed at the ①, ②, and ④ positions, and, using no defense, the play can be practiced quite a number of times in a few minutes, enabling players to learn the passing and cutting techniques required by the play. As the techniques are learned, defense can be added to the drill. Virtually any 5-man play can be broken down to enable drill on the essential elements of the play.

9. As the overall team offense is learned, use full-court scrimmage to simulate game conditions.

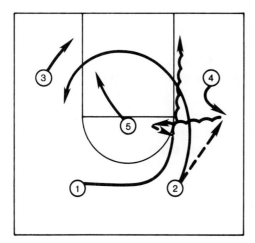

Diagram 9.1 *A basic single-post play termed the "second-guard play."* ②passes to ④and cuts as shown. ④dribbles to the free-throw line and hands off to ①who drives for a lay-up or close jump shot. ③and ⑤move into rebound position.

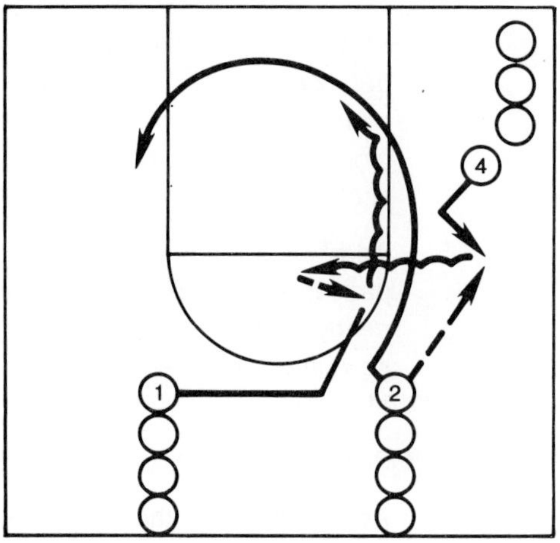

Diagram 9.2 This is an example of a break-down drill designed to teach the "second-guard" play. Two lines are formed at the guard position with one line at forward position. ②passes to ④and cuts. ④drives to free-throw line and makes flip pass to ①. ①drives for a lay-up or jump shot. Two balls can be used for more action.

Discussion Questions

1. When should team offense be selected?
2. Should the offense be adjusted to the personnel or the personnel be adjusted to the offense?
3. Should the offense be changed during the middle of the season if it is not proving successful?
4. What type of offense is more suitable for a group of small players?
5. Many high school teams face zone defenses a majority of the time. How much attention should be given to the team's man-for-man offense?

Projects

1. Study a game film. Select one team, determine their offense, and determine how many of the major essentials for a sound team offense are used.
2. Select an offense and write a brief paper outlining the characteristics of each position in the offense. Use three reference sources.
3. Observe a practice session conducted by a local coach. Write a brief paper on how the coach teaches the offensive portion of practice.

Suggested Readings

Brown, Bruce. "Developing a Total Team Concept in Basketball." *Athletic Journal,* September 1979, p. 28.

Ebert and Cheatum, *Basketball*, pp. 111–15.

Hankinson, *Progressions*, pp. 224–25.

Layton, Terry. "You Must Read the Defense." *Scholastic Coach,* September 1976, pp. 17ff.

Nitchman, Nelson. "1979–80 Basketball Offense." *Athletic Journal*, June 1980, p. 16.

Stewart and Sholz, *Complete Program,* pp. 55–57.

Tarkanian and Warren, *Winning Basketball*, pp. 32–42.

Van Gundy, Bill. "Variety in Offensive Initiation." *Scholastic Coach,* October 1978, pp. 34ff.

Wooden, *Modern Basketball*, pp. 149–51.

chapter ten

The Single-Post Offense

The single-post offense is the most popular offense in the game of basketball. More than half of the high school and college teams in the United States, it is estimated, use some form of this offense, and virtually every team in professional basketball uses it. Whether it be a freelance style of play, a set-play system, or a continuity offense, the popularity of the single-post offense attests to its strengths and advantages.

Figure 10.1 *The single-post offense with the center at the high-post position.*

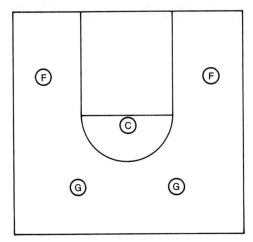

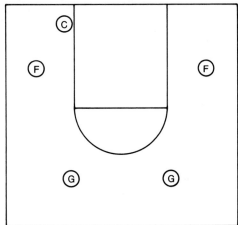

Diagram 10.1 *Basic single-post formation with center at the high-post position.*

Diagram 10.2 *Basic single-post formation with center at the low-post position.*

Positioning of Players

The single-post offensive alignment is diagrammed in diagram 10.1. The guards Ⓖ initiate play patterns from a balanced position behind the free-throw circle. The forwards Ⓕ are used at several positions along the sideline, but most often at a sideline position at the free-throw line extended. The center Ⓒ plays either at a high-post position, as shown in diagram 10.1, or at a low-post position, illustrated by diagram 10.2.

Qualifications of Players

The guards are the quarterbacks of the offense and usually are the team's smaller players. They also are usually faster and the best ball handlers—necessary abilities since it is their job to advance the ball downfloor and initiate play patterns. A guard's general qualifications include speed, outside shooting ability, ballhandling and passing, driving ability, and leadership. Leadership is extremely important, because even teams with excellent talent require leadership at the guard position.

The forwards generally are taller than the guards and may be slower, but they must be good rebounders and should be good side and corner shooters. Forwards need to be able to feed the pivot and drive toward the baseline and into the free-throw area for shots.

The center is most often the tallest player on the team and should be the better scorer from the pivot area. In fact, one of the advantages of the single-post offense is that it gives a talented post player considerable room to maneuver offensively without too much congestion. The post player should also be a good rebounder and possess the ability to feed off to cutters. Outside shooting ability is not essential, but it makes the post player more effective, since he or she can pull taller opponents away from the basket.

Single-Post Plays

Diagrams 10.3 through 10.25 show successful single-post plays. Again, take care not to choose too many plays for the offense. A selected few well-executed plays far surpass a larger number that are poorly executed. Also, get ready to run checks on each of the plays to counter any defensive switch or move by the defense. Of course, all of the plays diagrammed can be run from either side of the floor and should be practiced from both sides.

California Reverse Action

Pete Newell won a national championship while coaching at the University of California using a single post continuity offense that was termed the California Reverse Action. The basic pattern is shown in diagrams 10.9a and 10.9b.

The UCLA Basic Single-Post Play

Coach John Wooden won his 10 national championships at UCLA using a single-post offense with the center normally at the high-post position. As any outstanding coach does, he adapted the offense to his personnel and changed to a low-post offense when he had Kareem Jabbar and Bill Walton. His basic high post offense is diagrammed in diagrams 10.19 through 10.23.

Kentucky's Famous Second Guard Play

During his very successful tenure as head coach of the Kentucky Wildcats, Coach Adolph Rupp developed a play that became known as the Kentucky Second Guard Play. His offense included a number of excellent single-post plays, but the second guard play became the "bread and butter" of his offensive attack. Diagram 10.24 illustrates the basic play, and diagram 10.25 shows an alternate method of execution.

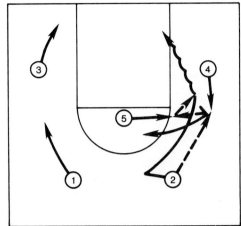

Diagram 10.3 *A split-the-post play from the high-post position.* ① feeds ⑤. ① and ② split the post with ①, the passer, cutting first. ⑤ feeds the open player, most often ②, who drives for the basket. ③ and ④ must be alert for the offensive rebound.

Diagram 10.4 *A split-the-post play from the side involving the guard and forward.* ② passes to ④ and sets up as shown. ⑤ slides over and receives pass from ④. ④ cuts first and ② cuts close, taking a pass from ⑤ and driving to the basket.

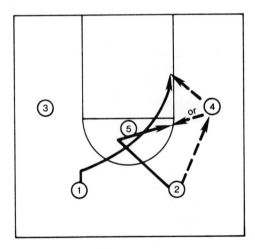

Diagram 10.5 *A variation of the high-post split.* ② feeds ④ and screens for cutter ① as shown. If ① is open, ④ makes the pass for the shot. After the screen, ② cuts back toward the ball and receives the pass from ④ if ① is covered. The cut-back maneuver is very effective if the defense is switching.

Diagram 10.6 *Another variation of the high-post split.* As ① feeds ⑤, ④ cuts toward the baseline. If ② is not open, ⑤ feeds ④ coming off screen set by ①.

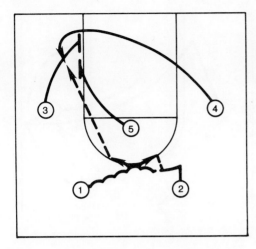

Diagram 10.7 ③ and ⑤ set double-screen for ④ as ① makes dribble hand-off to ②. ② makes pass to ④ for shot behind double-screen. If defense switches, ⑤ can roll out toward basket and take pass from ②.

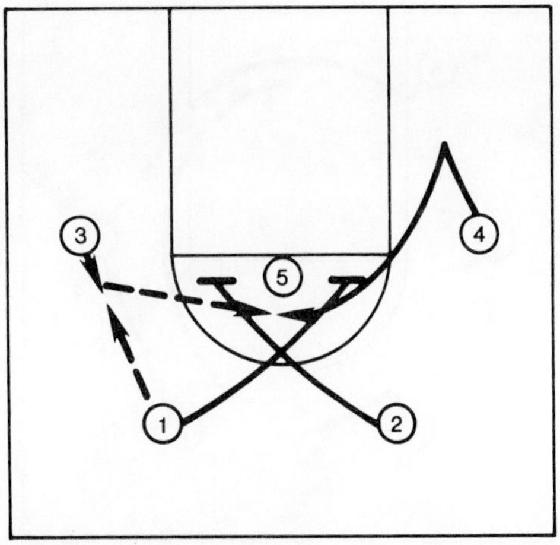

Diagram 10.8 ① passes to ③. ① and ② begin a split-the-post move but stop beside ⑤ and set a triple-screen for ④. ④ takes pass from ③ for shot behind triple-screen.

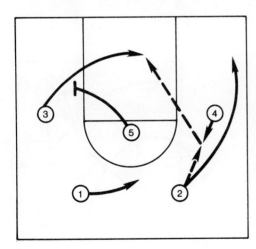

Diagram 10.9a *A simple continuity pattern often referred to as the "California reverse action."* ② feeds ④ and cuts outside to corner. ⑤ sets screen for cutter ③ as ① moves to top of circle. If ③ is open, ④ feeds ③ for shot.

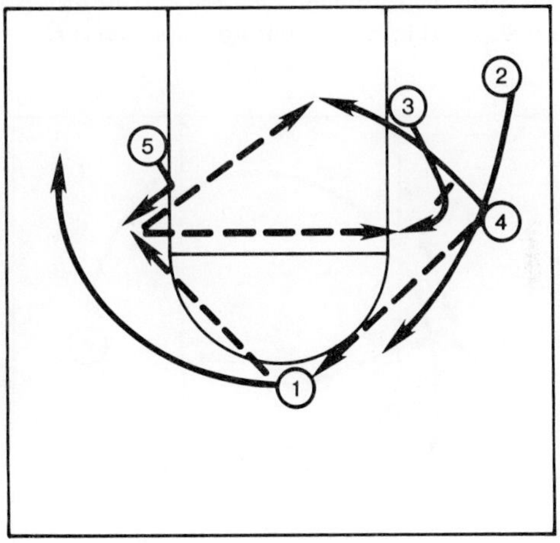

Diagram 10.9b If ③ is not open, ④ passes to ① at top of circle who hits ⑤ and cuts outside. ③ sets screen for ④ cutting for basket as ② comes out to top of circle. ⑤ feeds ④ if open. An effective option against a switch is for ⑤ to pass to ③ after the cut by ④.

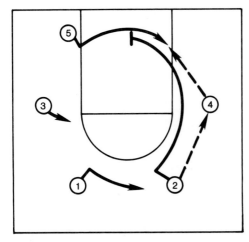

Diagram 10.10 ②passes to④, fakes screen for①and cuts down middle. If open, ②receives pass for shot. If not open, ② continues on through lane and sets screen for ⑤. This is a good method for feeding a pivot player. It can also be very effective against the switching defense, because it forces a small guard to switch onto a taller center.

Diagram 10.11 ②passes to④and cuts outside for a return pass.④flip passes to ②and cuts into the lane to set a screen for ③.②may pass to⑤at the low post or to③for a jump shot.

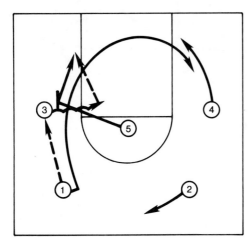

Diagram 10.12 *A screen-and-roll play.*① passes to③and cuts as shown.⑤sets screen for③who drives off screen. If defense switches,③passes to⑤rolling for the basket.

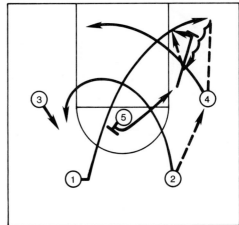

Diagram 10.13 ②passes to④as⑤sets screen for cutter①.⑤cuts toward ball after cutter goes.④may pass to①on cut, or to⑤. If neither is open,④passes to①in corner and clears through.⑤sets screen for①who dribbles off screen and looks for⑤rolling out to basket.

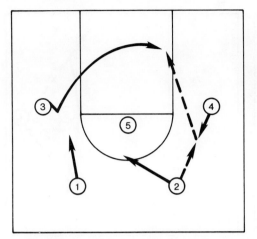

Diagram 10.14 *A simple play to take advantage of a forward who is effective at the low post.*

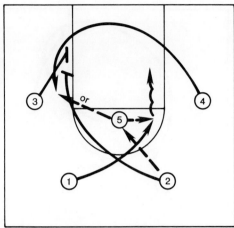

Diagram 10.15 ②passes to⑤as④clears out. ②and①split post. ②and③set double-screen for④. ⑤may hit①for a drive or④for a shot behind double-screen.

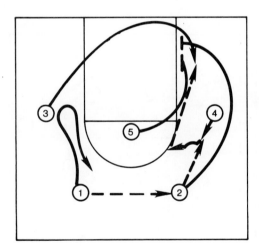

Diagram 10.16 ①passes to②who passes to④and cuts outside. ②and⑤set double-screen for③. ④sets up the defense by dribbling toward middle of floor, then passes to③for shot behind double-screen.

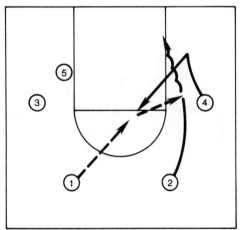

Diagram 10.17 This is an excellent play when the defensive player guarding②is preventing a pass from①to②.④cuts into the free-throw area, takes pass from①, and feeds②cutting for basket.

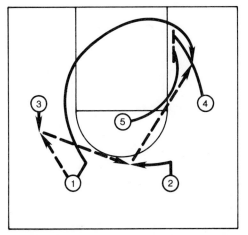

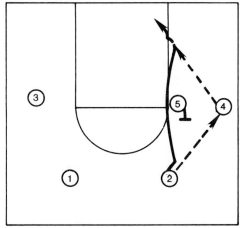

Diagram 10.18 *A double-screen play for the guards.* (1) passes to (3) and cuts to basket. (4) and (5) set double-screen. (3) passes to (2) who passes to (1) for shot behind double-screen.

Diagram 10.19 *UCLA basic play.* (2) passes to (4) and cuts to basket off screen set by (5). The first option of the play is for (1) to take a pass from (4) for a lay-up.

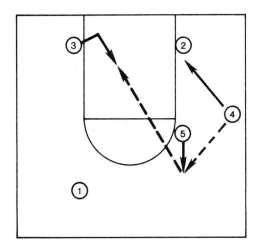

Diagram 10.20 If (2) is not open, (5) steps out and receives a pass from (4). (5) looks to pass to (3) flashing into the pivot area. (5) can shoot if open and has shooting ability from this range.

Diagram 10.21 As (3) is flashing into the pivot, (4) is setting a screen for (2). It is very important for (2) to set the defensive player up for the screen by faking into the lane. If (5) does not pass to (3), (5) looks to pass to (2) for the jump shot.

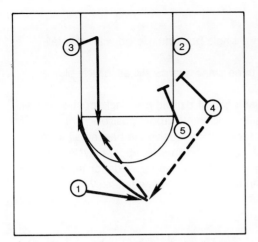

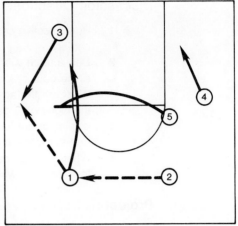

Diagram 10.22 If the defense prevents the pass from ④ to ⑤, ① cuts and receives the pass from ④. As ① receives the pass, ③ cuts up the lane and to the free-throw line. ① passes to ③ and cuts outside while ④ and ⑤ screen for ②. ③ can pass to ①, turn for a shot or drive, or pass to ②.

Diagram 10.23 As in all sound offensive plays, the pattern can be initiated from either side. If ④ is overplayed, ② can pass to ① who initiates the play with a pass to ③. ⑤ simply slides across the lane as the passes are being made and sets screen for ①.

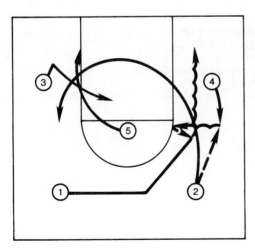

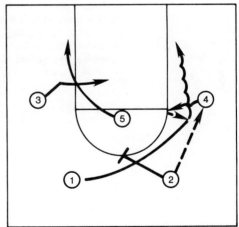

Diagram 10.24 *The famous Kentucky second-guard play.* ② passes to ④ and cuts to basket. ⑤ and ③ move into rebound position as ④ drives to free-throw line and hands off to ① for drive to basket.

Diagram 10.25 *An alternate method of executing the "second-guard" play.* ② passes to ④ and, instead of cutting to basket, sets screen for ① as ④ drives to free-throw line. ① cuts off screens set by ② and ④, takes hand-off, and drives to basket.

Discussion Questions

1. How effective can a single-post offense be without a tall center?
2. Can a team with three small guards still effectively play a single-post offense?
3. What are the advantages of playing the single-post center at the high-post position? At the low-post position?
4. Is it important for forwards to receive the basketball at the free-throw line extended to begin single-post plays?
5. What methods can be used to free forwards for the guard-to-forward pass when facing on overplay defense?

Projects

1. By studying various reference materials, compile at least 15 plays from a single-post pattern.
2. Write a brief paper outlining the qualifications of each position in the single-post offense.
3. Devise three breakdown drills for teaching the single post offense.

Suggested Readings

Bartow, Tom. "Incorporating One-On-One Guard Play in a Team Offense." *Athletic Journal,* September 1979, p. 44.

Ebert and Cheatum, *Basketball,* pp. 115–17.

Hankinson, *Progressions,* pp. 228–29.

Stewart and Sholz, *Complete Program,* pp. 69–73.

Tarkanian and Warren, *Winning Basketball,* pp. 105–6

Wooden, *Modern Basketball,* pp. 170–79.

chapter eleven

The Double-Post Offense

The double-post offense enables a coach to play two tall post players at the same time. Whereas neither may be strong enough to play forward in a single-post offense, the double-post offense allows both to play near the basket and to take advantage of their post scoring ability and rebounding ability. Though positioning two players in the post area may reduce driving opportunities by the outside players, the advantage of added scoring opportunities from the post area and two players always in offensive rebound position more than offset the disadvantage.

Positioning of Players

Diagram 11.1 illustrates the double-post set-up with the post players tight. ① is the point guard and best ball-handler. ② and ③ are the wing players, while ④ and ⑤ are the post players. The post players play along each lane line, moving anywhere from the baseline to the free-throw line and changing sides in screens for each other.

If the post players can shoot from the corners, they may be played wide (diag, 11.2), which opens the middle, allows the chance for better driving by the perimeter players, and allows flash-pivoting opportunities. This situation is sometimes referred to as a "spread" offense.

Qualifications of Players

The good point guard possesses the same qualifications as the good single-post guard—speed, ball-handling ability, and driving ability. It is the point guard's responsibility to be the key playmaker and initiate offensive patterns. The wing players are good outside shooters and have the ability to feed the

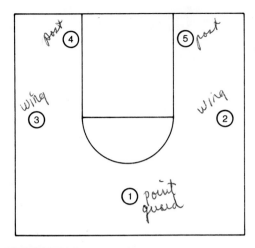

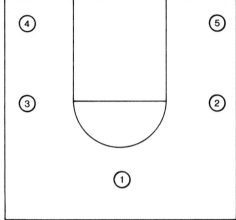

Diagram 11.1 *The double-post offense with post players tight.*

Diagram 11.2 *The double-post offense with post players spread wide.*

post. The smaller wing player is used as the second guard and must help bring the ball downcourt against full-court pressure. The larger wing player is assigned offensive rebounding duties.

Both post players should be good post scorers, good rebounders, and should be able to feed cutters. Outside shooting ability by the post players allows for more attack variability, since the wide post or spread formation can be used effectively and taller opponents taken outside.

Figure 11.1 Post players must present big "targets" to enable passers to get the ball inside. This is an important fundamental on any post offense.

Many smaller players are good post players—the double-post offense affords an excellent opportunity for using them. If your team, like most teams, has one player more adept at guarding a post player, assign him or her to the taller post players. And assign a team member less familiar with defensing the post position to the smaller post player. This allows for increased scoring opportunities by the small post player and presents quite a defensive problem to the opposing team.

Double-Post Plays

As in the previous chapter the plays given in diagrams 11.3 through 11.20 are intended to present a variety sufficient to allow the discerning coach to select a few that best fit his or her personnel.

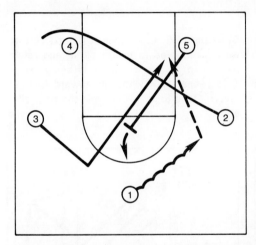

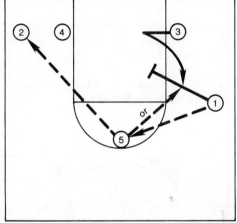

Diagram 11.3 ①dribbles to wing, and ②clears. ③cuts off screen by ⑤for a pass from ①.

Diagram 11.4 If ③is not open, ①passes to ⑤at top of circle. ⑤can pass to ②for a shot or to ③coming off screen set by ①. If ②receives ball, ④may be open for inside feed from ②.

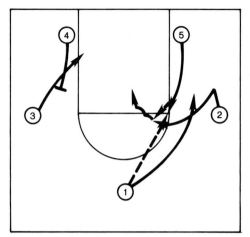

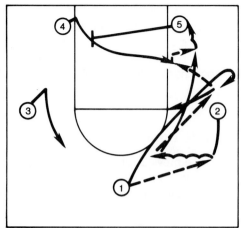

Diagram 11.5 *A "split-the-post" play.* ① passes to ⑤ coming out to meet pass. ① and ② split off ⑤ with ① cutting first. As ⑤ feeds ②, ③ cuts off back screen set by ④. ② may shoot or pass to ③. ① must cut back for defensive balance.

Diagram 11.6 ① passes to ② and cuts to wing. ② dribbles to top of circle and return passes to ①. As this pass is being made, ⑤ screens for ④ who cuts toward ball. ① feeds ④ and joins ② in a split-the-post situation.

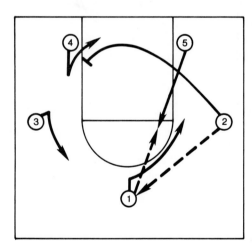

Diagram 11.7 ② passes to ① and cuts through lane in front of ⑤. ⑤ cuts toward ball and receives pass from ①. ① cuts outside ⑤. ⑤ may pass to ①, may fake pass and drive the middle, or may pass to ④ cutting off screen set by ②.

Diagram 11.8 ① passes to ② who passes to ⑤. ⑤ dribbles to lane, forming double-screen with ② for ① cutting outside. When ① receives ball, a drive to basket may be open. If not, ① looks to pass to ④ coming off screen set by ② and ⑤.

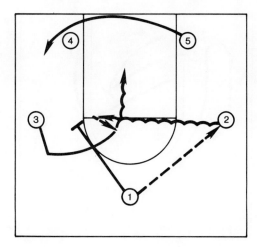

Diagram 11.9 ①passes to②and sets screen for③.②drives toward free-throw line forming double-screen for③.⑤clears to opposite side.③takes hand-off from② and can shoot or drive to basket.

Diagram 11.10 ③makes dribbling screen for①, hands off, and cuts away.①dribbles off screen set by④and looks for jump shot or pass to④rolling to basket.

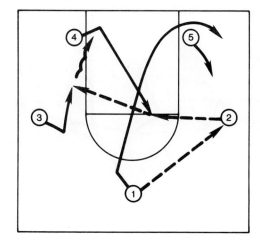

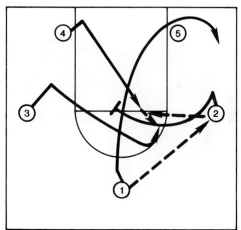

Diagram 11.11 This play is excellent when the defensive player on③, the offside guard, is turning the head to look at the ball.① passes to②and cuts down middle.④cuts to free-throw line to take pass from②.③ cuts for basket, taking pass from④for shot.

Diagram 11.12 This is a variation of the play in diagram 11.11.①passes to②and cuts. ④cuts to free-throw line for pass from②. ②cuts over top of④.③fakes cut to basket and cuts to top of④for a shot over the screen.

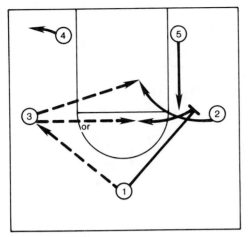

Diagram 11.13 ①passes to ③ and joins ⑤ in setting double-screen for cutter ②. ③ may pass to ② or to ① coming back toward ball, dependent on the reaction of the defense.

Diagram 11.14 ①passes to ③ and cuts to corner for a return pass. ④ sets screen for ⑤ who cuts toward ball. If defense switches, ④ rolls out under the basket for pass from ① .

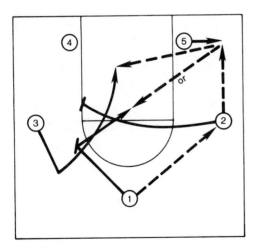

Diagram 11.15 ①passes to ② who passes to ⑤ . ① and ② set screen for ③ . ⑤ may pass to ③ or to ① , dependent on the reaction by the defense.

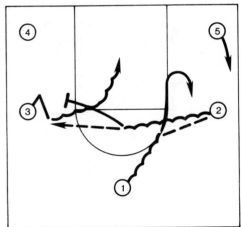

Diagram 11.16 *The three-man guard weave with post players wide.* The weave presents many freelance options. Here, ①passes to ② and cuts down middle. ② dribbles, passes to ③ , and sets screen for ③ who drives the middle.

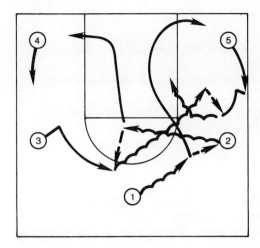

Diagram 11.17 The five-man weave can be used effectively from the spread formation. It gives opportunities for driving and flash-pivoting by all players. Here, ①, ②, and ③ exchange passes, with ③ passing off to ⑤ for a drive to the basket.

Diagram 11.18 1 passes to ③ who passes to ④. After passing to ③, ① cuts and sets screen for ② and ⑤. ② cuts first with ⑤ cutting close off the cut by ②. ④ passes to ② or ⑤, dependent on the reaction by the defense.

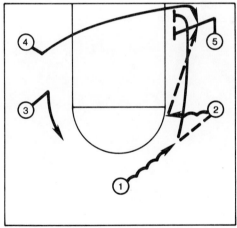

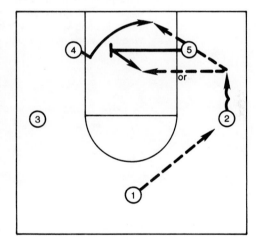

Diagram 11.19 *A double-screen for a post player.* ① passes to ② and cuts to set double-screen with ⑤. ② dribbles toward middle and passes to ④ coming off screen set by ⑤ and ①.

Diagram 11.20 ① passes to ② who looks to pass to ④ coming off cross-screen set by ⑤. ② often needs a dribble in this situation to improve the passing angle.

Discussion Questions

1. Can a team with a tall player effectively use a double-post offense?
2. What are the key advantages of the double-post offense? Disadvantages?
3. Does pressure overplay defense affect the double-post more or less than the single-post offense?
4. What is the advantage of playing the post players wide? Tight?

Projects

1. By studying various reference materials, compile at least 10 plays from a double-post formation.
2. Write a brief paper outlining the qualifications of each position in the double-post offense.
3. Devise three breakdown drills for teaching the double-post offense.

Suggested Readings

Ebert and Cheatum, *Basketball,* pp. 118–19.

Edwards, Mark. "Washington State's Double Low Post." *Scholastic Coach,* October 1979, pp. 21ff.

Hankinson, *Progressions,* pp. 229–30.

Tarkanian and Warren, *Winning Basketball,* pp. 76–89.

Wooden, *Modern Basketball,* pp. 179–82.

chapter twelve

The Tandem Post, or 1–3–1, Offense

The tandem post, or 1–3–1, offense has become progressively more popular in recent years. Like the double-post offense, it enables a coach to use two tall players in the lineup who may not have perimeter skills. Placing one player at the free-throw line opens up the area under the basket for more driving opportunities and more one-on-one scoring opportunities by the low-post player and positions a screener at the high post. As in any offense, any number of set plays are available for use with the formation.

The attack has the distinctive advantage of easily being adapted to both man-for-man and zone defenses. Most teams use the 1–3–1 attack against certain zones. When another offensive set is used against the man-for-man, confusion may result in trying to change into the zone attack and vice versa.

Figure 12.1 *The 1–3–1 offense initial set-up.*

Diagram 12.1 *The basic set-up of the 1-3-1 offense.*

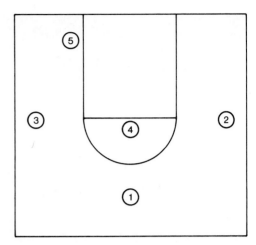

The danger of confusion is virtually eliminated when this attack is used against both types of defenses. Thus, advocates of this offense possess sound arguments for its use, particularly for junior and senior high school teams.

Positioning of Players

Diagram 12.1 illustrates the basic offensive setup. ① is the point guard who initiates play patterns. ② and ③ are the wing players and set up along the sideline, while one post player, ④, sets up at the free-throw line and the other post player, ⑤, is positioned along the baseline near the basket.

Qualifications of Players

The point guard is a playmaker, almost solely responsible for setting up plays, who possesses the essential qualities of a single or double-post guard. His or her leadership ability should be good enough to completely direct the offensive attack.

The wing players have a combination of guard and forward abilities. They should be able to shoot from the sides and corners as do single-post forwards, but both players do not have to possess the rebounding ability required of a single-post forward. Since some plays send them to the guard position, their ball-handling ability must be superior to that of the single-post forward.

The post players are the better rebounders and better post scorers. The baseline post player should be the best post scorer. If the post player at the free-throw line is a weak scorer, use that player solely as a screener and

Figure 12.2 The point guard on a 1-3-1 offense must be an excellent ball-handler and playmaker.

rebounder. Many teams have a good rebounder who is a weak scorer, and this offense allows this player to still be a great advantage to the team. The offense is even more effective when the post players can interchange from the high- and low-post positions.

Tandem Post, or 1–3–1, Plays

Diagrams 12.2 through 12.14 illustrate tandem post plays for man-for-man defenses. Plays from this alignment for attacking zones will be discussed in chapter 16.

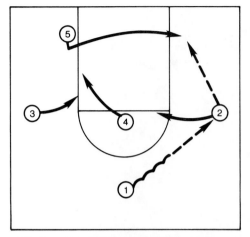

Diagram 12.2 *A simple feed to the low post player for a one-on-one post maneuver.*

Diagram 12.3 ①passes to②and cuts off screen set by④for a lay-up.

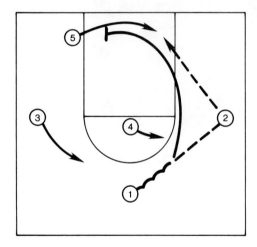

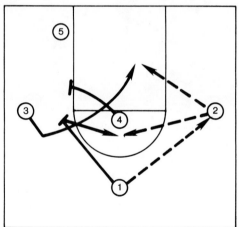

Diagram 12.4 ①passes to②and cuts for basket. If no pass is made to①,①sets screen for⑤. If defense switches, a small player will be switching to a tall player.

Diagram 12.5 ①passes to②and joins ④in setting double-screen for③.②passes to③or to①cutting back toward ball. Double-screens are far more effective when one of the screeners becomes a scoring option.

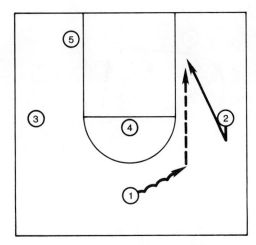

Diagram 12.6 This simple reverse or "back-door" play is important to all offenses but particularly to the 1-3-1 offense. Since so many 1-3-1 plays involve passing to a wing player, the defense often overplays these wings. The reverse reduces the effectiveness of the pressure defense.

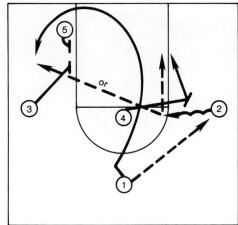

Diagram 12.7 ①passes to②and cuts. ④sets screen for②who dribbles off screen and looks to pass to④rolling out, or to①behind double-screen set by③and⑤.

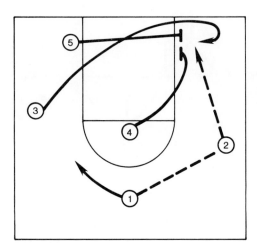

Diagram 12.8 ①passes to②who passes to③coming behind double-screen set by④and⑤.

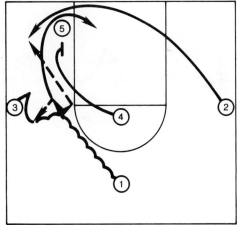

Diagram 12.9 ①makes dribble hand-off to ③as④and⑤set double-screen along free-throw lane. ③dribbles toward top of circle and may pass to②or①, who have crossed on the baseline side of the double-screen.

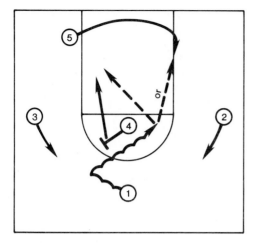

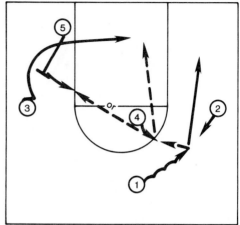

Diagram 12.10 ④moves to top of circle and sets screen for dribbler ①. ①has three options: a shot, pass to ⑤, or a pass to ④rolling to basket.

Diagram 12.11 ①passes to ④who may pass to ③cutting off rear screen set by ⑤. If defense adjusts, pass may be made to ⑤ who will be in a good one-on-one position.

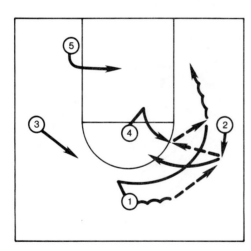

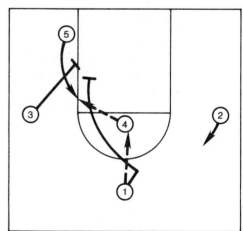

Diagram 12.12 *A split-the-post play.* ① passes to ②who feeds ④moving to a side-post position. ①and ②split the post, with ②cutting first. ④passes to ①for shot or drive.

Diagram 12.13 ①passes to ④and cuts to join ③in setting double-screen for ⑤. The screeners cannot hold the screen but must move on through the lane before the three-second violation.

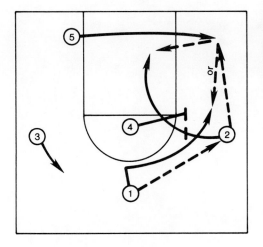

Diagram 12.14 ①passes to ②who passes to ⑤cutting along baseline. ②cuts to a position beside ④, forming a double-screen for ①. As ①cuts off screen, ②continues on for basket. ⑤may pass to either ① or ②.

Discussion Questions

1. How does the 1–3–1 offense differ from the double-post?
2. Does the point player on the 1–3–1 need any different skills than the ball-handling guard on a single- or double-post offense?
3. What are the key advantages of the 1–3–1 offense? Disadvantages?
4. Is there a problem with defensive balance from the 1–3–1 offense?
5. How can the 1–3–1 offense counter the overplay defense?
6. What adjustments are necessary to use the 1–3–1 offense against a zone?

Projects

1. By studying various reference materials, compile at least 10 plays from a 1–3–1 formation.
2. Write a brief paper outlining the qualifications of each position in the 1–3–1 offense.

Suggested Readings

Ebert and Cheatum, *Basketball,* pp. 119–20.

Fengler, Hank. "Patterned Phase of One-Guard Offense." *Scholastic Coach,* November 1977, pp. 38ff.

Healey, William A., and Hartley, Joseph W. *Ten Great Basketball Offenses,* pp. 83–102. West Nyack, N.Y: Parker Publishing, 1970.

Land, Harry L. "Double Stack to 1–3–1 Continuity." *Scholastic Coach,* January 1976, pp. 70ff.

Stier, William H. "1–3–1 High Post Continuity." *Scholastic Coach,* November 1979, pp. 33ff.

chapter thirteen

The 1-4 Offense

The 1–4 offense evolved recently from the 1–3–1 offense. It is very similar to the 1–3–1 in that a point, two wing players, and two post players are used. In fact, many teams who use the 1–3–1 as their basic offense also use several plays from the 1–4 formation. The essential difference is that the 1–4 offense stations both players in the high-post area as play patterns are initiated. This frees the underbasket area and makes the pressing defense more susceptible to "backdoor" plays.

Positioning of Players

Diagram 13.1 illustrates the positioning of players in the 1–4 offense. ① is the point guard, ② and ③ are the wing players, and ④ and ⑤ are the post players. As in the 1–3–1 offense, ② is termed the small wing and ③ the big wing.

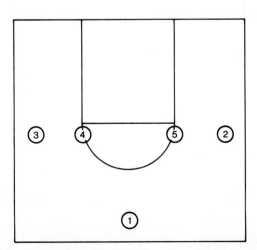

Diagram 13.1 *Basic set-up for the 1-4 offense.*

Qualifications of Players

The qualifications for the 1–4 offensive positions are basically the same as for the 1–3–1 offense. The point guard must possess excellent ball-handling and leadership skills, for he assumes the full responsibility for directing the offense. The wing players are good outside shooters and good ball-handlers. The small wing must have enough ball-handling ability to help downcourt advancement of the ball against full-court pressure, while the big wing must have sufficient rebounding ability in order to share rebounding responsibility with the post players. Both post players should be good rebounders and scorers from the post area and should possess the ability to pass to teammates cutting for the basket.

1–4 Offense Plays

Diagrams 13.2 through 13.12 give plays from the 1–4 formation. Since the 1–4 and 1–3–1 are so similar, virtually all of the plays shown for the 1–3–1 can be adapted for the 1–4 offense.

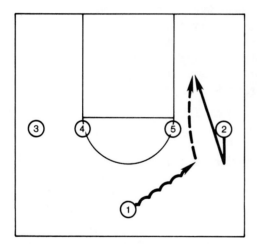

Diagram 13.2 *A reverse or "backdoor" play.*

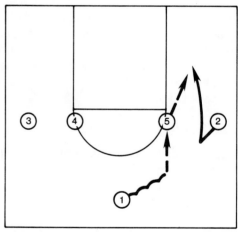

Diagram 13.3 *Another method for the reverse or "backdoor" play.*

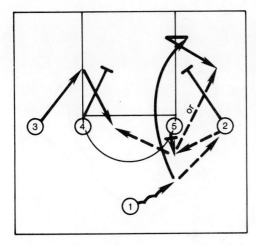

Diagram 13.4 ① passes to ② and cuts off screen set by ⑤. ② passes to ① if open. If ① is covered, ② passes to ⑤ who can pass to ③ coming off screen set by ④ or to ① coming off screen set by ②. ④ should not set the screen until ⑤ has ball possession.

Diagram 13.5 ① passes to ② and cuts off screen set by ⑤ looking for pass from ②. After cut by ①, ⑤ moves out to set screen for ②. ② dribbles off screen and looks to pass to ⑤ rolling out to basket or to ① coming off double-screen set by ③ and ④.

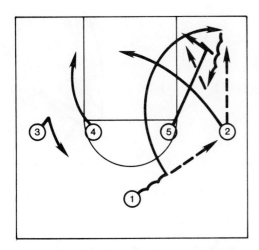

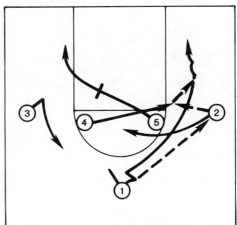

Diagram 13.6 ① passes to ②, cuts off screen set by ⑤, and on to corner. ② passes to ① and cuts through to basket. ⑤ slides down and sets screen for ① who dribbles out looking for either the shot or a pass to ⑤ rolling to basket.

Diagram 13.7 ① passes to ② who passes to 4 coming off screen set by ⑤. ② and ① run split-the-post play with ② cutting first. ④ passes to ① who shoots or drives for a lay-up.

The 1-4 Offense   149

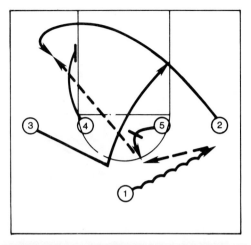

Diagram 13.8 ①dribbles to right wing as ②clears. ④rolls down, and ⑤sets screen for ③cutting to basket. ①passes to ③if open or to ⑤who relays to ②for shot.

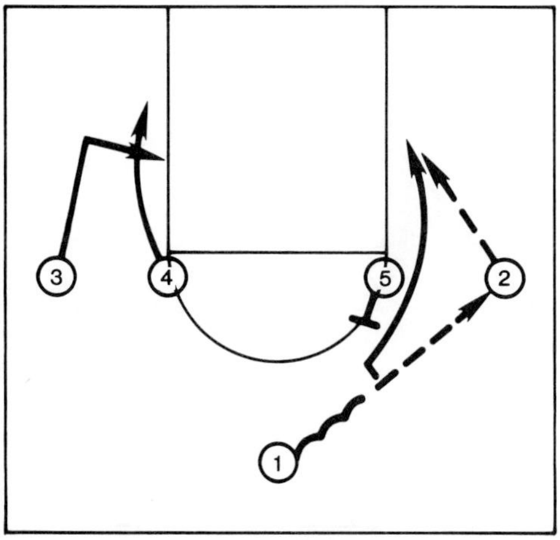

Diagram 13.9a ①passes to ②who cuts off screen set by ⑤. ②passes to ①if ①is open.

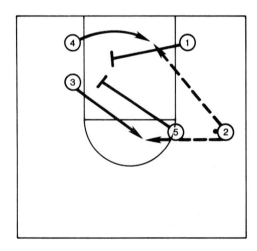

Diagram 13.9b If ①is not open on previous cut, ⑤and ①set screens for ③and ④cutting toward ball. ③and ④may change direction, with ③cutting low and ④cutting high.

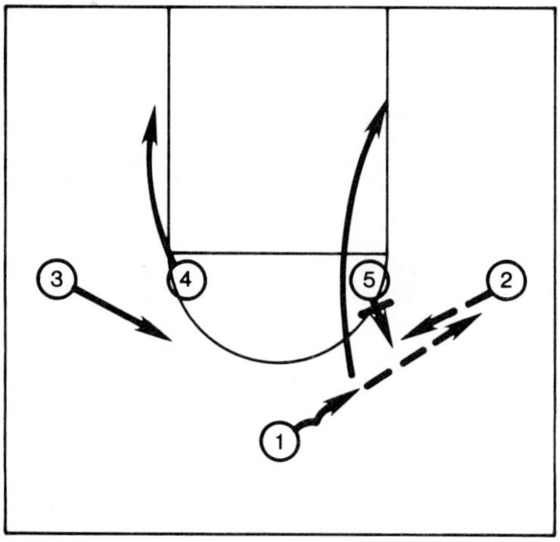

Diagram 13.10a ①passes to ②and cuts off screen set by ⑤. ②passes to ①if ①is open or to ⑤at the top of the circle.

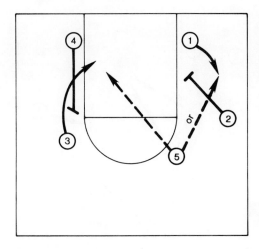

Diagram 13.10b As ⑤ receives ball from ②, ② sets downscreen for ①, while ④ sets rear screen for ③.

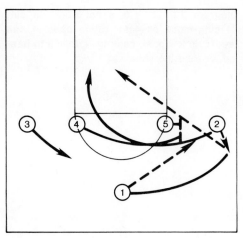

Diagram 13.11a ① passes to ② and cuts outside. ④ and ⑤ set double-screen for ② cutting for basket. ① looks to throw lob pass to ②.

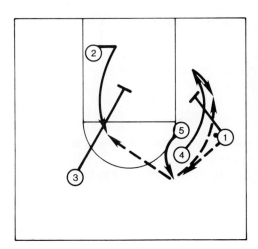

Diagram 13.11b If ② is not open, ④ cuts for basket as ⑤ moves to top of circle for pass from ①. ③ sets downscreen for ②, and ① sets downscreen for ④.

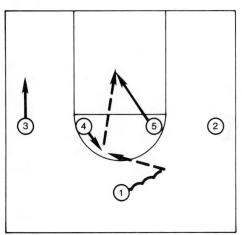

Diagram 13.12a If the strongside post is being overplayed, ① can pass to ④ who can quickly make a "backdoor" type pass to ⑤.

Diagram 13.12b If ⑤ is not open on cut, ① cuts close off ④ for return pass. ① can feed ⑤ in low post, pass to ④ rolling to basket, or take the shot.

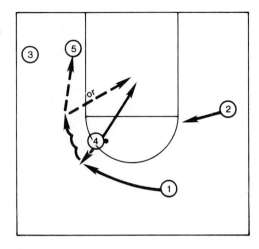

Discussion Questions

1. What is the difference between the 1–4 and 1–3–1 offense?
2. Compare the 1–4 and 1–3–1 offenses concerning attacking the overplay man-for-man defense.
3. What adjustments are necessary to use the 1–4 offense against a zone?
4. Should post players station themselves high prior to the initiation of the offense, or should they break up from a low-post position?

Projects

1. By studying various reference materials, compile at least 10 plays from a 1–4 formation.
2. Write a brief paper outlining the advantages and disadvantages of the 1–4 offense.

Suggested Readings

Ceravolo, Joe. *Basketball's 1–4 Offense,* West Nyack, N.Y: Parker Publishing, 1967.
Stewart and Scholz, *Complete Program,* pp. 73–74.

chapter fourteen

The Shuffle Offense and Wheel Offense

The shuffle offense was originated by Bruce Drake while he was coaching at the University of Oklahoma. It is a continuity offense that eliminates one of the distinct disadvantages of set plays—that of having to set up after a cut or play maneuver has failed to score. The shuffle begins with an overload to one side of the court, and, after its basic options have been executed, players are aligned in an overload on the opposite side of the court, and it is not necessary to set up again.

The wheel offense is a version of the shuffle. Coach Garland Pinholster of Oglethorpe University probably did more than any other coach to perfect this particular pattern. The wheel also begins with an overload, but it differs from the shuffle in that the first cutter has a double-screen instead of a single-screen.

Figure 14.1 *Initial shuffle set-up.*

Diagram 14.1 *Basic initial positions for the shuffle offense.* The overload may be set on either side of the floor.

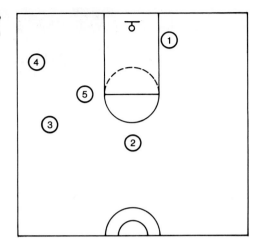

Since both offenses are continuity patterns, all players must learn to play each position, although either can be adapted to keep a tall player in the post position. Either the shuffle or the wheel is an ideal offense for the team with balanced height, good shooting, and good ball-handling.

Positioning of Players for the Shuffle Offense

The basic shuffle set-up is illustrated by diagram 14.1. ① is the key feeder position and is stationed along the lane close to the basket. ② is about a yard back of the top of the circle, while ③ sets up one step ahead of ② and approximately two yards from the sideline. ④ plays near the sideline and about two yards from the baseline. ⑤ sets up along the lane near the free-throw line.

② and ③ are normally the guards, ① and ④ the forwards, and ⑤ the center. However, since the continuity requires all players to learn each position, they can change at the coach's discretion. Any changes, such as initiating the offense with a guard at the "five spot," can make the offense even more difficult to defend.

Qualifications of Players for the Shuffle Offense

Since all players play each position, the shuffle offense is more suited to a team with balanced height, particularly for a team without tall centers and forwards. All players must be able to handle the ball and pass well. Rotation

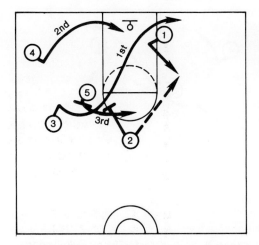
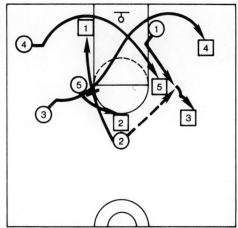

Diagram 14.2 *Basic shuffle pattern.* As ② passes to ①, ③ cuts off screen set by ⑤. This is the first option. ④ delays until ③ has cut by ⑤, then cuts along the baseline and flashes into the pivot area. This is the second option. ② sets screen for ⑤ who cuts to the top of the circle for the third option.

Diagram 14.3 *The continuity.* Circles indicate original positions, while squares indicate new positions after the three options have been run without a score. ③ cuts and becomes the new ④ player. ④ becomes the new ⑤ player, ⑤ becomes ②, ② becomes ①, and ① becomes ③.

to an outside position requires good shooting ability. This same rotation sends players inside and requires adequate rebounding skills. Players must also develop cutting skills and be able to receive passes on the move.

The Shuffle Pattern and Variations

Diagram 14.2 illustrates the basic shuffle pattern with its three basic options. The cut made by ③ is the first scoring option, while the flash pivot by ④ into the post area is the second scoring option. The rotation to the top of the circle by ⑤ off the screen set by ② is the third scoring option. Once these options have been executed and no scoring attempt has been made, the offense is overloaded to the opposite side of the court and the three options are again executed by different players (diag. 14.3).

Diagrams 14.4 through 14.15 illustrate some other potential plays and some drills needed to help teach the offense.

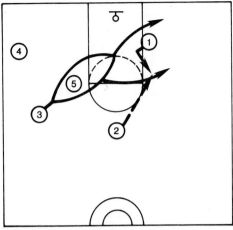

Diagram 14.4 ③ has three cutting paths in executing the first option. ③ may cut to either side of the post player, ⑤, or over the top of ①. In all cases, ③ becomes the new number 4 player if ③ does not get the ball for a scoring attempt.

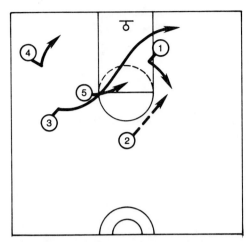

Diagram 14.5 *Counter for a switching defense.* If the defensive player on ⑤ is switching to the first cutter ③, ⑤ follows ③ for a possible scoring pass.

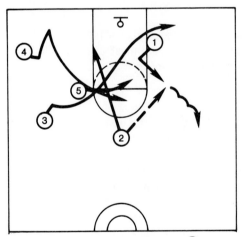

Diagram 14.6 *Continuity when ⑤ follows ③.* ⑤ becomes the new number 5 player on the opposite side. ② sets screen for ④, and ④ becomes new number 2 player. Other positions are the same as in basic pattern, with ① becoming 3, ② becoming 1, and ③ becoming 4. If a team has a tall center they prefer to keep in the post, this version of the shuffle enables them to do so.

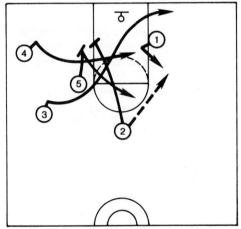

Diagram 14.7 Some shuffle teams like to screen for the second cutter, ④. After ③ cuts by ⑤, ⑤ slides down and sets screen for ④ who cuts off screen into the pivot area. ② then sets screen for ⑤ coming out for the third option. The continuity is the same as in the basic pattern.

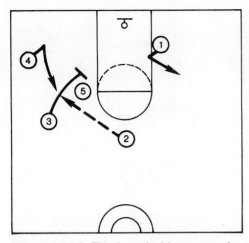

Diagram 14.8 This is a double-screen play that is effective when the defensive player guarding ④ is sagging into the lane. ② fakes pass to ① as ③ cuts to a position beside ⑤. ④ fakes baseline cut and comes out for shot behind double-screen.

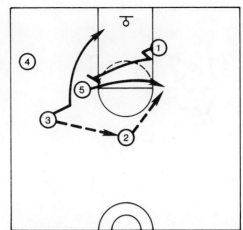

Diagram 14.9 Since the ball must go to the 1 player to initiate the basic offense, many defenses try to overplay the 1 player to prevent this key feeder receiving the ball. When such a defensive maneuver is faced, ① may cut across lane and set screen for ⑤ who cuts out to become the new 1 player. ① becomes the new 5 player and sets a screen for the first cutter, ③.

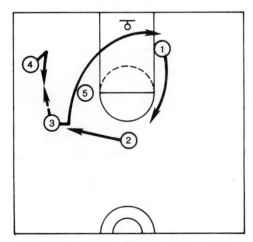

Diagram 14.10 The offense must have plays to the strongside to be successful. A variety of various single-post plays may be used. The revolving maneuver shown here is very effective. ③ passes to ④ and cuts as shown. ④ may return pass to ③, drive the baseline, or drive off ⑤. ④ may return the ball to the new number 3 player. ② has cut to become the new number 3 player, while ① has become the new 2 player, and ③ has become the new 1 player. If the ball is passed to the new number 3 player, the regular shuffle pattern may be executed.

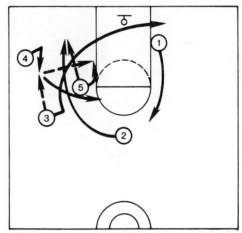

Diagram 14.11 *Strongside play.* ③ passes to ④ and cuts through. ④ passes to ⑤. ④ and ② split the post, with ④ cutting first. ② receives pass from ⑤ for shot or drive as ① hustles out for defensive balance.

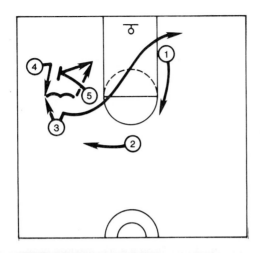

Diagram 14.12 *Strongside play.* ③ passes to ④ and cuts over top of ⑤. ⑤ sets screen for ④ who drives toward free-throw line. ⑤ rolls out for basket. If defense switches, ④ passes to ⑤ for shot.

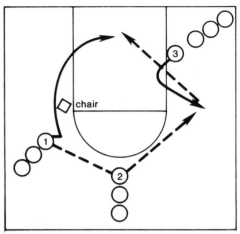

Diagram 14.13 *First option lay-up drill.* ① passes to ② who passes to ③. ③ passes to ① cutting for a lay-up. Use two balls for more lay-up practice. Players rotate lines clockwise.

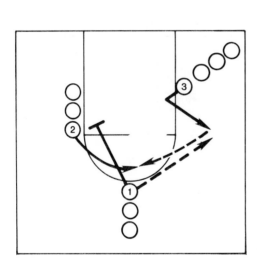

Diagram 14.14 *Third option shooting drill.* ① passes to ③ and screens for ②. ② takes pass at top of circle for shot. Use two balls for more shooting practice. Players rotate lines clockwise.

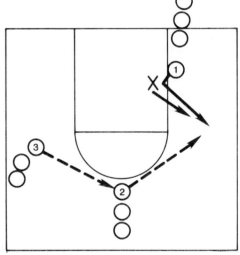

Diagram 14.15 *Wing pressure drill.* Most teams try to prevent the pass from ② to ①. Considerable practice must be given to the timing for this pass and for the possible reverse action by ①.

Positioning of Players for the Wheel Offense

The initial formation for the wheel offense is shown in diagram 14.16. The essential difference between the initial formation of the wheel and the shuffle is that ④ is stationed in a double-screen position beside ⑤. This double-screen makes the first cut of the offense more difficult to defend. The cut made by ③ is made on the baseline side whenever possible. This baseline cut is out of the vision of the defensive post player, making it more difficult for that player to defend.

The basic wheel pattern is shown in diagrams 14.17 to 14.19, and diagram 14.20 illustrates how the offense may be adapted to leave the offensive post player in the post area.

Most teams using the wheel offense also use a concealment pattern to get into the basic wheel formation. The offensive players may set up in a 2-1-2 or single-post alignment and cut into the wheel formation. A concealment makes the offense more effective and is shown in diagram 14.21.

Diagrams 14.22 through 14.27 show other potential plays for the offense as well as basic drills for teaching.

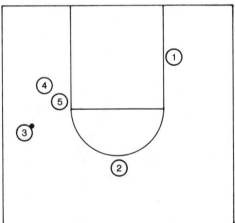

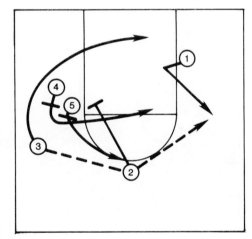

Diagram 14.16 *Basic formation for the wheel offense.* It is very similar to the shuffle, except ④ sets up alongside ⑤, and ③ sets up slightly deeper.

Diagram 14.17 *Basic wheel pattern.* ③ passes to ② who passes to ①. ③ cuts off double-screen set by ④ and ⑤ and stops momentarily in the lane. ④ cuts over top of ⑤, and ⑤ cuts to top of circle off screen set by ②.

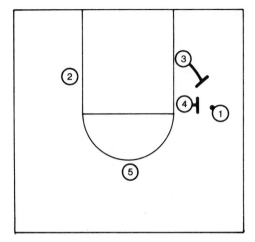

Diagram 14.18 *The continuity.* If no scoring opportunity develops, ③ and ④ set double-screen for ①, and pattern is ready to be run to opposite side.

Diagram 14.19 *The continuity.* ① passes to ⑤ who passes to ②. ① cuts off double-screen and stops momentarily in the lane. ③ cuts over top of ④. ④ cuts to top of circle off screen set by ⑤.

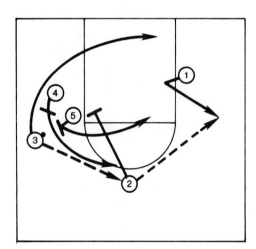

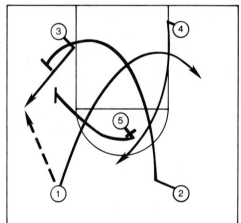

Diagram 14.20 *The wheel with ⑤ remaining at the "five" position.* This is easier to teach and allows a taller player to remain at the post position.

Diagram 14.21 *Concealment formation and cuts to set up the wheel offense.* Players are aligned in a single-post formation. ① passes to ③. ② cuts off screen set by ⑤ and ④ comes to top of circle off screen set by ①. After screen, ⑤ slides across for double-screen for ③.

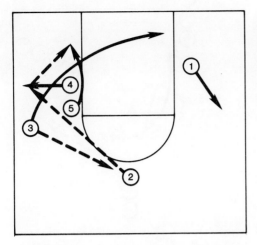

Diagram 14.22 This is a play designed to take advantage of defensive player guarding ⑤ who is jamming the lane. ③ passes and cuts. ② fakes pass to ① and passes to ④ who passes to ⑤ for a post move. Wheel teams term this play a "reverse."

Diagram 14.23 *A strongside play.* ③ passes to ④ and cuts through. ⑤ screens for ④. ④ drives toward middle and may shoot or pass to ⑤ rolling to basket.

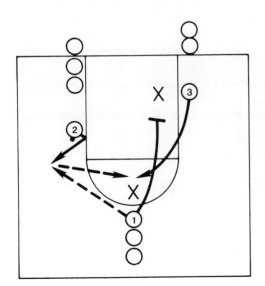

Diagram 14.24 *Drill to teach screen technique.* ① passes to ② and sets screen for ③. Emphasis must be on setting a legal screen on the defensive player.

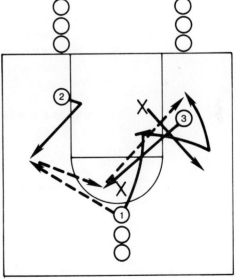

Diagram 14.25 *Wing pressure drill.* ① passes to ② and screens for ③. ③ receives pass and passes to ① either at the free-throw line extended or reversing.

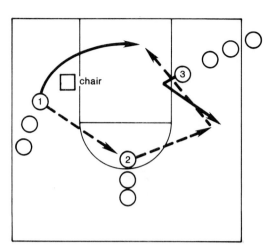
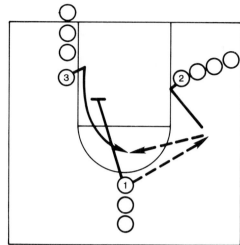

Diagram 14.26 *Wheel first-cut lay-up drill.* ① passes to ② who passes to ③. ③ passes to ① for a lay-up. Use two balls and rotate players clockwise.

Diagram 14.27 *Top circle shooting drill.* ① passes to ② and sets screen for ③. ③ uses V-cut, then moves to top of circle for shot. Use two balls and rotate players clockwise.

Discussion Questions

1. What are the essential differences between the shuffle and wheel offenses?
2. What are the advantages and disadvantages of the shuffle and wheel offenses?
3. What rebounding problems are inherent in both the shuffle and wheel?
4. Is there a problem with defensive balance with either the wheel or shuffle?

Projects

1. Compile a list of advantages and disadvantages of the shuffle or wheel offenses.
2. Devise three breakdown drills for teaching the shuffle or wheel offenses.

Suggested Readings

Ebert and Cheatum, *Basketball*, pp. 122–24.
Gourdouze, Frank. "The Double Shuffle Offense." *Athletic Journal*, November 1979, p. 20.
Hankinson, *Progressions*, pp. 225–28.
Healey and Hartley, *Basketball Offenses*, pp. 145–66.
Tarkanian and Warren, *Winning Basketball*, pp. 97–105.

chapter fifteen

The Passing, or Motion, Game

The Passing, or Motion, Game, one of basketball's most versatile offenses, is being used successfully by leading teams throughout the nation. It combines movement of the ball, player movement, shot selection, and team play to result in one of the game's most difficult offenses to defend.

The Passing Game has been a basketball offense for a number of years, but only recently has it begun to receive nationwide interest. Henry Iba of Oklahoma State was among the first to use the offense successfully. Don Haskins used it to win the 1965 NCAA championship at Texas Western. North Carolina's Dean Smith and Indiana's Bobby Knight were two of the first coaches in the East to use it with any success; Smith and Knight have perhaps done more to stimulate interest in the offense than any other coaches.

Just what is the Passing Game? This offense is not a set play offense. It actually may be called a freelance offense, but it differs from the normal freelance offense in that it is disciplined—it gives *player freedom with control*. The offense emphasizes movement of the ball, movement of personnel, shot selection, and team play. At the same time, it minimizes dribbling and one-on-one individual play. The players move within the offense under a set of rules. Since the players do have a great amount of freedom to cut and move around the court, it is very important that they know these rules and abide by them. If players violate the rules, the offense turns into a helter-skelter, undisciplined, freelance attack.

Advantages of the Passing Game Offense

The advantages of this offense are as follows:

1. *It is easy to teach.* Many coaches find they need only half the teaching time for the passing game than they need for a more patterned offense. This enables them to spend more time on defense and other vital areas of the game.

2. *It is not affected by pressure defenses as much as pattern offenses are.* Since the ball can be passed to any player, and the player may move in any direction, it is quite easy to find a pressure release.

3. *Players can interchange position.* Big guards can move inside to play a post, and post players, if sufficiently mobile, can move outside into the perimeter. Obviously, this freedom can cause considerable problems to the opposing defense.

4. *It is easier to take advantage of a defensive opponent in foul trouble or who is weak defensively.* In a pattern offense, an attack on such an opponent usually means that your team stops running the offense and tries to get the ball to one player while the other players are idle. Not so in the Passing Game. You can plan to attack a particular opponent and yet still have good ball and player movement.

5. *It can be run from any initial formation, and more than one formation can be used successfully during a game.* The same basic rules apply whether the offense is initiated from a 1–3–1, single-post, 1–2–2, stack, or other formation.

6. *The Passing Game develops team play.* The success of the offense is dependent on patience, good shot selection, and unselfish team play. In the passing game, it becomes easy for a player to give up the ball, because he or she knows that with proper movement the ball will be returned. This is not the case with all offenses; in fact, in many offenses players are afraid to give up the ball for fear they won't get it back. The Passing Game when run properly does not do this. Players get the ball back after giving it up—a fact that helps create good team play.

7. *Players like it.* This offense does not restrict players to a particular pattern but rather enables them to use various offensive maneuvers to get open and to score. They sense more freedom in the Passing Game than in a pattern offense, yet the rules keep them under control.

8. *It eliminates the need to set up after an unsuccessful fast-break attempt.* Players easily can flow directly into the offense at the end of a fast-break attempt. This quick movement from the break to the offense puts the defense at a definite disadvantage and often results in a score before the defense can get set up themselves. The offense that always has to back the ball out to set up gives the defense opportunity to set up also.

9. *The offense is difficult to scout.* Players have freedom to move, cut, and screen as they choose, within the rules. Therefore it is impossible for a scout to be able to chart what each player will do in a particular situation.

10. *It improves your defense.* This is one of the more important advantages. When your offense is a strict pattern, you get no defensive practice while running that pattern against your own defense. Your own defensive players know the pattern and tend to "play the play." For example, if the defender is guarding a player who is to make a shuffle cut, the defender often beats the cutter through simply because of knowing the play in advance. This cannot be true of the Passing Game, since the offensive player is not restricted by a pattern and has a choice of what to do. Therefore, the defensive player must use basic defensive fundamentals to be able to do the job properly. When you spend 20 minutes practicing the Passing Game against your defense, your defense actually is getting 20 minutes of practice also. Your team defense is bound to improve by virtue of the passing game.

11. *It allows good offensive rebounding.* Your better rebounders can be designated as rebounders and given that responsibility on all shot attempts. Thus, when a shot is taken there is no need for hesitation. This is not true of all pattern offenses, since some determine responsibility by position on the floor.

12. *Team ball-handling improves.* There are several reasons for this: (1) The offense requires more movement of the ball than most pattern offenses and therefore players get more ball-handling practice while running the offense. (2) Players are not required to pass the ball to a particular player as required by a pattern; instead they pass it to the open player. If a player is closely guarded, they simply pass it to someone else. (3) The offense emphasizes making the *easy* pass. In fact, this is one

of the most important rules of the passing game. As the coach constantly stresses this rule, players learn what an easy pass is, and they learn that what may be an easy pass for one player is not necessarily true for another player.

13. *It makes defensive help very difficult.* Most man-for-man defenses depend a great deal on defensive help for success. Many pattern offenses fail to move all five players enough to prevent the defensive players from giving considerable help to each other. This is not possible when the Passing Game is run properly. The constant movement of all players makes defensive help very difficult.

14. *It teaches players how to play basketball and makes complete players out of them.* Pattern-oriented players tend to become stereotyped. As long as they are playing the pattern they have learned, they are fine. But they may be virtually lost in a situation where their pattern is not being used. Players actually can learn to be dependent on the pattern to get them open for shots. Not so with the Passing Game. Players become well-schooled in offensive fundamentals. They learn to move without the basketball, screen for teammates, cut to the basket, and a variety of other offensive moves. A player who knows this offense is a far more complete player than one harnessed by a stereotyped pattern offense.

Disadvantages of the Passing Game Offense

The Passing Game offense does have some disadvantages, of course:

1. *Players have to be taught to move without the ball.* Few players possess this skill—they learn it only after considerable coaching. There are many, many players throughout the country who are great as long as they have the ball, but there are far fewer players who are great without the ball.

2. *Floor balance is not constantly maintained.* With the freedom of movement the players have, they sometimes get congested into a particular area—the post area, especially. Wing players who cut to the basket often want to hang too long in the pivot area, jamming the middle. A coach must constantly be on the alert to correct this error.

3.   *It is not as easy to set up one particular player.* If a team has
      one superstar who is far better than any other player on the
      team, it can be difficult to make certain he or she gets enough
      shots and scoring attempts. The coach of the patterned
      offense can call a particular play to get the star player the ball,
      whereas the coach of the Passing Game cannot. However, the
      freedom of movement inherent in the offense may make this
      superstar more difficult to guard, particularly since help for the
      defense is so limited.

Keys to the Passing Game Offense

1.   *Movement of the ball.* When the offense is initiated, keep the
      ball moving. Each player should hold the ball two seconds to
      give things a chance to develop, then *move it.* The more the
      ball is moved, the more difficult it is for the defense.

2.   *Player movement.* We're talking again about moving without
      the ball—a basic fundamental skill players must learn.
      Remember, without proper player movement, the defense can
      prevent good ball movement. Ball movement and player
      movement are dependent on each other.

3.   *Shot selection.* Good shots are absolutely necessary. Excellent
      ball and player movement are useless without good shot
      selection. Just what determines a good shot? As discussed in
      chapter 9, the key factors are a player's shooting ability, the
      amount of defensive pressure, and whether rebounders are in
      position. As stated earlier, what may be a good shot for one
      player may be a bad one for another. If even a great shooter
      puts the ball up from as close as the free-throw line under a
      great deal of defensive pressure, odds are the shot will be a
      bad one; and when no rebounders are in position, all shots
      except close ones are bad.

4.   *Team play.* Since movement of the ball and movement of
      players are so important to the Passing Game's success, team
      play becomes even more important. Encourage and praise
      team play, and criticize players who tend to play as individuals.

Passing Game Formations

The Passing Game can be initiated from virtually any formation—the single-
post, double-post, 1–3–1, or various stack formations. The basic success
of the offense depends on its rules, how well they are taught to the team,
and how well they are enforced by the coach.

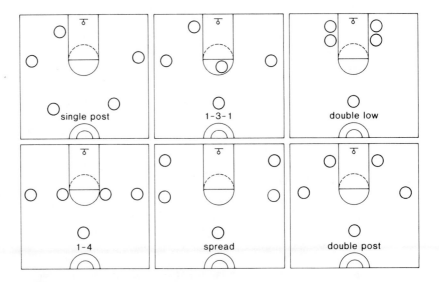

Diagram 15.1 *Passing game formations.*
The passing game can be initiated from virtually any formation.

Passing Game Rules

1. *You must move every time a pass is made.* As simple as this sounds, it requires constant emphasis if the Passing Game is to be learned properly.

2. *Move with a purpose.* Players must be taught that when they move they must move with a purpose, not aimlessly. They move to screen for a teammate. They cut to the basket looking to get open. They move to fake a screen and then cut to the basket. Always move with a purpose.

3. *Look to pass first, shoot second, and drive third.* Since the passing game emphasizes team play, players must think *pass first, shot second.* This is not to say they should not be aware of a shot opportunity or a drive opportunity; they must be very aware of these opportunities and take them when they come. However, emphasis on the pass first enables you to create the team play concept that results in better offensive play.

4. *Take no more than two dribbles after the offense is initiated.* The point player can use as many dribbles as necessary after crossing the center line in order to initiate the offense— however, once it is initiated, discourage more than two dribbles. This enables continued enphasis on the pass and

team play rather than on excessive dribbling and individual play. When a player takes a third dribble in practice, blow a whistle and call a violation giving the other team the ball.

5. *You must make at least four passes before a shot is taken unless the ball goes to the low-post area.* This rule does not apply to the fast-break situation. It applies after the offense has been initiated. The coach should *require* four passes—not ask for it. Four passes help instill the feeling that if a player gives up the ball it will be returned. If one player is allowed to shoot after two passes, another player will want to do the same thing, and before long, the advantage gained by team play is down the drain. This is not to say that a close shot should be passed up prior to the fourth pass. Not at all. Any time the ball gets into the low-post area, the offensive player should make the move to score.

6. Any time you are overplayed by the defense, cut to the goal or screen for a teammate. *Never fight pressure.* This is the basic rule that gives the Passing Game its effectiveness against pressure defenses. For example, a wing who is overplayed may cut to the basket and screen for another player who may be free to receive the pass. Or the wing may continue on through and receive the ball on the other side of the court from perhaps the high-post player. You can't say exactly what a player will do. You *can* say a player will not fight pressure.

7. *Always make the easy pass.* This may be the most important rule. Constantly stress this. If a player makes a difficult pass and gets it through for a basket, don't praise the pass. Criticize it instead, for a difficult pass gets thrown away in that situation far more than it gets completed. As players learn to make the easy pass, their turnover rate decreases greatly.

8. *After receiving the pass, face the goal and hold the ball at least two seconds before you pass.* Players often have a tendency to receive the ball and pass it too quickly. The two-second pause gives things a chance to develop on the inside and gives the passer time to see them.

9. *You may screen on the ball after four passes are made.* A screen on the ball at the beginning of an offensive pattern is one of the easiest plays in basketball to defense. However, once the defense has had to worry about various cuts to the basket and other offensive maneuvers, a quick screen on the ball is not as easily defensed.

Perimeter Play Rules

1. When you pass the ball: (a) cut to the goal—the cutter may turn out either way, to the ball or away from the ball, (b) screen away from the ball, (c) look to screen down, (d) set a rear screen, or (e) screen on the ball after four passes have been made. As mentioned earlier, a screen on the ball after one or two passes is one of the easiest plays to defend. On the other hand, once the ball has been passed enough to get the defense moving and worrying about various cuts and screens, a quick screen on the ball can be more difficult to defend.

2. When the ball is passed to a post player: (a) screen for the closest player, (b) look to cut off a screen by a teammate, or (c) cut to an open spot. Avoid cutting close to the post player with the ball and giving your defensive player an opportunity to help out defensively. The most important thing to remember when the ball goes to the post player is to move. Don't stand still. *Move!* Movement minimizes defensive help and results in more offensive scoring situations.

3. Maintain a position approximately 15 feet away from another perimeter player. We call this our spacing rule.

Post Play Rules

The following are rules for a single-post Passing Game:

1. Post players may set up at low, medium, or high post
2. The low-post player sets up away from the ball.
3. When receiving the ball in the low post, look to score first and to pass to a perimeter player second.
4. Screen away for a perimeter player and then cut toward the ball.

The following are rules for a double-post or 1–3–1 Passing Game:

1. The high-post player sets up ball side, and the low-post player sets up away from the ball.

2. When the high-post player receives the ball, the player quickly pivots, looks inside to the low post, then looks to the weak side. This is one of the tougher parts of the offense. When the high-post player receives the ball near the top of the circle and faces the basket, that player really is looking down the defense. The low-post player is in a fine one-on-one situation,

since it is difficult for defensive help to come from the wings. The high-post player can pass the ball to the inside to the low post, to the weak-side wing and let the wing pass it inside, pass back to the strong side, feed a cutter, or drive to the goal. Since the high-post player is in the middle of the court with the dribble alive, that player is in a choice offensive position, one that is tough to defense.

3. When the low post receives the ball, the low post looks to score first, to pass to the high-post player going down the lane second, and to a perimeter player third.

4. Take the ball to the goal and be conscious of drawing the foul by pump or head faking.

5. When the ball is passed to the high post, the low post player attempts to flash pivot as close to the goal as possible. The low-post player should receive the next pass every time if the defense allows it.

6. When the ball is passed to the low post, the high-post player cuts down the lane opposite the low post looking for a pass. This prevents the defensive player on the high post from helping on the low post.

Rebounding and Defensive Balance Rules

1. All players are designated either rebounders or defensive players once the shot is taken. The three best rebounders should always rebound. The point guard should always be responsible for backcourt defense. The second guard must be somewhat versatile and be able to change responsibilities from game to game. When playing against a real fast-breaking team, the second guard must stay back for defense. When playing against a more controlled opponent, the second guard must be ready to go to the offensive board.

2. Everyone is responsible for getting back on defense once the opponents have the ball. Though bigger players are designated rebounders, they still must feel a responsibility for getting back on defense.

3. When the ball is passed to the post area, designated rebounders must think REBOUND . . . designated defenders must think DEFENSE to stop the break. If they wait until the post player shoots before they move toward their responsibility, it will be too late.

Drills for Teaching the Passing Game Offense

A number of breakdown drills can be used to teach the offense. The type of drill depends somewhat on the type of formations selected for the passing game. Actual breakdown drills are shown in diagrams 15.2 through 15.7.

Though breakdown drills are very good in teaching players the basic fundamentals of the Passing Game and its options, the most effective method for teaching this offense is playing 5-on-5. In 5-on-5 play, players move as they have been taught to move in the breakdown drills. However, the 5-on-5 play develops the timing and cohesion necessary for all of the positions to blend together.

In playing 5-on-5, it is important to create a number of situations and use different restrictive rules to help teach the offense. For example, 5-on-5 practice may begin by not allowing a shot—instead counting the number of passes before the defense touches the ball. This teaches ball-handling, movement, and the rules of the offense. Another practice might require 10 passes before a shot. Other situations or restrictions for teaching the offense include the following:

1. Do not allow a shot until there has been a screen on the ball. In this situation, players must abide by the rule of making at least four passes before setting a screen on the ball. They could make more passes. However, they cannot shoot until they have created the ball-screen situation. And once they have created that situation, they do not automatically take a shot off it. Rather they can take the next good shot available.

2. Do not allow a shot until there has been a rear screen—either a screen away from the ball or a screen on the ball.

3. Do not allow a shot until a low-post off-ball screen has been set.

4. Play 5-on-5 with no dribbles allowed.

5. Set up a particular player. For example, assume that the player is being guarded by someone with four fouls. No one is allowed to shoot until the ball is given to that player in a low-post situation who attempts to score and draw the fifth foul or take advantage of the player in foul trouble refusing to play defense. Set up outside players as well as inside players.

6. No shot can be taken outside the lane.

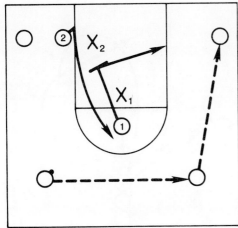

Diagram 15.2 *High-low post play breakdown drill.* Perimeter players pass the ball outside, while ① and ② screen for each other and attempt to score against X₁ and X₂. This drill is excellent tor teaching the passing game from the 1-3-1 formation.

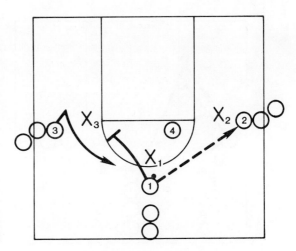

Diagram 15.3 *Perimeter Drill.* ①, ②, and ③ use passing game rules to attempt to score against X₁, X₂, and X₃. Post player ④ has no defense and cannot score but can receive passes and return pass to perimeter players. This drill is also good for teaching the 1-3-1 passing game.

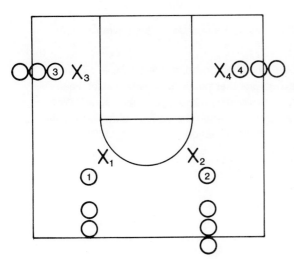

Diagram 15.4 *Perimeter play drill using four perimeter players.* This drill is good for teaching the single-post passing game.

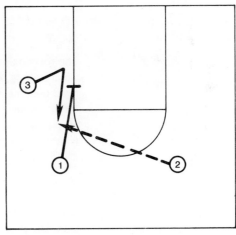

Diagram 15.5 *Receiving a screen and shooting drill.* ③ makes a V-cut and comes off screen set by ① for pass from ② and shot.

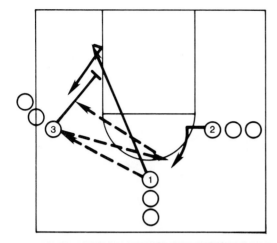 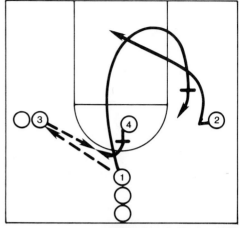

Diagram 15.6 *Passing game situation drill.* ① passes to ③ and cuts ballside. ③ passes to ② and sets screen for ①. ① receives pass for shot.

Diagram 15.7 *Passing game situation drill.* ① passes to ③ and cuts off post screen set by ④. ③ passes to ④ who may pass to ②, cutting off rear screen set by ①, or to ①.

Coaching Points

Several coaching points are very important in teaching the offense.

1. Regardless of the rules you select, keep them simple. Avoid complications.

2. The rules must be strictly enforced. If one player is allowed to violate a rule, expect another player to violate a rule. Then rules become rules no longer, but suggestions instead. Watch for violations carefully, and when they occur, blow the whistle, stop play, and correct the violation. Be consistent. Do it every time a rule is violated.

3. Teach shot selection. The team should be made to take good shots and thereby increase chances of winning. It is up to the coach to teach players what a good shot is. Remember, what is a good shot for one player may be a bad shot for another. Individual players must know in what situations they can best shoot, and it is up to the coach to teach them this. There is no place in the game, much less in the Passing Game offense, for the fall-away, off-balance "hope" shot.

4. Teach your players to move with a purpose. From time to time, blow your whistle and ask a player, "Why were you moving?" If players know you are going to stop and ask them, they will be more conscious of moving with a specific purpose in mind.

5. Run post play and perimeter play drills daily. Constant repetition is needed for good execution.

6. Stress off-ball fundamentals. Most players are well schooled in what to do if they have the basketball. But fewer players do a good job when they do not have the ball. Learning to move without the basketball is basic to the passing game. Screening, using screens, cutting, changing direction, and posting and releasing must be constantly stressed to develop good off-ball fundamentals.

Discussion Questions

1. What basic techniques are important in teaching the Passing Game?
2. What is the difference between a Passing Game with three perimeter players and one with four perimeter players? What are the advantages and disadvantages of each?
3. Can a team with a tall center use a 5-man Passing Game?
4. Are there any special rebounding problems with a Passing Game?
5. Why should ball-handling improve when using the Passing Game?
6. How does the Passing Game develop team play?
7. How does the Passing Game improve team defense?

Projects

1. By studying various reference materials, compile at least five drills for teaching the Passing Game other than those shown in this textbook.
2. Write a brief paper discussing the problems in teaching the Passing Game.
3. Interview a player who has played on a team using the Passing Game offense. Outline his or her likes and dislikes about the offense.

Suggested Readings

Fertig, Jack. "Man-to-Man Structured Motion Offense." *Scholastic Coach,* October 1977, pp. 46–50.

Foster, Bill. "Clemson's Passing Game." *Scholastic Coach,* November 1978, pp. 28ff.

Hankinson, *Progressions,* pp. 232–37.

Huckle, Bruce, "Continuous Unpredictable Motion Offense." *Scholastic Coach,* August 1979, pp. 58ff.

Korobov, Glen. "Motion Offense vs. the Zone." *Scholastic Coach,* August 1976, pp. 68–71.

———. "Stetson's Controlled 'Motion Offense' " *Scholastic Coach,* December 1975, pp. 40–44.

Loftus, John. "Motion Game Complementary Plays." *Scholastic Coach,* November 1977, pp. 36ff.

Potter, Dr. Glenn R. "Beat Pressure with a Six-area 'Passing Game' " *Scholastic Coach,* August 1978, pp. 80ff.

Stier, Wm. F. "Inside Motion Continuity Offense." *Scholastic Coach,* December 1978, pp. 22ff.

Tarkanian and Warren, *Winning Basketball,* pp. 110–16.

chapter sixteen

Zone Offense

A sound plan for attacking zone defenses is an important part of offensive preparation. All teams face a certain amount of zone defenses, and man-for-man attacks normally are ineffective against zone defenses.

Zone offense is probably more important to junior and senior high school teams than are methods of attacking man-for-man defense. This is simple because the great percentage of those teams employ the zone defense as their basic team defense. A high school team might prepare one of the better man-for-man offenses and be able to run it with precision, yet, they might find that they face only three or four man-for-man defenses during the entire season.

Zone defenses can be very difficult to penetrate, and a good zone attack pattern should be prepared and practiced well in advance to defeat the zone. Of course, the simplest method for defeating the zone is good outside shooting. If a team boasts shooters who can consistently score from 20 to 25 feet out, few zone defenses can defeat them. Unfortunately, few of us possess such shooters, and an attack must be ready that will penetrate the zone and obtain closer shots.

Zone Defense Attack Principles

Regardless of the type of zone defense you may face, certain basic zone defense attack principles should be observed in a team's zone offensive pattern:

1. Penetrate the seams or gaps of the zone. In other words, dribble penetrate between two defensive players, then pass to the open player (diag. 16.1).

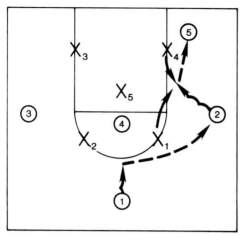
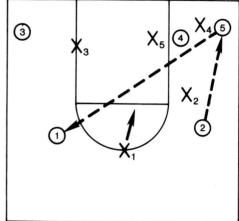

Diagram 16.1 This is an example of dribble penetration into the seams or gaps of a zone defense. ② dribbles between X₁ and X₄. As the defense converges, ② passes to ⑤.

Diagram 16.2 *An example of the "skip" pass.* ⑤ "skips" a pass to ② and passes to ① instead. This causes much movement by the defense and creates considerable problems to the defense.

2. Move the ball rapidly.
3. Minimize dribbling except when attacking the seams or gaps of the defense.
4. Play for the high percentage shot.
5. Develop offensive patience. The more patience, the more likely a defensive mistake.
6. Use ball fakes. Fake the pass in one direction, pass another. Fake the shot, pass.
7. Look to get the ball inside.
8. Assign definite rebounding responsibilities in order to obtain the second shot.
9. Pull the opponent's better rebounders away from the basket.
10. Use the skip pass (diag. 16.2). By skipping the closest pass receiver and passing to a player on the other side of the floor, the offense gives the zone defense more area to cover and opens up the zone for closer shots and better dribble penetration.
11. Attack areas guarded by weak defensive players.
12. Use the fast break to obtain shots before the zone can set up.
13. Control the ball when leading late in the game.

The Fast Break

The best method for getting the close shot against the zone defense is the fast break. To be strong, the zone defense must be able to set up around the basket, each player with an assigned area. By using fast-breaking tactics, the offense can get the ball downfloor and into a high percentage shooting area before the zone has time to organize. In addition to gaining more high percentage shots, offensive rebounding is stronger when shots are taken before the zone has formed.

Zone Attack Patterns

Since your team may not possess good outside shooting, and the fast break does not always materialize, you must prepare a set zone attack. Your attack may vary with the strengths of the offensive personnel and your particular coaching philosophy, but always direct your attacks at the weak areas of the zone.

Weak Areas of Zone Defenses

The weak areas of zone defenses vary with each type of zone. Diagrams 16.3 through 16.6 depict the weaknesses of the major types of zones being used in modern basketball.

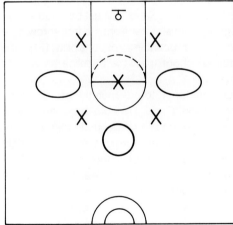

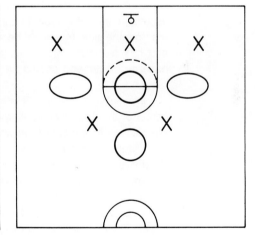

Diagram 16.3 Circles indicate major weak areas of a 2-1-2 zone defense.

Diagram 16.4 Circles indicate major weak areas of a 2-3 zone defense.

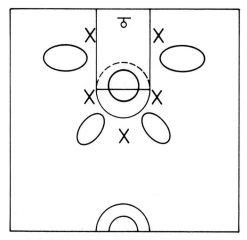

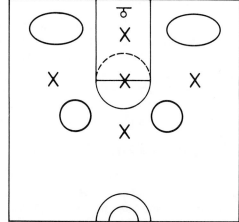

Diagram 16.5 Circles indicate major weak areas of a 1-2-2 zone defense.

Diagram 16.6 Circles indicate major weak areas of a 1-3-1 zone defense.

The 1-3-1 Attack

The most popular attack for the zone defense is the 1–3–1 attack. It is particularly effective against the 2–1–2 or "even-front" zone. Diagram 16.7 shows the basic formation for this attack. ① is the key ball-handler and must assume responsibility for directing the attack. ② and ③ must be good shooters from the side. ④ should be a good jump shooter from the free-throw area and has a major part of the offensive rebounding responsibility. ⑤ is the baseline player and should be able to shoot from the baseline as well as rebound.

In initiating the attack, it is important for ① to advance the ball down the center of the floor until meeting opposition. Once ① meets opposition, he or she passes to the side from where the defensive challenge is made.

Diagram 16.8 assumes the defensive challenge is made by the right defensive guard. Thus ① passes to ②. ④ and ⑤ move toward ② as shown. ② has several options. ② may shoot if unguarded, pass to either ④ or ⑤, or return pass to ①. If ② shoots, offensive rebounding responsibility is handled by ③, ④, and ⑤, with backcourt responsibility going to ①. The shooter, ②, remains in the area of the free-throw lane to take care of the long rebound or to prevent the defensive rebounders from making a quick pass-out to begin the fast break.

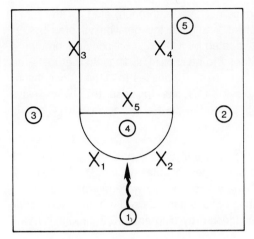

Diagram 16.7 *The basic formation for the 1-3-1 zone offense.* ① should be the key ball-handler, ② and ③ the better outside shooters, while ④ and ⑤ should be the better post scorers.

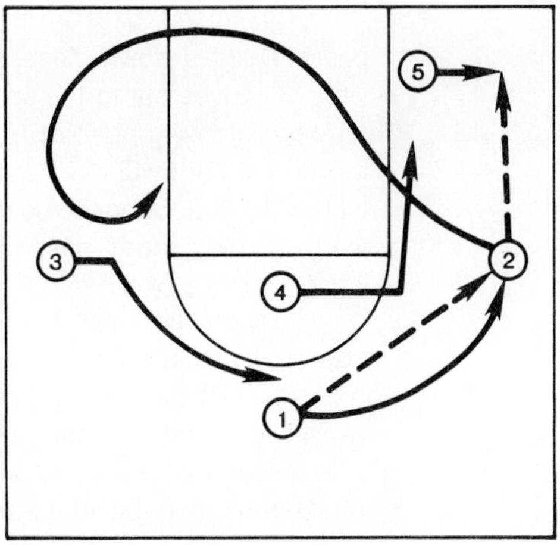

Diagram 16.8 *A 1-3-1 zone attack pattern.* ① advances down the center of the court. ① passes to ② who passes to ⑤ and cuts through. ④ cuts close behind ②. ⑤ passes to ④ or passes to ① filling spot vacated by ②.

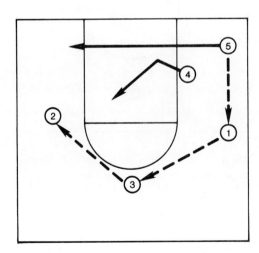

Diagram 16.8a *1-3-1 zone attack continuity.* ⑤ passes to ① and goes to opposite low block. ① passes to ③ who passes to ②. ② may shoot, pass to ⑤ low, or pass to ④ cutting into post area.

If ② passes to ⑤ on the baseline, ② cuts through, alert for the return pass. ④ slides down close behind ②, ① fills the position vacated by ②, while ③ moves out to the spot vacated by ①. ② continues on through to the opposite wing position. ⑤ looks to pass to ④ sliding into the post area behind the cut by ②. If this is not open, ⑤ passes to ① and goes immediately to the opposite low block. ① looks to pass to ③ who relays to ②. ② may shoot, pass to ⑤ at the low-post area, or pass to ④ cutting into the middle of the lane.

On the initial pass from ①, if ② does not elect to pass to ⑤ on the baseline, ② can return pass to ① who can quickly pass to ③. With quick movement of the ball, a good shot often is obtained for ③. If no shot is available, ③ has the same options that previously were available to ②.

A variety of plays and scoring options can be used with the 1–3–1 zone attack formation. Several are suggested by diagrams 16.9 through 16.14.

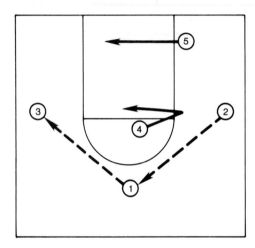 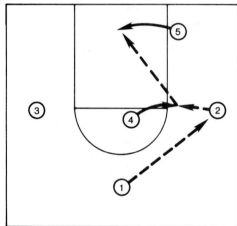

Diagram 16.9 If ② does not pass to ⑤ on baseline, ② can return pass to ① who quickly passes to ③ for a possible shot. If ③ does not shoot, ③ has the same options previously open to ② —a pass to either ④ or ⑤ or a return pass to ①.

Diagram 16.10 This shows an option open to ④ when receiving a pass from ②.

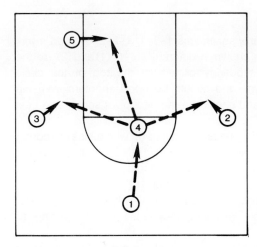

Diagram 16.11 This shows options open to (4) when receiving a pass from (1).

Diagram 16.12 Some teams like to cut player (2) through when the pass is made to (5), but like for (1) to remain at the top of the circle. In this case, (4) cuts to position vacated by (2), and (3) cuts to position vacated by (4).

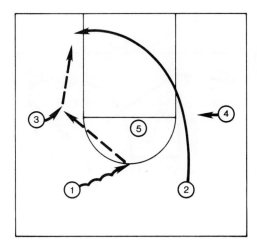

Diagram 16.13 *Cutting into the 1-3-1 attack from a single-post set-up.* (2) *should be the better shooter of the guards, since* (2) *will often be open for a shot on the baseline.*

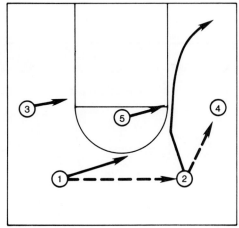

Diagram 16.14 *Another method for cutting into the 1-3-1 attack from a single-post set-up.*

The 2-1-2 Attack

The 2-1-2 attack is used primarily against the 1-3-1, 1-2-2, or "odd-front" zones. The attack formation is shown in diagram 16.15. ① and ② are the guards and should possess shooting ability from the top of the circle area. ③ and ④ are the forwards and should be good shooters from the corner areas. ⑤ is the center and should be the best pivot scorer and best offensive rebounder.

In initiating the attack, guard ① passes to guard ② who passes to corner player ④. As ④ receives the ball in the corner, ⑤ slides to the baseline, while off-corner player ③ cuts to the position vacated by ⑤. ④ may shoot, pass to ⑤ or ③ for a shot, or return pass to guard ②. If ④ return passes to ②, ② quickly looks for an opening for a pass to ③. If no opening exists, a quick return pass to corner player ④ may result in an opening to either ③ or ⑤.

If ② elects to pass to guard ①, center ⑤ slides out to the left corner position to receive a pass from ①. As ⑤ receives the pass, forward ③ at the free-throw line assumes the responsibility originally held by ⑤ and slides to the baseline. ④ cuts into the free-throw area to the position vacated by ③. The continuity is shown in diagrams 16.16 and 16.17.

Offensive and defensive responsibilities are easily delegated. Players ③, ④, and ⑤ are responsible for offensive rebounding, while ① and ② are responsible for defensive balance. If the opponents are a fast-breaking team, either ① or ② should press outlet pass receivers.

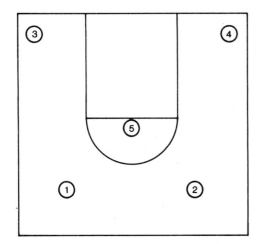

Diagram 16.15 *The basic 2-1-2 zone attack formation.*

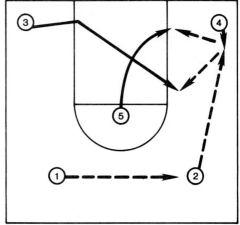

Diagram 16.16 *The 2-1-2 zone offense.* As ② passes to ④, ⑤ slides to the baseline, and ③ fills spot vacated by ⑤. ④ may pass to ③, ⑤, or return pass to ②.

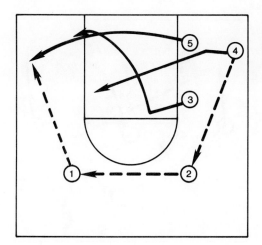

Diagram 16.17 *The 2-1-2 attack continuity.*
②passes to ①who passes to ⑤on the baseline. ③rolls low, and ④cuts into the position vacated by ③.

Screening the Zone

Many coaches have developed screening plays that can be used successfully against zone defenses. Screens are established to prevent defensive players from sliding to cover opponents in their respective zone areas. Diagrams 16.18 through 16.20 illustrate screen plays that have been found effective against zone defenses.

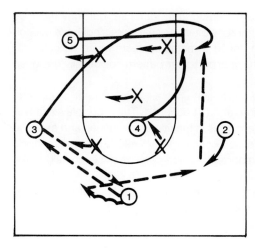

Diagram 16.18 *The use of a double-screen against a zone.* ①passes to ③, causing the zone to shift left. ③return passes to ① as ④ and ⑤ set double-screen. ① dribbles left, then passes to ②who passes to ③ for shot behind double-screen.

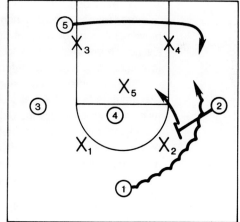

Diagram 16.19 *The use of a single screen against a zone.* ①dribbles around screen set by ②. ①may have a shot or a pass to ②or ⑤, dependent upon the movement by the rear zone defenders.

Diagram 16.20 *Another example of screening the zone.* (1) *dribbles right as* (2) *and* (3) *slide to baseline.* (5) *sets screen for* (3). (1) *makes long "skip" pass to* (3) *for shot. If X₃ rushes hard to prevent shot,* (3) *may pass inside to* (5) *posting.*

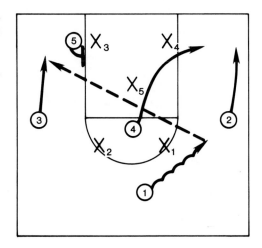

Attacking the Match-up Zone Defense

The match-up zone defense combines both zone and man-for-man principles. As in a regular zone defense, defensive players are assigned areas to guard; however, they must guard an opponent in the area man-for-man. If no opponent is in their area, they must move to another area. All of their movements and adjustments are guided by a set of rules designed to combat offensive maneuvers.

Teams seldom may face a match-up zone defense, but they must be prepared for one. A team's normal zone offense usually does not have enough movement, cuts, or screens to cause a match-up team much difficulty adjusting. Therefore it is wise to have a particular pattern specifically designed to combat the match-up defense.

Key principles in attacking the match-up are (1) movement of players, (2) attempts to get the ball inside, and (3) patience. The more player movement, the more difficulty the defense has in making adjustments, and as these adjustments are made, the defense becomes vulnerable to passes to inside players. Patience is extremely important, for the defense will eventually make a mistake if the offense has sufficient patience.

An effective match-up offense combining movement of players, screening, and inside posting is shown in diagrams 16.21 and 16.22.

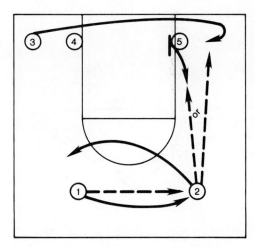

Diagram 16.21 *Match-up zone attack.* ① passes to ② who passes to ③ cutting off screen by ⑤, or to ⑤ if defense makes a mistake in adjusting. ② and ① exchange positions.

Diagram 16.22 *Match-up zone attack continuity.* If ③ does not shoot, ③ passes to ① and cuts along baseline off screen set by ④. ① passes to ② who will pass to ③ or ④, dependent on the adjustment by the defense.

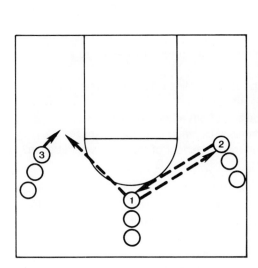

Diagram 16.23 *"Step-up" zone shooting drill.* As ① passes to ②, ③ steps closer to basket. ② return passes to ① who passes to ③ for jump shot. Players rotate lines.

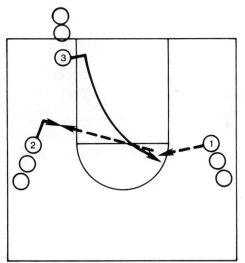

Diagram 16.24 *Post reverse-pass zone shooting drill.* ③ cuts to high post for pass from ①, pivots to face basket, then passes to ② for shot. Only post players work at the ③ line, with perimeter shooters working at ① and ②. The drill is run from both sides of the court.

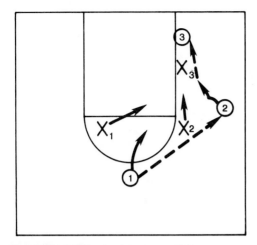 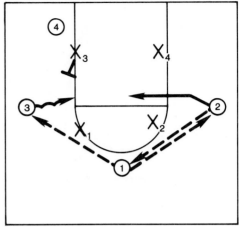

Diagram 16.25 *Strongside zone drill.* **Three offensive players work against three defensive players. Object of drill is for ② to penetrate and practice passing to post player ③ who then makes scoring move.**

Diagram 16.26 *Gap penetration zone drill.* **Four offensive players work against four defensive players. Offense moves ball, and players practice dribbling into gaps and passing to players spotting up for shot.**

Discussion Questions

1. How much practice time should be spent on zone offense?
2. Should one zone offense be used for all types of zone defenses?
3. How are rebounding responsibilities different in zone offenses and man-for-man offenses?
4. Discuss defensive balance from a zone offense.
5. How important is offensive patience to a zone offense?
6. Which is more important, movement of the ball or penetration?

Projects

1. By studying various reference materials, diagram a pattern for attacking an even-front zone. An odd-front zone.
2. Diagram three breakdown drills for teaching zone offense.
3. Write a brief paper on rebounding from a zone offense.
4. Select a zone offense and write a brief paper on the qualifications of each position.
5. Interview a local coach in regard to his or her philosophy on movement against a zone defense.

Suggested Readings

Davis, Dr. Tom. "Attacking the 2–3 Zone." *Pro-Keds Coaches Digest,* 1980, pp. 2–3.

Ebert and Cheatum, *Basketball,* pp. 124–36.

Froelich, Clyde W. "Two-Guard Tandem Post Vs. The Diamond and One." *Scholastic Coach,* November 1975, pp. 52–53.

Hankinson, *Progressions,* pp. 243–51.

Kitchens, Rich. " 'Revolver' Zone Offense." *Scholastic Coach,* October 1975, pp. 68ff.

Kornblith, Fred. "Triangulating vs. the Zone Defense." *Scholastic Coach,* October 1978, pp. 57ff.

Lehr, Robert E. "Combatting the Odd Front Zone Defenses." *Pro-Keds Coaches Digest,* 1980, p. 11.

Munoz, Hector. "Getting the High Percentage Shot Vs. The Zone." *Scholastic Coach,* December, pp. 28ff.

Nagel, Jack. "Shallow Guard Zone Attack." *Scholastic Coach,* December 1977, pp. 22ff.

Richards, Jack. *Attacking Zone Defenses in Basketball.* West Nyack, N.Y.: Parker Publishing, 1977.

Robinson, Jim. "Beating the 2–3 Zone." *Scholastic Coach,* November 1977, pp. 42ff.

Sheridan, Bill. "Beating the Wide 1–3–1 with a 1–4." *Scholastic Coach,* October 1975, p. 49.

Staak, Bob. "All-Purpose Rotation Zone Offense." *Scholastic Coach,* January 1978, pp. 108ff.

Stewart and Scholz, *Complete Program,* pp. 84–92.

Swepston, Greg. "Mop the Zone Defense." *Scholastic Coach,* December 1975, pp. 32ff.

Tarkanian and Warren, *Winning Basketball,* pp. 137–67.

Wooden, *Modern Basketball,* pp. 182–87.

chapter seventeen

The Fast-Break Offense

A majority of teams in present-day basketball use some type of fast break in their offensive plans. Some go to the extreme, earning themselves the label of "race horse" teams—those who run every time they get ball possession. Most teams, however, release their fast break only when the opportunity presents itself favorably. This latter type probably is more sound, although some great teams have worn the race horse label.

The primary problem with many fast-breaking teams is that, in their eagerness to fast break, they tend to let up on defense. They want the opponent to shoot quickly so they can get the ball. These teams are very susceptible to the opponent who plays ball control. The fast-breaking team's lack of defense usually gives the ball-controlling opponents easy shots, and, when they do get the ball, they may make ball-handling mistakes in their eagerness to run. Actually, *the better a team plays defense, the better their fast break should be.*

Team Qualities Necessary for the Fast Break

A team must have certain qualities for successful use of the fast break:

1. *Rebounding strength.* The majority of fast-break opportunities arise from missed shot attempts, and the ability to control the defensive board greatly increases the number of fast-break opportunities.
2. *Speed.* At least three players with good speed are necessary.
3. *Good ball-handling.* A team must have good ball-handling, or fast play usually results in more lost balls and bad passes than scores.

Figure 17.1 The key to the fast break is the speed with which the outlet pass is made after gaining possession of the ball. Here, the rebounder is looking for an outlet pass receiver before he hits the floor.

4. *Physical condition.* Excellent physical conditioning is necessary for a fast-breaking game.

When to Fast Break

Fast-breaking opportunities may be found after the following situations:

1. A missed field goal or free throw by the opponents.
2. A successful field goal or free throw by the opponents.
3. A loose ball or interception of a pass.
4. A jump-ball situation.

Fast-Break Technique After Rebound

The basic fast-break technique after rebounding a missed shot attempt involves three major phases:

1.   The release
2.   Filling the lanes
3.   The scoring move

The Release

The key to the fast break is the speed with which the outlet pass is made after gaining possession of the ball. Every second's delay gives the defense more opportunity to retreat into defensive position. If the player can rebound the ball and immediately pass it out to waiting guards, the break has an excellent chance of developing.

Two conditions are essential for the pass to be made quickly.

1.   The rebounder must immediately look for an outlet pass receiver.

2.   A receiver must be in the proper outlet position. This means that at least one of the guards must be near the sideline, approximately even with the top of the circle. This is often the hardest essential to make happen.

The question may arise as to why the outlet pass receivers should be near the sideline in preference to the center of the court. The answer is simply that the player responsible for the defensive balance of the opponents usually is at the center of the court and the other defenders are retreating down the center. Outlet passes to the center of the court are more susceptible to interception than are passes to the sideline.

Filling the Lanes

Diagram 17.1 divides the court into three lanes. Since the majority of fast-break opportunities involve 3-on-2 or 3-on-1 situations, it is important for an offensive player to cut into each of the three lanes. Start filling these lanes as soon as you get the ball. The players not rebounding the ball or in outlet pass position immediately begin breaking downfloor in an attempt to fill the lanes. The culmination of filling the lanes comes after the outlet pass receiver has taken the ball and either passed or dribbled to the middle lane. The lanes should be filled by the time the ball gets to midcourt or shortly thereafter.

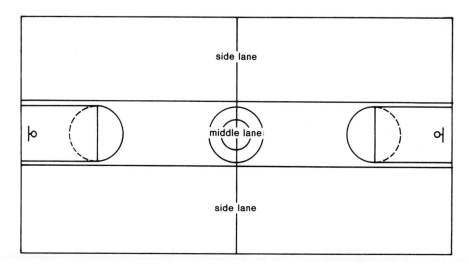

Diagram 17.1 *The three lanes to be filled on the 3-on-1 or 3-on-2 fast-break situation.*

The Scoring Move

As mentioned above, the ball is taken to the middle lane where passing opportunities to the left and right are available. If the ball is kept in one of the side lanes, a passing opportunity is eliminated.

Once the ball reaches the middle lane, keep it there and advance to the free-throw line by the way of a dribble. The dribbler usually meets opposition at the free-throw line. When this happens, the dribbler stops and passes to a teammate in a side lane cutting for the basket.

The opposition uses either the vertical or horizontal defense if it is a 3-on-2 situation. If the defense is vertical, pass the ball to the side lane. If the defense is horizontal, the clever dribbler may have an opportunity to drive in for an easy lay-up.

The Trailer

The use of a trailer on the break increases scoring potential. If the ball is passed to the side lane and the defense adjusts quickly, a trailer cutting to the basket may be open for a pass and a subsequent lay-up. Diagram 17.2 gives a recommended pattern for a fast break after a rebound and includes the use of the trailer when the initial scoring move is stopped.

The 2-on-1 Situation

The 2-on-1 situation happens less often than the 3-on-2 and involves different cutting paths. The two offensive players advance the ball in the path shown by diagram 17.3, with neither player going to the middle. Once the ball has

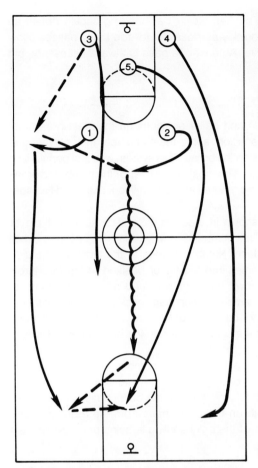

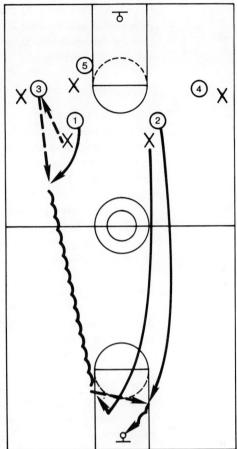

Diagram 17.2 *The fast break after a rebound.* As ③ takes the rebound, ④ and ⑤ start down opposite sidelines to fill the lanes. ① and ② have cut to outlet pass positions. ③ passes out to ① who passes to ② in the middle lane. ② advances the ball to the free-throw line area, with ④ and ① filling the side lanes. ⑤ becomes the trailer when ④ fills the side lane ahead of ⑤. Upon meeting opposition, ② passes to ① for a possible shot. When the defense rushes to prevent the shot, ① passes to the trailer, ⑤. The rebounder, ③, is responsible for defensive balance.

Diagram 17.3 *The 2-on-1 situation.* This may occur after numerous situations. Here, ③ makes an interception and passes out to ①. When ① realizes a 2-on-1 situation is available, ① drives hard toward the basket but does not go to the middle of the court. When ① meets defensive opposition, ① passes to ② for the shot. The 2-on-1 situation should receive regular drill practice.

been advanced close to the basket, clever ball-handling should obtain an easy shot. Take the shot as quickly as possible, for too many passes allow time for defensive help to arrive. At least one pass is always necessary, but seldom more than two.

The Numbered Fast Break

While most teams fill the lanes and trailer positions on their fast break with the first players who get into position, some teams number their players and assign specific lanes and areas on the break. This system was first popularized by Marshall University years ago. The most noted user of the numbered break today has been Sonny Allen in his tenures at Old Dominion, SMU, and Nevada-Reno.

The numbered break is shown in diagram 17.4. The number 1 player always receives the outlet pass. Number 2 always fills the right lane, while number 3 always fills the left lane. Number 4 goes to the block on the side of the ball, while number 5 comes into the trailer position at the free-throw line. If the ball is advanced down the right side and no shot is obtained, number 2 can pass back to number 1 who can quickly pass to number 5 for a shot. If number 5 does not have a shot, number 5 can look to number 3 in the left lane or to number 4 inside. Of course, the ball can be advanced down either sideline.

There is a definite advantage in having the number 1 player handle the outlet pass every time. The best ball-handler on the team can be designated as this pass receiver. Although this might make the outlet pass a little slower, it cuts down on turnovers both on the outlet pass from the rebounder and on the break itself, since most of the ball handling is being done by the best ball-handler.

Fast-Break Technique After Successful Field Goal or Free Throw

The technique for breaking after a successful field goal or free throw by the opponents is quite different from the ordinary rebound fast-break situation. The ball must be taken out-of-bounds, thus allowing more time for the defense to retreat. The defensive retreat is primarily made down the middle of the court, and therefore the ball can be passed down the sidelines. The ball must be taken out of bounds hurriedly, passed in to a waiting receiver, and advanced rapidly. Theoretically, the defense should be in position to prevent such a break opportunity. However, when forwards hustle down the sideline they often find themselves ahead of their respective defensive opponents who often retreat to defensive position at three-quarter speed. Diagram 17.5 illustrates an effective technique for breaking after either a successful field goal or free throw.

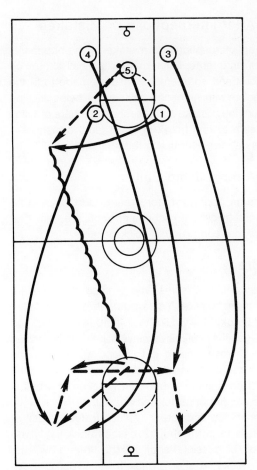

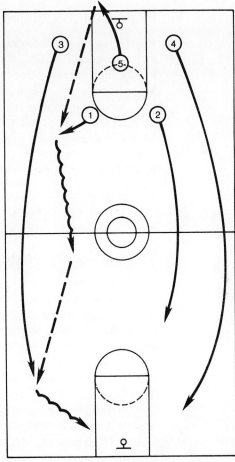

Diagram 17.4 *The numbered fast break.* The outlet pass always goes to the number 1 player. The number 2 player always fills the right lane, and the number 3 player always fills the left lane. The number 4 player always goes to the block on the side of the ball, and the number 5 player always comes into the trailer position at the free-throw line.

Diagram 17.5 *Fast break pattern after successful field goal by opponents.* As ball goes through net, ⑤ quickly takes ball out-of-bounds, while ③ and ④ sprint down the sidelines. ⑤ passes to ① who drives hard downcourt passing to ③ if ③ is open. If ③ is not open, ① may pass to ② who may pass to ④. This pattern can also be used successfully after successful free-throw attempts by opponents.

Fast-Break Technique After Interceptions or Mistakes

Reaction is the key to turning an interception or a mistake by the opponents into a successful fast break. If an interception is made, the ball should be advanced immediately downcourt and an attempt should be made to fill the lanes. Using 5-on-5 drills in practice with intentional bad passes helps develop the quick reaction needed to turn the mistake into a score. Adequate practice on filling the lanes allows a team to fast break in an organized manner—whether ball possession comes after a rebound or an interception.

Fast-Break Technique After a Jump Ball

The jump-ball situation creates an opportunity for prearranged plays to be run to advance the ball downcourt quickly into scoring position. Diagram 17.6 and 17.7 show two such plays that can produce quick baskets.

The Secondary Fast Break

Most fast-breaking teams today count on some type of secondary break if the primary fast break does not materialize. Years ago, when teams failed to get a quick shot on the fast break, they would back the ball back out and set up. This enabled them to get their offensive players into an organized position, but it also gave the defense time to get organized as well. The secondary break gets the players into an organized position quickly at the end of a primary fast break. If no primary break shot is taken, the ball is moved quickly, and immediate scoring opportunities are sought.

The numbered break diagrammed in diagram 17.4 illustrates the use of a secondary break. When ② fails to get a shot, ② passes back to ① who looks to ④ inside or to ⑤ for a possible shot at the free-throw line. When ⑤ receives the pass, ⑤ looks to shoot, pass to ④ inside, or pass to ③ on the baseline. If ③ receives the ball, ③ may have a shot or a pass to ④. All of this action is referred to as the secondary portion of the fast break. Diagram 17.8 and 17.9 show two other plays that can be used in secondary action.

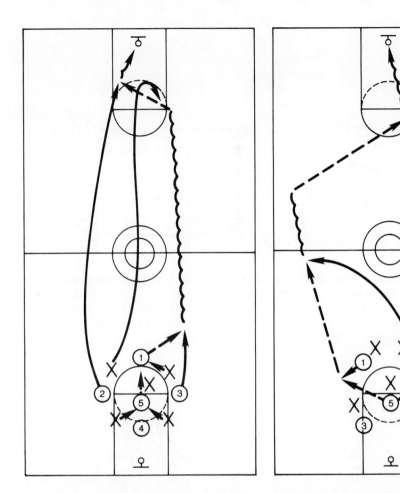

Diagram 17.6 *A fast break opportunity from a jump-ball situation using the "diamond" jump formation.* ⑤ taps to ①. *On the tap,* ② *and* ③ *break downcourt.* ③ *receives pass from* ① *and a 2-on-1 situation is often obtained. This play should be attempted only when control of the tap is virtually certain.*

Diagram 17.7 *A fast-break opportunity from a jump-ball situation using the "box" jump formation.* ⑤ taps to ① *and cuts downcourt, as* ② *cuts to the sideline at midcourt.* ① *passes to* ② *who passes to* ⑤ *for the scoring attempt. This play is effective because the opponent jumping with* ⑤ *usually looks to see where the ball is tapped, allowing* ⑤ *to get ahead on the break downcourt.*

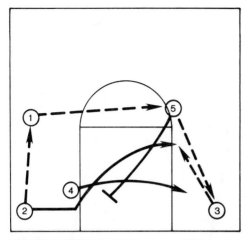

Diagram 17.8 *Secondary-break action at the end of a fast-break attempt.* If ② does not have a shot, ② passes to ① who relays to ⑤. ⑤ passes to ③ and sets screen for ②. ③ can pass to either ② or ④ for shot.

Diagram 17.9 *Secondary-break action at the end of a fast-break attempt.* ② passes to ① who passes to ⑤. ⑤ can pass to ② cutting off screen set by ③, or to ④ in the post area.

Fast-Break Drills

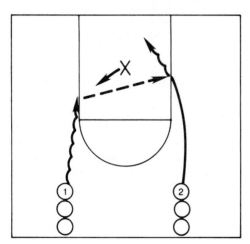

Diagram 17.10 *The frontcourt phase of the 2-on-1 situation.* ① advances the ball until challenged by defense, then passes to ② for shot attempt or return pass. Offensive players go to ends of lines. Change defensive player often to allow each player to practice the defensive phase of the 2-on-1 situation.

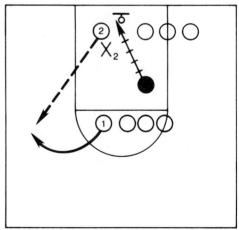

Diagram 17.11 This is an outlet pass drill used to teach players to make the outlet pass quickly and to afford practice in making the pass by an opponent. The coach attempts a shot. ② rebounds and passes by X_2 to ①, who has cut to outlet pass position. ② goes to defense, and X_2 goes to end of rebounding line. ① goes to end of outlet pass line.

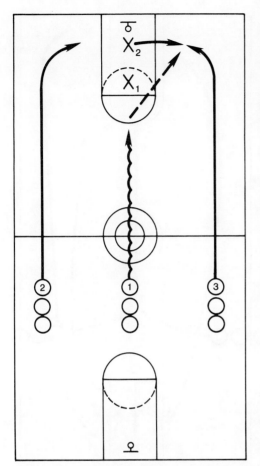

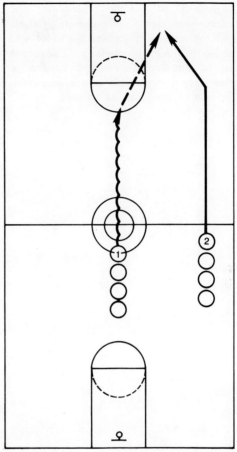

Diagram 17.12 *3-on-2 drill.* ① advances the ball until meeting opposition. ① passes to ③ who may shoot, pass to ②, or pass back to ①. Players rotate lines, and the defense is changed often.

Diagram 17.13 This is a drill designed to teach the pass and angle cut for a fast-break lay-up. ① drives to free-throw area and passes to ② driving for basket. Use two basketballs. As ② shoots, the next two players proceed toward basket.

Diagram 17.14 *Full-court fast-break drill.*
Coach shoots ball. As ② rebounds, ① starts
down left sideline. ② passes out to ④ who
passes to ③ in the middle lane. ③ advances
ball to free-throw area and passes to
either ① or ④ in the side lanes. Rebounder,
②, hustles downcourt as a trailer.

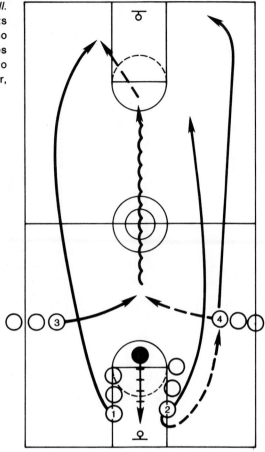

Discussion Questions

1. Can a team of small players fast break effectively?
2. Which is more important in a successful fast break, speed or reaction?
3. Can a controlled offense blend with a fast break?
4. Discuss the differences between the freelance type of fast break and the numbered fast break.
5. Should the freelance type of fast break result in more scoring than the numbered fast break?

Projects

1. Compile a list of advantages and disadvantages of the fast break.
2. Diagram at least five fast-break drills.
3. Teach a fast-break drill to the class.
4. Study a game film and write a critique on a selected team's fast-break methods. Include in your critique the number of fast-break opportunities, number of scores, and number of turnovers, and ascertain whether or not the fast break was an advantage or disadvantage.

Suggested Readings

Ebert and Cheatum, *Basketball,* pp. 137–39.

Gilbert, Dale A. "Quick Transitions Make A Difference." *Scholastic Coach,* December 1977, p. 34ff.

Hankinson, *Progressions,* pp. 200–12

Harter, Dick. "Oregon's Fast Break." *Scholastic Coach,* December 1975, p. 20ff.

Russo, Rich, "Organizing the Consistent Fast Break." *Athletic Journal,* October 1971, p. 8.

Stewart and Scholz, *Complete Program,* pp. 106–30.

Tarkanian and Warren, *Winning Basketball,* pp. 56–72.

Weinstein, Paul. "Fast Breaking Off a Free Throw." *Scholastic Coach,* November 1979, p. 54ff.

Wooden, *Modern Basketball,* pp. 153–67.

Yow, Kay, and Finch, Nora Lynn. "Developing the Transition Game." *Pro-Keds Coaches Digest,* 1980, pp. 34–37.

chapter eighteen

Attacking Pressing Defenses

One of the many improvements in modern basketball has been the rapid strides made by pressing defenses. Not only have the man-for-man pressing defenses become more effective, but the various types of zone presses have become popular as well. In addition, varying positions of pick up—full-court, three-quarter-court, and half-court—are used extensively. The sound basketball team must be prepared to meet all types of pressing defenses.

Scoring Is the Primary Objective

A common mistake many teams make when facing a pressing defense is failing to attack it. Many times their only objective is advancing the ball past the midcourt line and setting up their offense. However, the larger area the defense has to cover, the weaker that defense should be—*if attacked properly*. The primary objective is to *score*, not just to advance the ball past midcourt. If the objective is scoring, then the offense should attack the defense—pass and cut, screen and go for the basket, get the 3-on-2 situation or better the 2-on-1. In general, be a constant scoring threat and the effectiveness of the press will be reduced.

Objective May Vary with Time Remaining

The objective to score and the resulting plan of attack may change depending on the stage of the game and the score. If the press is faced early in the game, it is obvious that the offense must continue to score. If the offense has an 8- or 10-point lead and 5 or 6 minutes to play, the primary objective must still be to score. Failure to do so and a few ball-handling mistakes may lead to defeat. However, with a small lead and little time remaining, game strategy may dictate a freeze or a stall. In such situations, the primary objective may be to advance the ball past midcourt and go into a stall or freeze pattern.

Attack plays may be modified according to the situation. If the objective is to score, screens and crosses on the ball can be sound moves. Although double-team opportunities are presented to the defense, the screens create situations that more often result in scoring plays. When the objective is simply to advance the ball downcourt and protect a small lead late in the game, screens and crosses on the ball are unsound, because the defense must not be given a chance for the double-team situation.

Press-Attack Formations

A number of different formations can be used for attacking the various types of pressing defenses, and some of these formations are diagrammed in this chapter. The same basic formation is recommended for attacking the zone press as for the man-for-man press, or a team may run into considerable difficulty when facing one of the smarter opponents who continually change from one type of press to another.

Although the basic *formation* is the same, the basic *principles* vary. As a general rule, the dribble can be an effective weapon against a man-for-man press, whereas the zone press is best attacked by sharp passing.

Full-Court Man-for-Man Press Attack

The attack for the man-for-man full-court press can be divided into three phases:

1. The throw-in from out of bounds
2. Midcourt advancement
3. Frontcourt scoring moves

The Throw-in

Most teams using the full-court man-for-man press attempt to prevent the ball from coming inbounds. Consequently, it is imperative for a team to have set plans for making the throw-in successfully.

Diagrams 18.1 through 18.5 show several methods for making the throw-in. In diagram 18.1, one player, quick and a good ball-handler, is positioned in bounds near the free-throw line from where a cut may be made in any of several directions. This player is responsible for making the fakes and cuts needed to get free for the throw-in. It is important that the offensive manuever begin near the center of the backcourt so a wide choice of cutting directions are available. Should the cut begin from the near sideline, the choice of directions would be reduced greatly.

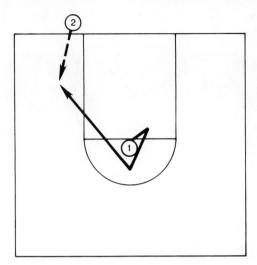

Diagram 18.1 *The in-bounds throw-in.* ① may be positioned at the free-throw line where fakes and cuts may be used to get open. ① should be a fast player and good ball-handler.

Diagram 18.2 *The use of the screen-and-roll in making the throw-in.* ① sets a screen for ③ and rolls out toward ball as ③ cuts by. If defense switches, ① should be open.

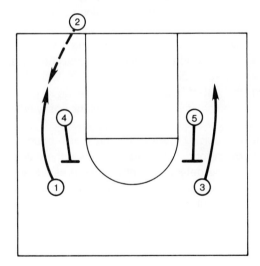

Diagram 18.3 *The use of rear screens in making the throw-in.* ④ and ⑤ set screens for ① and ③, who cut toward ball for throw-in.

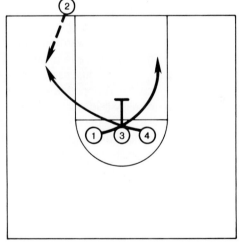

Diagram 18.4 *The use of a three-player alignment for the throw-in.* ③ steps forward to form screen. ① and ④ criss-cross off ③, with ① cutting first. A variety of screens and cuts may be used off this set-up.

Diagram 18.5 ① may cut to an out-of-bounds position, receive a pass along the endline from ② , and return pass to ② . It is important to remember that the ball must be in-bounded within five seconds.

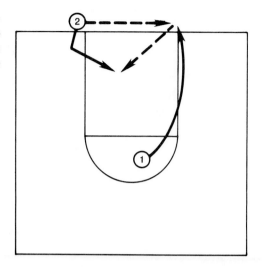

Diagram 18.2 shows the use of a two-player screen-and-roll maneuver for the throw-in, while diagram 18.3 illustrates the use of a rear screen to free pass receivers. Diagram 18.4 depicts a three-player alignment which allows a variety of screens and cuts. In diagram 18.5, the player in bounds simply steps out of bounds, takes an out-of-bounds pass along the endline from the initial out-of-bounds player, ① , and either return passes to ① cutting up the middle or to a teammate cutting from the frontcourt. This can be an effective throw-in technique, but it is important to remember that the pass must be made in bounds within five seconds.

For a successful throw-in, the out-of-bounds player must be a good passer. A poor passer in this situation can make the opponent the costly gifts of easy field goals.

The coach must determine how quickly to make the throw-in in bounds. In general, the more of a set throw-in formation used, the slower the ball is in-bounded, and the easier it is for the defense to set up their press. Many teams use a rebounder near the basket to take the ball out quickly after a score and make a fast throw-in without setting up a particular formation. Teams who can take the ball out quickly and use the threat of a full-court pass are very difficult to press.

Midcourt Advancement

Most teams advance the ball against the full-court man-for-man press by using one of their better dribblers. How quickly this advancement is made is determined by the position of the defensive player when the pass is received. If the defensive player maintains good defensive position between the pass receiver and the opposite basket, the pass receiver should pause for a second

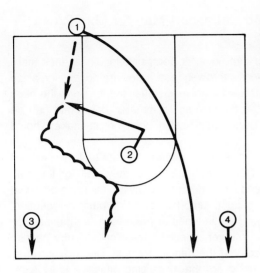

Diagram 18.6 *Clearing the floor to allow the good dribbler to advance the ball downcourt.* As ②receives the throw-in, ①cuts hard downcourt to clear the backcourt area and allow the dribbler to use any path needed in advancing the ball downcourt.

or so to give teammates an opportunity to clear out of the way. The pass receiver can then advance the ball downcourt by dribbling and can initiate the team offense as quickly as possible. However, if in an effort to steal the basketball the defensive player gets out of position, the pass receiver advances the ball at full speed down the middle of the court looking for the outnumbered offensive situation similar to a fast break.

Occasionally a team's best ball-handler is overmatched by the quickness of the defensive opponent. In this case, a very good strategic manuever is to bring a ball-handling forward or center downcourt to receive the ball, allowing this taller player to advance the ball downcourt. Defensive forwards and centers are seldom excellent full-court pressers in the one-on-one situation.

Frontcourt Scoring Moves

Whether or not the offense looks for a good scoring opportunity once the ball has been advanced to the frontcourt depends on whether or not an outnumbering offensive situation exists. If, as the ball is being advanced downcourt, all five defensive players have maintained good positions on their respective opponents, the best offensive method simply is to go into your regular offensive patterns. However, if one or more of the defensive players has gotten out of defensive position, an outnumbering situation exists, and scoring moves similar to the fast break should be attempted as quickly as possible. As a general rule, a team has far less outnumbered situations when attacking the man-for-man press than they have when attacking the zone press.

Three-Quarter-Court and Half-Court Man-for-Man Press Attack

When teams pick up at either three-quarter court or midcourt in their man-for-man press defense, no specific throw-in techniques are necessary, since no challenge is made on the throw-in. However, after the throw-in, the pass receiver should turn to face the defense so teammates downcourt can be seen and the defense read. The team's best dribbler or playmaker should be the pass receiver.

Teams using these pressing defenses accept the fact that they will not be able to steal the ball from the dribbler. Instead, they wait for the ball-handler to pick up the dribble and then attempt to deny a pass to an offensive teammate, hoping to get a 5-second jump-ball count, a pass interception, or a throw-away. When attacking these types of presses, a team uses their regular man-for-man offense. However, special moves called entry passes should be practiced daily to combat the denial attempts. Denial techniques have become so good in recent years that practicing offensive entry techniques only once or twice a week is not sufficient. Daily practice develops skill against these defenses and enables a team to take advantage of the overplay or denial attempts by the defense.

Diagrams 18.7 through 18.10 show some particular entry techniques that have been used from various offensive alignments. These techniques must be initiated before the ball-handler dribbles into the passing area and the dribble is picked up. Most entry techniques begin about the time the ball-handler reaches the center line. This is termed "early offense." If offensive players wait until the ball-handler has picked up the dribble to begin their offensive entry techniques, the denial tactics cause them far more difficulty.

Zone Press Attack

Full-Court 1-2-1-1 Attack

The full-court 1-2-1-1 attack is the most commonly used full-court zone press. Most teams place one of their taller players on the throw-in player to discourage the long downcourt pass. The other defensive players play their specific areas with the intent of making the throw-in come near the endline and near the corner where a double-team situation can be established. In fact, the success of this type of zone press depends a great deal upon the defense's ability to force the ball-handler into a double-team situation near the corner of the court. Therefore the offensive player receiving the in-bounds pass should make every effort to cut into position to receive it as far away from the corner as possible.

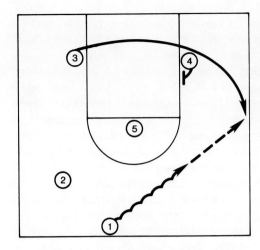

Diagram 18.7 *An entry technique against pressure.* ③ *cuts off screen set by* ④ *to receive the pass at the forward position from* ① .

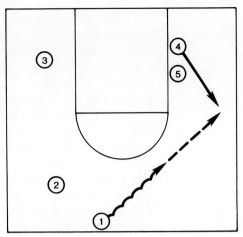

Diagram 18.8 *An entry technique.* ④ *and* ⑤ *double-stack.* ④ *pops out of the stack for the pass from* ① .

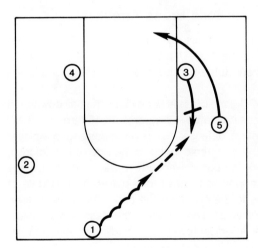

Diagram 18.9 *An entry technique.* ③ *sets rear screen for cutter* ⑤ *. Defender on* ③ *usually gives defensive help on* ⑤ *, leaving* ③ *free for an entry pass.*

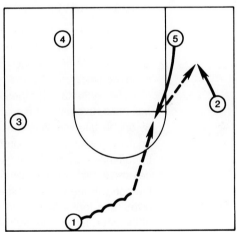

Diagram 18.10 *Using a flash-post and backdoor play as an entry technique.* ① *passes to* ⑤ *flashing to the high post.* ⑤ *looks to pass to* ② *cutting backdoor.*

There are varying patterns for advancing the ball to midcourt and for frontcourt scoring. Regardless of what pattern a coach might select, techniques for advancing the ball must be centered around sharp passing, with a minimum of dribbling. Dribbling into the double-team situation is unsound and results in lost balls and jump-ball situations. As the ball is received inbounds, the pass receiver turns and faces the defense. As defensive players advance to double-team, the pass receiver makes a sharp, crisp pass to a teammate. If possible, make this pass just before the double-team situation is established. If the pass is not made until a good double-team has been set, harrassment by the defensive players may force a bad pass. Potential pass receivers must cut to meet passes. Lob passes absolutely must be avoided. After making a pass, a cut down the middle by a passer often results in an opening for a return pass and a frontcourt scoring situation.

Once the ball has been passed to a teammate downcourt, the defense should be out numbered, and 4-on-3, 3-on-2, and 2-on-1 play situations occur. The offense should take advantage of these outnumbering situations and attempt to *score.*

Diagrams 18.11 through 18.14 illustrate basic patterns commonly used for attacking the full court 1-2-1-1 press.

Three-Quarter-Court 2-2-1 Zone Press Attack

Most teams using this type of zone press do not employ as many double-team situations as teams using the 1-2-1-1 press. Instead, they attempt to keep pressure on the passer and force bad passes without resorting to the double-team.

The best attack for the 2-2-1 zone press is to advance the ball downcourt with pass reversal techniques as illustrated in diagrams 18.15 through 18.17. By dribbling toward one side of the defense, then reverse passing to a player on the other side of the court, who in turn dribbles to the side of the defense, the offense can gradually work the ball downcourt—always looking for any defensive mistake and always looking to pass to a player in the middle of the court. If the ball is passed to the middle of the court, the pass receiver pivots and looks to pass downcourt. The threat of the pass to the middle of the court forces the defense to adjust toward the middle and leaves openings for passes down the sideline after pass reversal.

This method of advancing the ball downcourt against the 2-2-1 press is often termed "walking the ball downcourt." It is a more cautious attack than those used for zone presses that rely greatly on double-team tactics. The pass reversal techniques, however, are safer ball-handling methods than are long passes downcourt, and, although it may result in slower advancement, far fewer ball-handling mistakes are made. Since most teams do advance the ball more slowly against the 2-2-1 press, the press is often called a container press.

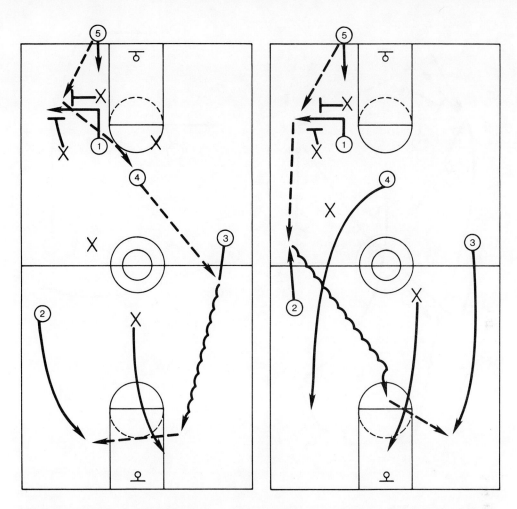

Diagram 18.11a *Full-court 1-2-1-1 zone press attack.* ⑤ makes inbounds pass to ①. ① pivots to face defense and passes to ④ in middle of court. ④ quickly pivots to face defense and passes to ③ on the opposite side of court, who advances for a 2-on-1 situation with ②. Passes to the center of the floor and reverses of the ball to the opposite side of the court are difficult for the zone press to handle.

Diagram 18.11b *Full-court 1-2-1-1 zone press attack.* ① takes the inbounds pass and faces the defense. ① passes to ② who quickly advances for a 2-on-1 situation with ③.

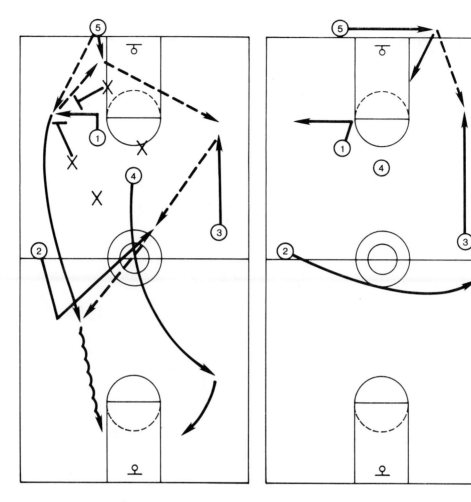

Diagram 18.11c ⑤makes inbounds pass to ①and steps in bounds on the ballside of the goal. ①cannot pass to ④or to②. ① return passes to ⑤, acting as a safety valve behind the ball. ⑤reverses the ball to③ on the opposite side of the court. ③can advance the ball on a controlled dribble or pass to②cutting into the middle after ④has cleared. If②receives pass, ②pivots and passes to ①. ①advances quickly for a possible 2-on-1 situation with ④.

Diagram 18.12 If the defense prevents⑤ from inbounding the ball to either ①or④, ⑤quickly runs the baseline and passes to ③.②cuts across court giving③ the same options that were available to ①on the opposite side of the court.

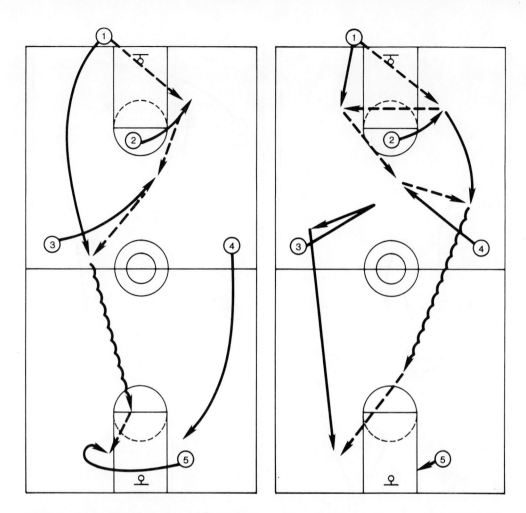

Diagram 18.13 This shows a 1-2-1-1 full-court zone press attack sending the center, ⑤, downcourt. ① inbounds ball to ② who passes to ③ cutting to the middle. ③ pivots to face defense and passes to ① on the opposite side of the court. ① advances quickly downcourt for possible outnumbering situation.

Diagram 18.14 If ③ cuts to the middle and is defensed, ② can return pass to ①. ③ clears out, and ④ cuts to the middle. ① passes to ④ who pivots to face defense and passes to ②. ② advances quickly downcourt for a possible fast break situation.

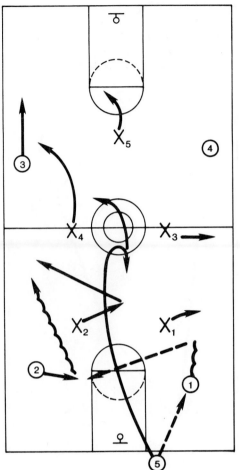

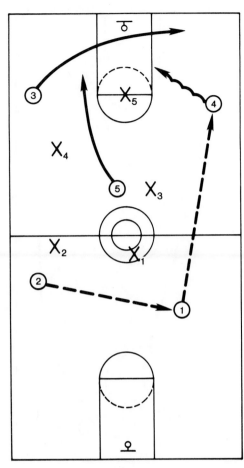

Diagram 18.15 *2-2-1 zone press attack.* ① advances ball carefully toward midcourt and, when challenged by the defense, passes to ② who advances.

Diagram 18.16 *2-2-1 zone press attack.* When ② is challenged, ② passes back to ① who can usually pass down the sideline to ④. ③ crosses under the basket and ⑤ fills the left lane as ④ drives toward the basket.

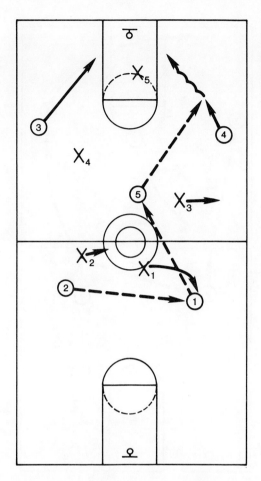

Diagram 18.17 *The 2-2-1 zone press attack.* When ① receives the return pass from ②, ① has the option to pass to the middle to ⑤. If ⑤ receives the pass, ⑤ pivots and attempts a quick pass to either ④ or ③.

Half-Court Zone Press Attack

Most teams employing the half-court zone press use either a 1-3-1 or a 1-2-2 formation. Both can be attacked in a similar manner. Diagram 18.18 recommends an appropriate attack for these types of presses. The same basic principle of attacking the full-court zone press applies when attacking the half-court zone press. Dribbling is held to a minimum, the lob pass is avoided at all times, and the offense *attacks* the defense.

Pressing Defense Attack Suggestions

1. Have an organized plan of attack for both man-for-man and zone presses.
2. Practice daily against pressing defenses to develop skill and confidence.

Diagram 18.18 *Half-court 1-2-2 zone press attack.* When meeting the half-court press, the ball-handler stops before getting to the center line and makes at least one cross-court pass. When ② receives the pass from ①, ② looks to pass to either ⑤ or ③.

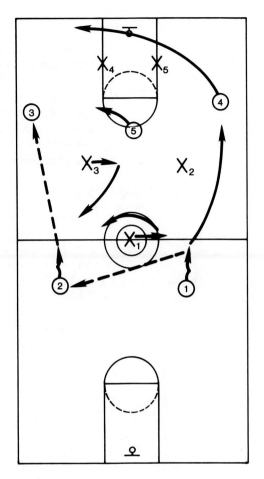

3. Regular practice on 4-on-3, 3-on-2 and 2-on-1 front court scoring plays is necessary.
4. The player taking the ball out of bounds must be a good passer.
5. The dribble must be used sparingly against the zone press.
6. Stay out of corners.
7. Pass receivers must meet the pass.
8. Avoid lob passes and bounce passes. Both are too slow and susceptible to intervention.
9. When protecting a small lead late in the game, avoid screens on the ball that allow the defensive double-team.

Discussion Questions

1. Discuss the philosophical difference between a control team's press offense and a fast-breaking team's press offense.
2. Discuss the various formations for attacking full-court pressing defenses.
3. How does an offensive attack for the three-quarter-court zone press differ from the attack for a half-court zone press?
4. Discuss the essential differences between attacking the full-court man-for-man press and the full-court zone press.
5. How much practice time should be devoted to press offense?
6. Is it more important to take the ball quickly out of bounds against a press or to wait for the team's best passer to take the ball out of bounds?

Projects

1. By studying various reference materials, compile an offense for attacking the man-for-man press and for attacking the zone press.
2. Interview a local coach about his or her philosophy in attacking pressing defenses.

Suggested Readings

Damon, Dr. Lyle. "Press Offense," *Pro-Keds Coaches Digest,* 1980, pp. 22–24.

Hankinson, *Progressions,* pp. 251–55.

Jack, Stan. "Beat the Press-Simply." *Scholastic Coach,* October 1975, p. 38.

Krause, Jerry, and Conn, James H. "Transition Offense vs. Half-court Trapping Defenses." *Scholastic Coach,* October 1975, p. 36ff.

Kresse, John. "50 Tips on Beating Pressure." *Scholastic Coach,* December 1978, pp. 42–46.

LaRicca, Robert. "Triple-Stack Press Breaker." *Scholastic Coach,* October 1975, pp. 40–42.

Lopez, Bill. "Full-court Zone Press Breaker," *Scholastic Coach,* December 1978, p. 32ff.

Master, George D. "Make Press Time Lay-up Time. *Scholastic Coach,* August 1978, pp. 60–61.

Mims, Ray. "Press Buster." *Scholastic Coach,* November 1978, p. 21.

Phillips, Bucky. "Junior High Press Breaker." *Scholastic Coach,* September 1977, p. 34ff.

Somogyi, John. "Gap Offense vs. Full-court Pressure." *Scholastic Coach,* November 1975, p. 30ff.

Stewart and Scholz, *Complete Programs,* pp. 57–58, 92–100.

White, Jim. "Beat the Full Court Press." *Pro-Keds Coaches Digest,* 1980, pp. 8–9.

Wooden, *Modern Basketball,* pp. 187–90.

chapter nineteen

Out-of-Bounds Plays

Types of Out-of-Bounds Plays

Out-of-bounds plays may be divided into three categories:

1. Endline out-of-bounds plays.
2. Sideline out-of-bounds plays.
3. Out-of-bounds plays for special situations.

The most commonly used out-of-bounds plays are attempted on the endline under the offensive basket. Such plays are more difficult to defense and often result in a score. Since the ball is taken out under the offensive basket, one slight mistake by the defense can result in a lay-up or close jump shot.

Many teams use sideline out-of-bounds plays, while others simply make the throw-in and proceed with their regular man-for-man or zone offense. Sideline plays can be very effective, because they allow an easy opportunity for such a play to be called and set up. A play that is not a part of the team's regular half-court offense can present a situation the defense is less ready to meet, resulting in a quick score.

Most situations in which a special out-of-bounds play is needed occur late in the game when the defense is using pressing tactics to get the ball. These special situations can occur anywhere on the sideline or the endline on the defensive end of the floor. These special plays are designed for when the defense is pressing in an effort to come from behind and using denial tactics to prevent the throw-in. Therefore, the first objective of the special play is to get the ball in bounds successfully. If one of the options on the special play results in an easy lay-up, all the better.

Figure 19.1 *Setting up an end-line out-of-bounds play.*

Another special out-of-bounds situation occurs when only a few seconds remain and a team is behind by one or two points. A pre-arranged, practiced out-of-bounds play has a far better chance of obtaining a score than one a coach might hurriedly diagram at a time-out.

Many sound out-of-bounds plays have been developed, and a number of them are diagrammed in this chapter. In any out-of-bounds play, the importance of a good passer taking the ball out cannot be over emphasized. A weak passer can cause many mistakes, missing open teammates and making bad passes that result in interceptions.

Select out-of-bounds plays that are best fitted to your material. Use only a few—too many out-of-bounds plays result in none being learned.

Keying Out-of-Bounds Plays

A well-coached team calls their out-of-bounds plays so the defense does not know exactly what play is to be run. If a team simply verbally calls number "one" and executes a play, then calls the same play in the same manner again, the defense can anticipate exactly what is coming. On the other hand, if the defense has a system for calling plays to disguise them, the play has a better chance of success. For example, a number one play could be called "twenty one," or "thirty one," or "forty one." Or, a number one play could be called "thirteen," "fourteen," or "fifteen." A number two play could be called "twenty one," "twenty two," or "twenty three." Disguising the call helps prevent the defense from anticipating the play.

Execution Suggestions

1. Out-of-bounds plays must receive regular practice so no player is uncertain as to an assignment.
2. A good passer takes the ball out of bounds.
3. The passer does not step out of bounds immediately on the official's signal but rather calls the play before stepping out and receiving the ball so teammates have time to set up in proper formation.
4. The passer gives a quick signal to begin the play. Usually this is done with a slap of the ball immediately upon receiving it from the official.
5. It is important to stress that the ball must touch an in-bounds player within five seconds after the official hands the out-of-bounds player the ball.

Endline Out-of-Bounds Plays

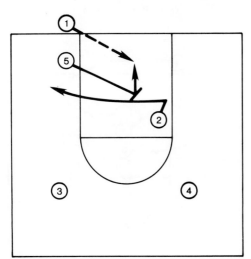 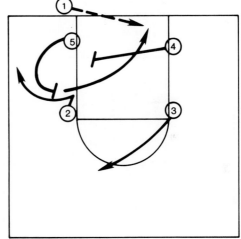

Diagram 19.1 ⑤, the center, sets screen for guard ②. ② cuts, and ⑤ rolls for possible pass from ①. If defense switches, a small player will switch to ⑤.

Diagram 19.2 *Box formation.* A screen-the-screener play. ⑤ sets screen for ② as ④ sets screen for ⑤. ⑤'s defender often is checking ② and lets ⑤ get lay-up.

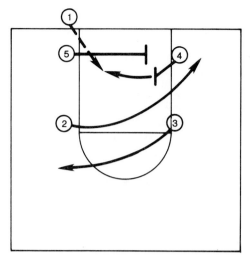

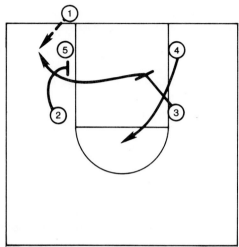

Diagram 19.3 *Box formation.* Another screen-the-screener play to counter the play shown in diagram 19.2. ②cuts early. ④sets screen on right side of lane as ⑤sets screen for ④.

Diagram 19.4 *Box formation.* ③ sets brush screen for ④and quickly cuts off double-screen set by ②and ⑤.

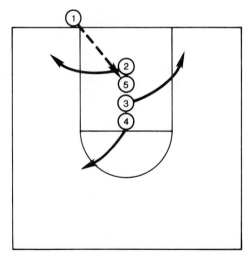

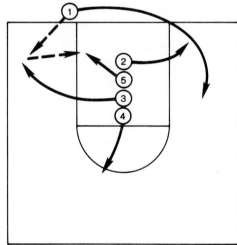

Diagram 19.5 *Vertical formation in lane.* ②, ③, and ④cut as shown. ①passes high pass to ⑤for shot.

Diagram 19.6 ②,③, and ④cut as shown. ①passes to ③who looks to pass to ⑤in post.

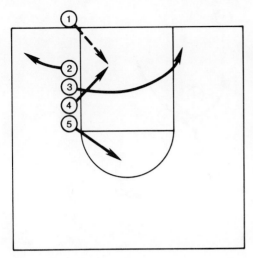

Diagram 19.7 *Vertical formation outside lane.* ②, ③, and ⑤ cut as shown. ④ cuts down middle for pass from ①.

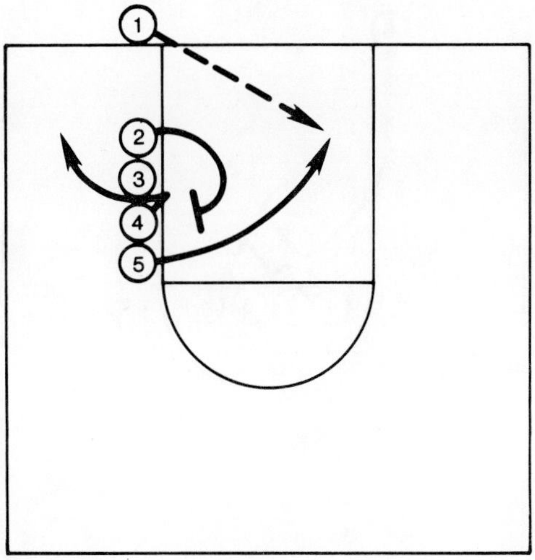

Diagram 19.8 *Vertical formation outside lane.* ② sets screen for ⑤. ④ and ⑤ cut simultaneously. ① can pass to either ⑤ or ④.

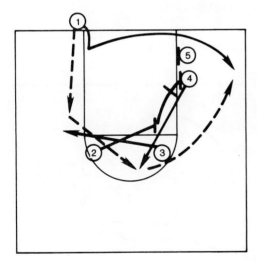

Diagram 19.9 ① passes to ③ cutting off screen set by ②. ③ passes to ④ cutting off screen also set by ②. ④ passes to ① coming off double-screen set by ② and ⑤.

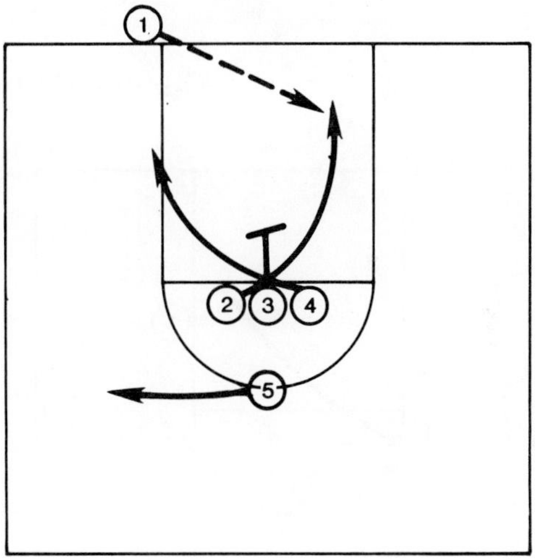

Diagram 19.10 ③ steps forward, and ④ and ② split off ③, with ④ cutting first.

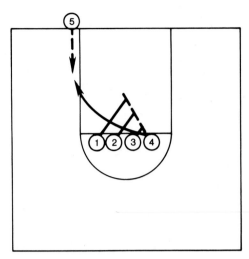

Diagram 19.11 ①, ②, and ③ set triple-screen for ④.

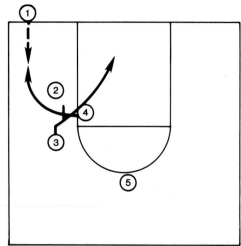

Diagram 19.14 ① passes to ③ cutting off screen set by ②. ③ passes to ⑤ also cutting off screen set by ②. ⑤ passes to ② who passes to ① cutting off double-screen set by ③ and ④.

Sideline Out-of-Bounds Plays

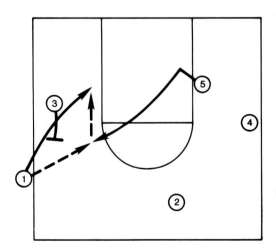

Diagram 19.13. ① passes to ⑤ cutting to ball. ⑤ passes to ① cutting off screen set by ③.

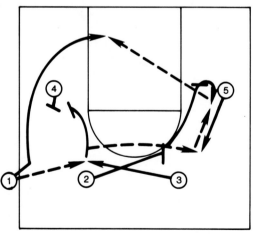

Diagram 19.14 ① passes to ③ cutting off screen set by ②. ③ passes to ⑤ also cutting off screen set by ②. ⑤ passes to ② who passes to ① cutting off double-screen set by ③ and ④.

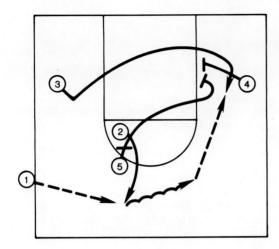

Diagram 19.15 ①passes to ②cutting off screen set by ⑤. ②dribbles over and passes to ③for shot behind double-screen set by ④ and ⑤.

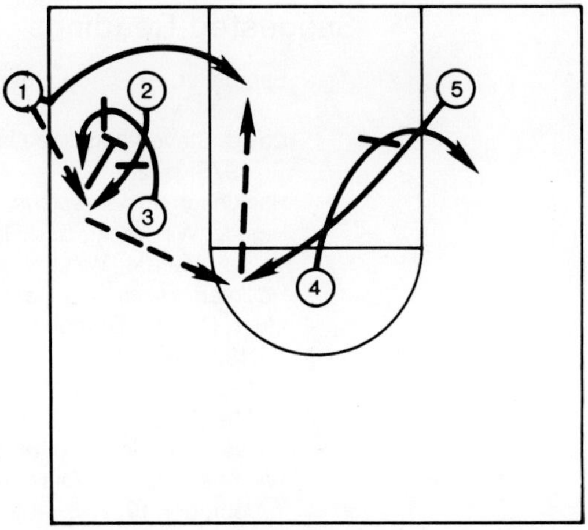

Diagram 19.16 *Special sideline play when ball is near corner.* ②sets rear screen for ③who cuts. ②steps to receive pass from ①and passes to ⑤coming off screen set by ④. ⑤may pass to ①cutting to basket or to ③coming off screen set by ②.

Discussion Questions

1. Should a team's objective be to score on out-of-bounds plays or just simply to get the ball in bounds?
2. Should the team's best passer always take the ball out of bounds?
3. How many endline out-of-bounds plays should be used? Sideline plays? Special situation plays?

Projects

1. By studying various reference materials, compile at least 10 underbasket out-of-bounds plays. At least five sideline out-of-bounds plays.
2. Write a brief paper discussing signals for out-of-bounds plays.

Suggested Readings

Burkhalter, Al. "Side Out-of-Bounds Plays." *Athletic Journal,* October 1979, p. 14.

David, Steve. "Sideline Out-of-Bounds Plays." *Scholastic Coach,* December 1975, p. 28ff.

Hankinson, *Progressions,* pp. 256–57.

Healey, William A., and Hartley, Joseph W. *The Winning Edge in Basketball,* pp. 21–104. West Nyack, N.Y.: Parker Publishing, 1973.

Holzman, *Holzman's Basketball,* pp. 182–94.

Miller, David. "Complete Inbounds System." *Scholastic Coach*, September 1978, p. 92ff.

Piscapo, Joe. "Out-of-Bounds Play for All Occasions." *Scholastic Coach,* March 1980, pp. 37–38.

Stewart and Scholz, *Complete Program,* pp. 375–84.

Williams, Carroll. "Out-of-Bounds Series from a Shuffle." *Scholastic Coach,* October 1977, p. 40ff.

Wooden, *Modern Basketball,* pp. 201–6.

chapter twenty

The Jump-Ball Situation

Control of the ball is paramount to the success of a basketball team, and jump-ball situations afford additional opportunities for ball possession. Except in collegiate men's basketball where the jump ball has been eliminated except to begin the game and each overtime period, at least eight to ten jump-ball situations generally occur during a game, and the team that gains possession of these toss-up situations greatly increases its chances for victory.

A jump-ball situation may occur at the center circle or at the offensive or defensive free-throw circles. The same basic techniques may be used to gain possession at all three positions, but greater emphasis must be placed on defense when jumping at the defensive circle, since the opponents can tap the ball into an immediate scoring position.

Jump-Ball Formations

Most teams use one of two jump-ball formations:

1. Box formation (diag. 20.1). This formation is strong defensively and may be used at any of the jump positions. It is particularly recommended when jumping at the defensive free-throw circle.
2. Diamond formation (diag. 20.2). This formation presents excellent offensive scoring situations but is weaker defensively than the box formation. Limit its use at the defensive jump circle to those situations when control of the tap is virtually assured.

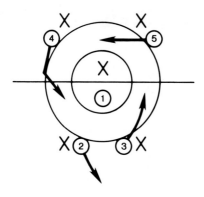

Diagram 20.1 *The box formation.* Cutting methods similar to those shown may be used to gain possession when the opposing jumper is expected to control the tap. Movement of the players may be clockwise or counterclockwise but all players must know their assignments, and the movement of all players must be coordinated.

Diagram 20.2 *The diamond formation.* ⑤ must carry the major defensive responsibility. As ⑤ drops back for defense, ③ and ④ must cut in front of the most likely receivers. ② may cut either left or right or guard against a back tap.

Both the box and diamond formations have considerable merit, and a variety of cutting moves designed to gain control and a number of plays designed to score may be successfully used from both formations. Diagrams 20.1 and 20.2 illustrate cutting methods from each formation that may be used in efforts to secure ball possession. These cutting methods are only necessary when the opposing jumper has the height advantage and should control the tap.

Jumping Technique

Prior to jumping, the jumper steps back to make certain all teammates are in position and to determine where to tap the ball. The jumper flexes the knees considerably for maximum spring and is alert for a quick toss by the official. On the toss of the ball, the jumper springs into the air and attempts to tip the bottom of the ball. Many jumpers make the mistake of tipping at the middle of the ball, which actually results in a loss of two or three inches on the jump.

Some disagreement exists on whether or not the jumper should use the inside or outside arm for the tap. Many coaches teach players to use the

Figure 20.1 The jumper should tip toward the bottom quarter of the ball.

inside arm, contending that more height is obtained this way. Other coaches teach the use of the outside arm, which requires a twist of the body on the spring. Advocates of this method contend the twist of the body increases the height of the jump. It is probably accurate to say that either method can be successful after sufficient jumping practice and depending on the preference of the player.

Figure 20.2 The players along the circle must have considerable practice at cutting moves designed to gain possession of the tipped ball.

Figure 20.3 Notice the alertness of all players around the jump circle.

Jump Signals

Many teams use a number of jump signals to advantage. One key reason for use of signals is to let teammates know the direction of the tap. Simply calling the name of the player to whom the tap may go is an option. Others call a word or number to indicate left or right, front or back, while others may touch one side of the body to indicate tap direction. The "clock" method, in which the jump circle is sectioned off like the face of a clock, is preferred by many. If a player calls "12," the intention is to tap the ball straight ahead to the 12 o'clock position, "3" means the player will tap to the right to the 3 o'clock position, and so on.

Signals also can be used when the jumper assumes either control or non-control of the tap. If the jumper is almost certain of tap control, he or she may call "sure" jump, and the team can be ready to initiate an offensive play to score. If the jumper is doubtful of ability to get the tap, the jumper may call "safe" jump, and teammates can be ready to go on the defensive, using practiced cutting methods to attempt to gain ball possession. Of course, calling a key to a special jump-ball play is another reason for use of signals.

When the opposing jumper has the height advantage, "inviting" him to tap to a certain teammate is a sound technique in gaining ball control. On the jump alignment, one opponent can be left open to encourage the opposing jumper to tap to this player. On the tap, players then converge on this opponent to intercept the tap. The technique is shown in diagram 20.3.

Diagram 20.3 *Influencing the direction of the tap.* On the jump alignment, ④ slides down toward X₃ to discourage a tap in that direction. ⑤ stays close to X₅. One side of X₂ is left open to invite the jumper, X₁, to tap to X₂. On the toss, ⑤ converges with ② onto X₂ in an effort to intercept the tap.

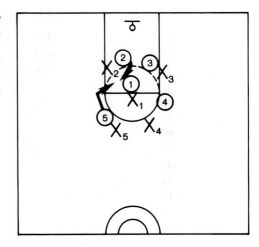

Jump-Ball Drills and Plays

Diagrams 20.4 and 20.5 give two drills very useful in practicing the jump-ball situation, while diagrams 20.6 and 20.7 illustrate two simple jump-ball plays. In addition, diagrams 17.6 and 17.7 in chapter 17 show two jump-ball plays that may result in fast-break opportunities.

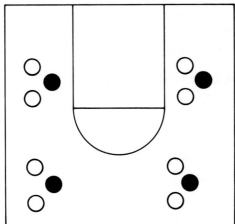

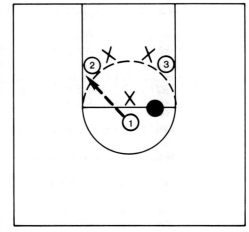

Diagram 20.4 *Three-man tapping drill.* Players are divided into groups of three. One player tosses the ball while the others jump. Players rotate tossing and jumping. This drill is excellent for teaching proper jumping technique and timing.

Diagram 20.5 *Tapping and receiving drill.* ① calls signal to indicate direction of tap. ① taps in direction indicated, with either ② or ③ practicing receiving the tap.

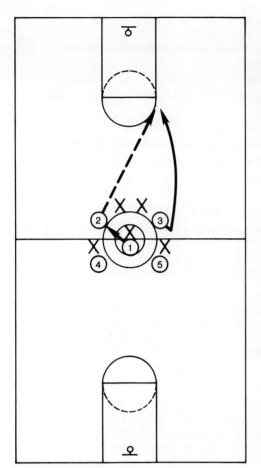

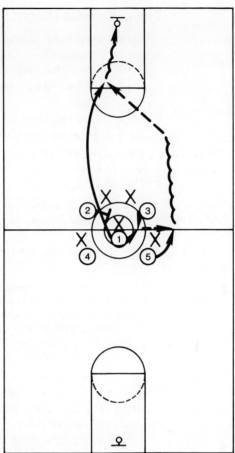

Diagram 20.6 *A very simple tip-off play.* As ① taps to ②, ③ cuts hard to the basket for pass. This play can also be used from the defensive jump circle.

Diagram 20.7 *A tip-off play.* ① taps to ③ who hands off to ⑤ cutting by. ② sets screen for ① who cuts to basket for pass from ⑤.

Discussion Questions

1. How much practice time should be devoted to jump-ball situations?
2. Should the jumper tip with the inside or outside hand?
3. Discuss types of signals that can be used in the jump-ball situation?
4. How important are jump-ball plays?
5. Are there any situations when the jumper should tip the ball on the way up?

Projects

1. Teach a jump-ball play to the class.
2. Chart a game or film and write a critique of jump ball methods.

Suggested Readings

Hankinson, *Progressions*, pp. 31, 86.

Healey and Hartley, *Basketball Offenses*, pp. 105–40.

Holzman, *Holzman's Basketball*, pp. 171–82.

Masters, George D. "Controlling the Tap." *Scholastic Coach*, November 1978, p. 61ff.

Stewart and Scholz, *Complete Program*, pp. 387–90.

Stiver, John. "Alignment for Center Jumps." *Athletic Journal*, September 1979, p. 72.

chapter twenty-one

Delay or Freeze Patterns

Unless the 24-second rule is placed into the high school and college rule book, teams will continue to use freezing or stalling tactics to preserve a lead late in the game. This situation presents opportunities for both the offense and defense to use tactical moves, and it is an important phase of the game. The offense must have practiced patterns ready to assure ball control, while the defense must have defensive maneuvers ready for a coordinated effort to gain possession.

When to Freeze

Several factors are involved in determining when to freeze:

1. The ball-handling ability of the offense
2. The pressing ability of the defense
3. The amount of lead
4. The amount of time remaining

When you analyze these factors for various teams and for various games, you come up with a variety of answers as to when to freeze. The team with tall, not-so-good ball-handlers certainly is apt to be less successful in a long freeze than the team with short and more clever ball-handlers. It may be far more wise to freeze the ball against the taller and slower team than against the shorter and quicker opponent. A 2-point lead with 5 minutes to go would hardly be the time to freeze in the normal situation, whereas an 8-point lead with the same amount of time remaining easily could dictate a freezing pattern. Thus, all these factors must be quickly and carefully considered and a wise decision reached.

Table 21.1 When to Freeze

Number of Minutes Remaining	Minimum Point Lead Desired
0–2	1–2
2–3	2–4
3–4	4–6
More than 4	6

Table 21.1 is presented as a general guide to freezing the ball. Remember, however, that consideration of the above factors may cause some variation.

Freeze or Stall

Patterns designed to control the ball to preserve a lead may be of a *freeze* or *stall* nature. The freeze is usually used late in the game with a small lead, when the primary objective is to hold on to the ball. The stall is normally used with a larger lead and considerable time remaining, when the objective is still to score. The stall game has been used successfully by clever ball-handling teams in the latter stages of a game to pull the defense away from the basket and to open up cutting and driving lanes that result in easy scores. The same basic pattern may be used in playing both types of games, but some of the principles may differ. For example, if a team leads by a point with 30 seconds to play, a screen on the ball is unsafe because it affords an opportunity for the defense to double-team the ball-handler. On the other hand, if a team is leading by 8 points with 5 minutes to play, a screen on the ball can be good basketball. Losing of the ball to a double-team situation is not disastrous here, and the offensive maneuver created by the screen often can result in an easy basket.

Substitution for Better Freeze Technique

Sometimes it is wise for the coach to make substitutions at the time to freeze or stall to remove the weaker ball-handlers, even though they may be good scorers and rebounders. The same is true of free-throw shooters. At this stage of the game, possession of the ball and good free-throw shooting is of paramount importance, and a mistake by a poor ball-handler or missed free-throw can mean defeat.

Prior to the game, the coach should decide which players to use if faced with the necessity to freeze the ball. A decision made well in advance is the best bet, rather than a choice made on the spur of the moment during the last minutes of a hotly contested game.

Freeze Principles

1. A team's better ball-handlers do most of the ball-handling.
2. Ball-handlers should save the dribble until needed.
3. The ball-handler should face teammates. Turning away from teammates affords an excellent opportunity for the double-team. Also, unless facing teammates, the ball-handler cannot see one who may become open under the basket.
4. Dribblers should keep their heads up to clearly see the defense and their teammates.
5. Ball-handlers should stay away from the corners where boundary lines can combine with a defensive double-team to cause loss of the ball.
6. Good free-throw shooters should handle the ball. Missed free-throw attempts in last-minute freezing situations can quickly result in defeat.
7. Make weak opposing defensive players come out to press for the ball.
8. Avoid screens and criss-crosses that allow the defense opportunities for double-team situations.
9. If a man-for-man press is being used by the defense to try to get the ball, a good dribbler can be used effectively. However, if zone-pressing tactics are being used, sharp passing is necessary and the dribble should be avoided.
10. If a stalling game is in order, use screens and cuts that afford scoring opportunities.

Freeze and Stall Patterns

There are quite a number of successful freeze or stall patterns. Although a coach needs to teach only one freeze or stall pattern, he or she should be familiar with other freeze patterns to be able to combat them defensively. Some of the more popular freeze patterns are:

1. High-post freeze
2. Four corners
3. Tease
4. Spread formation.

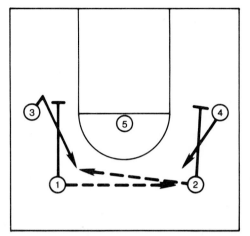 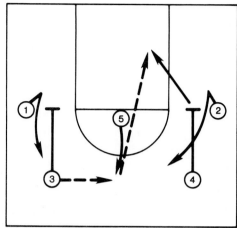

Diagram 21.1 *High-post freeze.* ① passes to ② and screens for ③. ② passes to ③ and screens for ④. Players stay even or above the free-throw line extended to leave the area near the basket open for back cuts.

Diagram 21.2 *High-post freeze.* If ③ cannot pass to ④, ③ looks to ⑤ popping out for pass as ④ sets screen for ②. If defensive player guarding ④ overplays toward ②, ⑤ may be able to pass to ④ for a lay-up.

High-Post Freeze

The high-post freeze is shown in diagrams 21.1 and 21.2. It involves a single-post type of offense, with the center at the high-post ready to break free for a pass if needed. The offense involves a great number of cross-court passes from the guard position as well as down-screens from the guard to the forward position. The high-post player remains at the high-post until needed. When perimeter players cannot find other perimeter players to pass to, they pass to the high-post player cutting to the area near the center line.

Four Corners

The "four corners" delay game has been popularized by Dean Smith of the University of North Carolina and is probably the most widely known delay pattern in the game of basketball. It can be used as a deep freeze late in the game or as a scoring offense. Smith has used it very successfully for long periods of time, and on occasion he will go into it in the first half of play. It is an offense that enables the teams' three best ball-handlers to do most of the ball-handling, with the two bigger players placed in the deep corners. Diagrams 21.3 through 21.7 give this pattern.

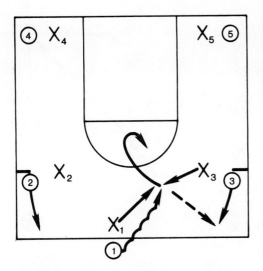

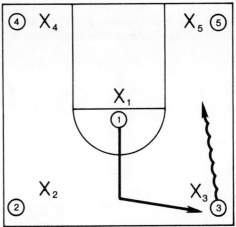

Diagram 21.3 *Four-corners freeze.* ① dribbles across midcourt and passes to ③ when X₃ helps defensively. ① then cuts to free-throw line as ③ faces the defense and saves the dribble until X₃ moves into defensive position. ② and ③ begin near the "hash" marks to give ① dribbling room but move to corners as ① penetrates.

Diagram 21.4 *Four corners.* ① holds at free-throw line until ③ establishes a dribbling direction. When ③ dribbles right, ① moves in path shown to corner.

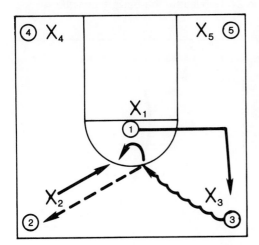

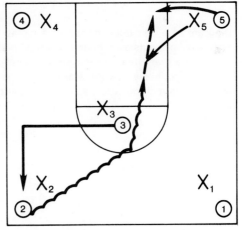

Diagram 21.5 *Four corners.* When ③ dribbles left, ① moves in path shown to corner. If X₂ helps defensively, ③ passes to ② in corner. ② faces defense and does not dribble until X₂ returns to defensive position.

Diagram 21.6 *Four corners.* When ② penetrates, a normal 3-on-2 situation may occur. When X₅ stops penetration, ② may pass to ⑤ for a lay-up.

Diagram 21.7 *Four corners.* If X$_2$ stops penetration by ② and X$_5$ sags off ⑤, ② passes to ⑤ and gets an immediate return pass.

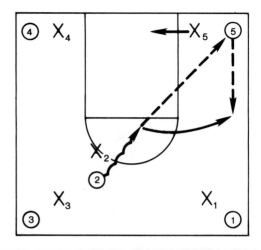

Tease Offense

The tease freeze offense is one of the newer freeze patterns. Coach Mel Gibson of the University of North Carolina at Wilmington has done more than any other coach to popularize this freeze pattern. The set-up is shown in diagram 21.8. By placing all five players close to the center of the court, the area near the basket is open for cuts into the scoring area. It is very difficult to get defensive help when a player loses an opponent, and a team must be well versed in defensive fundamentals when facing this particular freeze pattern. Diagrams 21.8 through 21.12 illustrate the basic technique.

Diagram 21.8 *The tease freeze.* All five players are even or outside of "hash" marks. This results in a great deal of room for back cutting. As ① dribbles toward stack, ③ pops out for pass and looks to pass to ① cutting to basket.

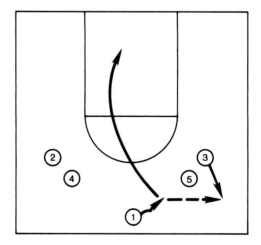

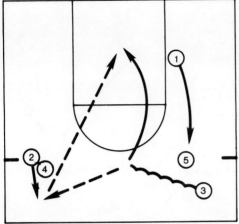

Diagram 21.9 *Tease.* ③ attempts to penetrate and, when stopped, passes to ② popping out of stack. ③ cuts to basket and receives pass from ② if open.

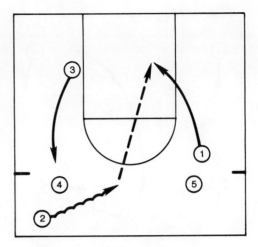

Diagram 21.10 *Tease.* If ③ is not open, ② begins penetration looking to pass to ① popping out of stack. If defensive player guarding ① overplays, ① back cuts for pass from ② .

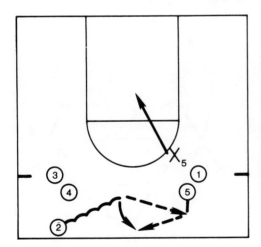

Diagram 21.11 If X₅ sags off ⑤ to stop back cuts, ⑤ pops out for pass from ② . ⑤ should hold the ball until X₅ returns to defensive position. It is very important to pass to ④ or ⑤ to keep their defensive players from dropping back toward the basket.

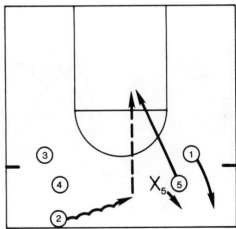

Diagram 21.12 If X₅ attempts any type of overplay, ⑤ cuts to the basket.

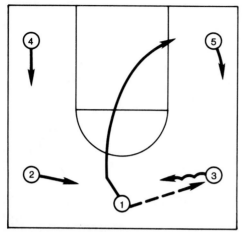

Diagram 21.13 *The spread formation as a freeze pattern.* ① passes to ③ and cuts down the middle looking for a return pass. ② begins move toward ball. ① takes position being vacated by ⑤.

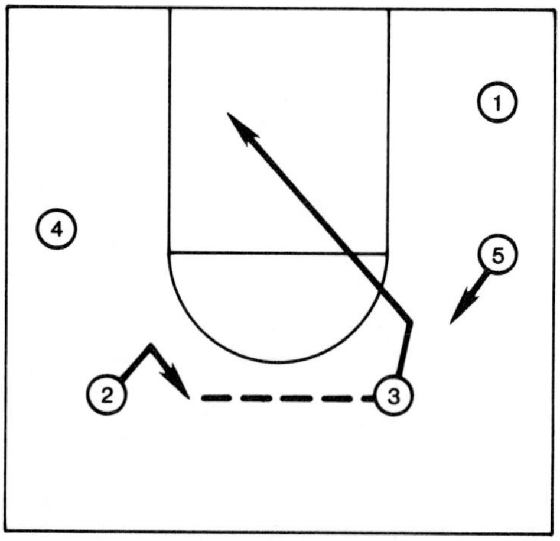

Diagram 21.14 *The spread formation.* ③ passes to ② and cuts down the middle. ⑤ moves toward ball as ③ continues on through to position being vacated by ④. This pattern is a continuity and involves continual movement by all players.

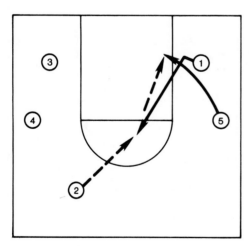

Diagram 21.15 *A back-door possibility from the spread formation.* If ⑤ is being overplayed, ① can flash to the high post for a pass from ②. ① then passes to ⑤ cutting to the basket.

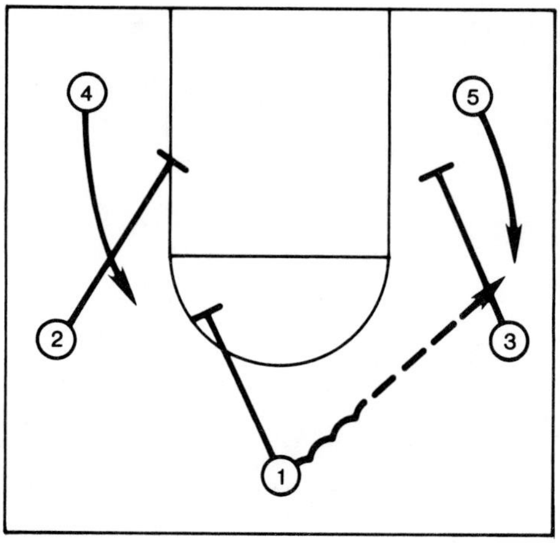

Diagram 21.16 Some teams use downscreens when using the spread formation freeze.

The Spread Freeze Pattern

The spread freeze is run from a 3–2 or 1–2–2 set up. It can be played with players wide, using no screens but considerable passing and quick cuts to the basket, as shown in diagrams 21.13 through 21.15, or it can be used with a considerable number of down-screens, as shown in diagram 21.16. The down-screens make the passing easier, but they also tend to congest the basket area and prevent an easy cut to the basket.

Discussion Questions

1. Should daily practice time be devoted to delay or freeze patterns?
2. Under what circumstances could a delay pattern be used early in a game?
3. How important are substitutions to a successful delay or freeze pattern?
4. Should the delay pattern and freeze pattern be the same?
5. Discuss specific differences between the delay and freeze.
6. Is it ever good basketball to delay or freeze the ball when trailing?
7. How can the poor free-throw shooter be incorporated in the freeze?

Projects

1. Teach a freeze pattern to the class.
2. By studying various reference materials, diagram a freeze or a stall pattern not outlined in this textbook.
3. Interview a local coach about his or her philosophy in freezing or stalling the ball.

Suggested Readings

Beecroft, John R. "Interchangeable 'Spread' Delay Offense." *Scholastic Coach,* October 1978, pp. 91–94.

Dougher, James D. "Holy Cross's Control Offense." *Scholastic Coach,* October 1977, pp. 40ff.

Gibson, Mel. "Double Stack Tease Offense." *Scholastic Coach,* October 1979, pp. 36ff.

Hankinson, *Progressions,* pp. 237–43.

Jackson, Jack. "Delaying . . . And Scoring." *Scholastic Coach,* November 1977, pp. 34ff.

Schmidt, James. "Angle-Stacked Triangle Stall." *Scholastic Coach,* October 1976, pp. 62–63.

Stewart and Scholz, *Complete Programs,* pp. 358–75.

Swartz, Steve. "The 1–2–2 Ball-Control Game." *Scholastic Coach,* November 1978, pp. 34ff.

Williams, Greg. "Auxiliary Delay Offense." *Scholastic Coach,* October 1976, p. 50.

Wooden, *Modern Basketball,* pp. 191–95.

part three

Team Defensive Formations and Techniques

chapter twenty-two
Selecting and Teaching Team Defense

The importance of sound team defensive play to championship basketball cannot be over emphasized. Good team defense can bring a victory when the offense is having the inevitable "off" night. In fact, the major difference between the average basketball team and those who trail at the end of a tournament lies in the ability to play defense. Few coaches would argue against the tremendous importance of team defense, but failure to emphasize team defense and to teach it properly is prevalent in basketball coaching. If I could emphasize only one point to the beginning coach, it would be the value of team defense and the role of the coach in its achievement. Players need little coaching to play offense, the fun part of the game. Few players, however, like to play defense, and most will not do so unless properly guided by an enthusiastic coach who teaches them the value of defense, using sound teaching techniques to help them master the defensive part of the game.

The building of a whole team defense begins with selecting the defensive maneuvers to be used for the season, and it includes a schedule of adequate practice time to develop these defenses. A coach may select a sagging type of man-for-man defense for the basic team defense, yet there will be times when a pressing defense is needed. A zone defense may be chosen as the basic defense, but again provision must be made for the pressing situation. The team that uses the man-for-man as their basic defense may want to learn a zone for use in special situations, such as when opposing a high-scoring center or when facing a weak outside shooting team. Thus, more than one team defense is needed for a season of play. Select these defenses in advance and make practice plans accordingly.

Selection of the Defense

Several factors are involved in selecting defenses to be used during the season:

1. The defensive philosophy and knowledge of the coach
2. The defensive ability of the players
3. The type of competition to be faced

The coach's defensive philosophy is tremendously important in selecting defenses. If, for example, the coach's philosophy centers around a belief in agressive man-for-man play, the coach may find it difficult to generate sufficient enthusiasm for teaching a zone defense.

The defensive ability of players on hand is certainly an important factor to be considered. A team of tall, slow players may find zone defense more effective than a man-for-man. A zone may also be more suitable for the smaller team that needs rebounding strength. The team with fast, medium-sized players may be able to gain more advantage from a man-for-man defense.

Not to be forgotten in the selection of a defense is the type of competition to be faced. As a general rule, the better the competition, the less likely a zone defense will be successful. Fewer college teams play zone defenses than do high school teams, because college shooters are more proficient, and a man-for-man defense can be more efficient. Fewer zones are played by the larger high schools than by the smaller ones, mainly because larger high schools face similar schools with a higher probability of better shooters. Smaller high schools have fewer players to choose from, and teams use zones more often to make use of their personnel as best they can. Thus, the success of zone defenses is closely related to the type of competition to be faced.

Team Defensive Essentials

Many types of team defenses are used in modern basketball. Various types of man-for-man and zone defenses exist, and combinations of both are seen often. Regardless of the type of defense a team may use, certain essentials are necessary for success:

1. Team members must have a desire to play defense.
2. All team members must use correct defensive stance and footwork.
3. All team members must maintain correct positioning.
4. Team members must talk to one another to be able to combat the variety of possible offensive situations.
5. Establish definite responsibilities and techniques for meeting the various types of possible offensive maneuvers.
6. Make definite rebounding assignments.

Desire

Team members must have a desire to play defense. Because of the nature of the game and the tremendous amount of publicity and public favor given to high scorers, most players prefer to play offense. The coach's job is to *sell* the importance of playing defense to the team and to instill in them the *desire* to play defense. Defense can be the great equalizer. When the offense is having a bad night—and this will invariably happen—good, sound defense can produce a victory. But good defense cannot be played unless team members *want* to do it. The idea of letting the other team shoot so that you can get the ball for a scoring attempt results in a long, dreary winter. The *worst* method of obtaining the ball is by taking it out of the opponent's basket! If a coach stresses defense at least on an equal basis with offense in practice sessions, if a coach cites outstanding defensive performances to the press, if awards at the end of the season include awards for best defensive players as well as offensive players, and if a coach distributes praise regularly to the good defensive players, then the desire to play defense *can* be instilled, and the seeds that are a prerequisite to a solid team defense can be sown.

Correct Defensive Stance and Footwork

All team members must use correct defensive stance and footwork. The player who stands erect in guarding an opponent or who uses incorrect footwork seldom does a good defensive job. Since a good team defense is dependent on not one or two players but on five working as a coordinated unit, improper stance or footwork by any one of the five can greatly reduce the effectiveness of the team defense.

Correct Positioning

All team members must maintain correct positioning. A player cannot expect to defense an opponent unless he or she maintains proper floor position. In man-for-man defenses, this means that the player is usually between the respective opponent and the basket. If the opponent breaks into the area near the basket, the defensive player must play between the opponent and the ball to prevent the opponent from receiving the ball in such a dangerous scoring position. If the team defense is a zone, each player must be in the proper floor position in the zone and must make the proper shifts with the movement of the ball. An incorrect shift results in improper position and a weakness in the team defense. One player out of position can nullify the work of four other players and weaken an otherwise sound team defense.

Talk

Team members must talk to one another to be able to combat the variety of possible offensive situations. Talk is a valuable asset to a good team defense. The player who does not yell out to teammates to warn them of special situations impairs the effectiveness of the team defense, even though he or she may be a good individual defensive player. Calls such as "watch the screen," "screen left," "switch," "stay," "rebound," and "slide through" are a few of many needed to insure correct defensive action for the variety of offensive screens and maneuvers that may be faced.

This defensive talk is not something that happens automatically—in fact, it is one of the more difficult facets of team defense to achieve. Coaches must *require* this defensive talk and should include practice drills in which players must yell out the proper defensive terms.

Techniques for Meeting Various Maneuvers

Establish definite responsibilities and techniques for meeting the various types of possible offensive maneuvers. A good team defense is prepared to meet all types of offensive formations, whether it be a single pivot, a double pivot or another offense. Definite techniques and responsibilities must be established for meeting the offensive maneuvers that go toward making up the opponent's offense. Work on the practice floor allows team members to get to know any adjustments in the team defense that may be needed for each formation. Definite techniques must be prepared for meeting the various types of screens, the split-the-post situation, the "give and go," the "shot over the screen," and other offensive plays. These techniques must be developed on the practice floor and cannot be left to chance during the game. Players who switch on a screen one time and then "slide through" on the identical screen the next have not mastered these techniques, which are absolutely essential to a sound team defense.

Rebounding Assignments

Make definite rebounding assignments. Rebounding assignments begin with a shot by the opponent. If the defense is a man-for-man, each defensive player must screen, or box out the opponent to get between opponent and basket. Failure to do this by any one member of the defense can result in an easy basket for the opponent. Correct blockout techniques usually bring three rebounders into the vicinity of the basket for the short rebound and two rebounders outside in a position to grab the long rebound. If the defense is a zone, players must be certain of rebounding areas and must attempt blockouts of opponents in their respective areas.

Discussion Questions

1. Should team defenses be selected prior to the beginning of practice sessions or after players have been evaluated?
2. What type of defense is best for a tall, slow team? Small, quick team?
3. Can a slow team use a pressing defense? What kind? Why?
4. How important is the coach's defensive philosophy to the selection of the defense?
5. How is a team's desire to play defense generated?
6. What percentage of practice time should be devoted to defense?

Projects

1. Study a game film and write a critique on team defensive play.
2. Observe a practice session conducted by a local coach. Write a brief paper on how the coach teaches the defensive portion of practice.

Suggested Readings

Ebert and Cheatum, *Basketball,* pp. 166–67.
Hankinson, *Progressions,* pp. 91–92.
Holzman and Lewin, *Holzman's Basketball,* pp. 93–96.
Tarkanian, Jerry, and Warren, William. "The Role of Quickness in Basketball." *Athletic Journal,* November 1979, p. 30.
Wooden, *Modern Basketball,* pp. 275–76.

chapter twenty-three

Man-for-Man Team Defense

Man-for-man defense differs from zone defense in that players are assigned specific opponents to defense rather than specific floor areas. Man-for-man defense requires aggressiveness and presents a real challenge to the players, because the ability to defense an individual opponent is the basic measuring rod of defensive worth to the team. It is a more versatile defense than the zone, for opponents can be defensed aggressively at half- or full-court, or the defense can sag away from the opponents and congest the dangerous area near the basket.

The man-for-man defense allows the coach to make defensive assignments on the basis of height, position, speed, and individual offensive ability of opponents. The team's best defensive guard may be assigned to the opponent's best scorer, or the poorest defender may be assigned the opponent's weakest scorer, or a slow defensive player may be assigned a slow opponent. This way defensive match-ups are facilitated, and definite responsibility can be charged for scoring by opponents. Individual pride in defensive ability can be more easily fostered, since each player has a specific opponent to guard and can judge his or her performance in terms of the points scored by that opponent.

Advantages of Man-for-Man Defense

1. Specific defensive responsibilities can be assigned to each opposing player.
2. Defensive pride can be fostered by the individual challenge presented by specific responsibility.
3. Defensive match-ups can be made based on size, height, speed, and ability.

4. The defense is flexible in that it can be played on any position of the court.
5. The defense can be played when the team is behind late in the game.
6. It affords good rebounding positions.
7. It enables better mental preparation.
8. Game adjustments can be made readily.

Disadvantages of Man-for-Man Defense

1. It requires superb physical condition of each player.
2. It is susceptible to screens and other offensive movements.
3. Individual defensive weaknesses are glaring.
4. Players may have a tendency to foul more in man-for-man defense than in zone defense.
5. The opponents can attack a star player and possibly get that player into foul trouble.
6. It is more difficult to hide a weak defensive player.

Defensive Positioning

Defensive positioning is the most important aspect of team defense. As long as good defensive positioning is maintained, the defense is strong. When defensive positioning breaks down, good scoring opportunities present themselves to the offense, and defensive fouls and other mistakes are made. Offensive screens and patterns are designed to force the defensive players out of position, enabling good shots and scoring opportunities. Therefore, it is the job of the coach to teach players the value of good defensive positioning—just what it is, how to maintain it when combating offensive screens and maneuvers, and how to help a teammate who is out of position. Good positioning takes a considerable amount of daily practice and constant emphasis by an enthusiastic coach.

For players to clearly understand defensive positioning, it is necessary to divide the court into zones or sides, as shown by diagrams 23.1 and 23.2. In diagram 23.1, zone C is the least dangerous area on the court, and unless the defense is a pressing style of defense, defensive players should drop off their opponents in this area. Zone B is a far more dangerous area of the court, and players should aggressively challenge their opponents in this area. Zone A is the most dangerous area of the court, and the constant goal of the team defense should be to prevent the ball from going into this area. Once it does go into zone A, all players should converge on the ball.

Diagram 23.2 divides the court into two sides. The side of the floor with the ball is called the "strong side," or "ball side." The side of the court away from the ball is called the "weak side," or "help side." The player guarding the ball should keep defensive pressure on the ball in most situations, while

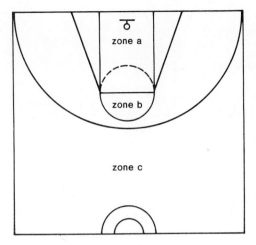

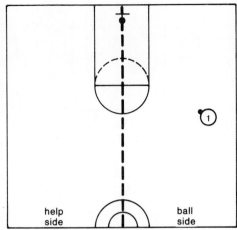

Diagram 23.1 *Floor zones for the man-for-man defense.* The defense must attempt to keep the ball out of zone A since it is the most dangerous area. Zone B is also a high percentage shooting area and requires pressure on the ball at all times. Zone C is the least dangerous area.

Diagram 23.2 The court is divided into two sides to help players understand and maintain defensive positioning. Players on the "ball side" of the court pressure the ball and deny penetrating passes. Players on the "help side" of the court sag away from their opponents toward the "ball side" of the court to give defensive help if needed.

Figure 23.1 Number 20 is in a *denial position* designed to prevent the opposing forward from receiving the basketball. It is important for the defender to use "split vision" to be able to see both the passer and the receiver.

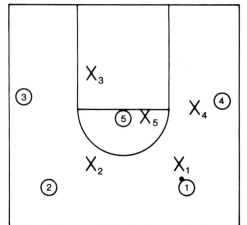

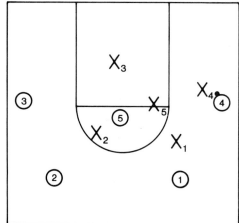

Diagram 23.3 *Defensive positions with the ball at the guard position.* X_1, X_4, and X_5 are on the "ball side" and play their opponents aggressively. X_2 and X_3 are on the "help side" and sag toward the "ball side" of the court.

Diagram 23.4 *Defensive positions with the ball at the forward position.* X_1, X_4, and X_5 are still on the "ball side" and play their opponents aggressively. Notice X_1 and X_5 have moved toward the ball. X_2 and X_3 are still on the "help side" but move further away from their opponents toward the ball.

"ball side" players guarding a player without the ball should overplay and attempt to prevent passes to their defensive opponents. Players guarding opponents on the "weak side" or "help side" of the court should sag considerably away from their respective opponents and toward the ball to be in position to give defensive help if needed. The distance players sag away from their particular opponents depends on how far their opponents are from the ball. Diagrams 23.3 and 23.4 show various positions on the floor dependent upon the location of the basketball.

Ball-You-Opponent Principle

The "ball-you-opponent" principle is very important in teaching proper "help side" defensive positioning. Defensive players must be constantly aware of the location of the basketball and their respective offensive opponents, and each must maintain a position between the two. Again, just how far away from the opponent depends on the location of the basketball. However, defensive players must maintain the ball-you-opponent position to prevent their opponents from being able to cut to receive the basketball.

Figure 23.2 The defensive player in the lane is observing the *ball-you-opponent principle*. He has sagged from the "help side" of the floor to the "ball side" in order to be able to help on a drive to the basket by the player with the ball.

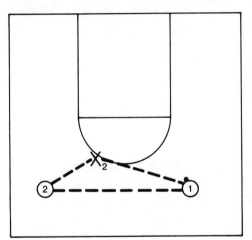

Diagram 23.5 *Ball-you-opponent position when guarding at the guard position.* Notice the imaginary triangle between the ball, opponent, and the defensive player.

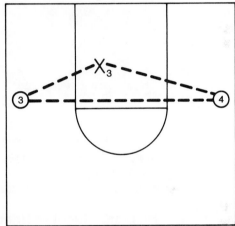

Diagram 23.6 *Ball-you-opponent position when guarding at the forward position.*

A study of diagrams 23.5 and 23.6 shows the correct ball-you-opponent position. Notice that a triangle is formed between the defensive player, the ball, and the defensive player's opponent. The base of the triangle is a line drawn from the opponent to the ball, with the defensive player forming the apex of the triangle. This imaginary triangle is maintained in all "help side" defensive situations.

Figure 23.3 Defensive player number 52 has violated the *ball-you-opponent principle* and has allowed number 45 to cut between him and the ball. Number 30 can now pass to number 45 in the low-post area.

Diagram 23.7 illustrates an example of incorrect ball-you-opponent position. X_2 has failed to move toward the "ball side" of the court and, by not doing so, the opponent being guarded by X_2 is in position to make a quick cut to the basket to receive the basketball. Also, X_2 is not in position to help stop any penetrating drive to the middle by ①.

Help-and-Recover Principle

Defensive players must be constantly aware of the necessity for helping their teammates in addition to guarding their respective opponents. Defensive help is needed particularly by the player guarding the basketball. Helping a teammate stop penetration of the ball and then returning to an assigned opponent is termed "help-and-recover." When the help-and-recover situation occurs, the defensive player gives aid quickly, and, when no longer needed, recovers quickly to the assigned opponent. This technique requires a great deal of practice from the various situations in which it may be needed. It also requires a great deal of alertness and hustle to be able to recover properly. Diagrams 23.8 and 23.9 show help-and-recover situations.

Figure 23.4 *A help-and-recover situation.* The defensive player guarding number 21 has shifted toward the ball to help his teammate stop penetration. If the ball is passed to number 21, the defender will quickly recover to guard number 21.

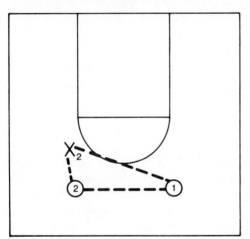

Diagram 23.7

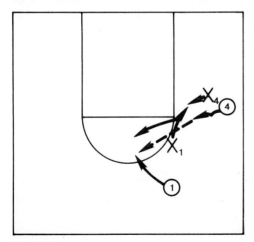

Diagram 23.9

Diagram 23.8

Diagram 23.7 *Incorrect ball-you-opponent position.* ② is in position to cut by X₂ for a pass from ① .

Diagram 23.8 *A help-and-recover situation at the guard position.* ① begins a drive. X₂ helps stop the penetration and returns to ② when ① picks up the dribble.

Diagram 23.9 *A help-and recover situation with the ball at the forward position.* As ④ begins to drive, X₁ helps stop penetration and returns to ① when ④ picks up the dribble.

Combating Screens

Since a considerable amount of screening is part of any offensive pattern, the good man-for-man team defense must be well prepared to combat screens. Screens can be countered in several ways, and the coach must determine a plan to combat these screens and to make certain each player clearly understands the technique. Most man-for-man defensive teams combat screens using one of three philosophies:

1. Switch opponents on all screens.
2. Switch opponents only when necessary.
3. Never switch opponents.

Teams who switch opponents find that they can combat screens relatively easily. However, switching opponents can result in smaller players having to guard larger players, slower players guarding faster players, and other mismatches. Therefore, few man-for-man defenses employ full switching techniques. Many teams switch only when necessary. This leads to some uncertainty and requires a great deal of communication between players to be successful. Far more teams today use the never-switch philosophy, feeling that proper defensive assignments can be made and maintained and that specific responsibility can be determined for scoring by an opponent.

For those teams who never switch or who seldom switch, three defensive techniques are needed to help combat screens. These are (1) the "fake switch" technique, (2) the "slide through" technique, and (3) the "over-the-top" technique. The fake switch is shown in diagram 23.10 and is actually another form of help-and-recover. The slide through is given in diagram 23.11 and is usually used against screens or crosses that occur outside of the high-percentage shooting range, or in zone C of diagram 23.1. When screens occur in zone B, or a potentially high-percentage shooting range, the over-the-top technique is needed, as shown in diagram 23.12. If the defensive player slides through in zone B, the offensive player can shoot the jump shot behind the screen when the slide through is occuring. By going over the top, the shot is prevented. Considerable practice is needed in each of these situations so that coordination between the defensive players is achieved.

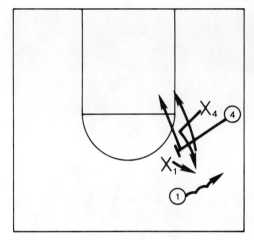

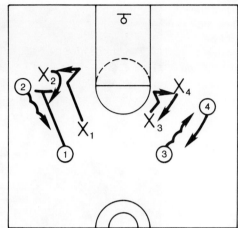

Diagram 23.10 *A fake switch used against a rear screen.* As ④ sets screen on X₁, X₄ steps out in ① 's path as if to switch. X₁ fights over the top of the screen. When ④ cuts for basket, X₄ goes also, attempting to stay between ④ and the ball.

Diagram 23.11 *The slide-through technique.* On the left, ① passes to ② and sets screen. As ② dribbles off screen, defensive player X₁ steps back and allows defensive player X₂ to slide through and remain with ②. On the right, ③ uses dribbling screen for ④. As ④ comes outside ③, X₃ steps back to allow X₄ to slide through and remain with ④.

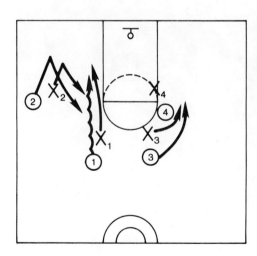

Diagram 23.12 *The over-the-top technique.* On the left, ① forms dribbling screen for ②. As ② cuts off screen, defensive player X₂ fights over the top of ① and between ① and ②. On the right, defensive player X₃ cuts between ③ and ④ as ③ cuts off ④ 's screen. If defensive players go behind screens this close to the basket, the offensive player can stop behind the screen for a good shot at the basket.

Figure 23.5 *Defensing the low-post player.* When the ball is even with the free-throw line, the defensive player should play on the top side of the low-post.

Figure 23.6 *Defensing the low-post player.* When the ball is on the baseline, the defensive player should play on the baseline side of the low post.

Figure 23.7 *Defensing the low-post player.* When the low post does receive the ball, other defenders should drop inside to help defense the low post. This is called "choking off" the low post.

Defensive Drills

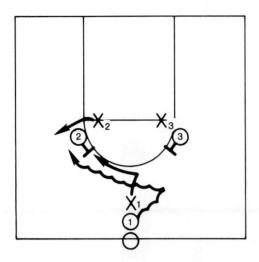

Diagram 23.13 *Over-the-top defensive drill.* ② and ③ set screens for ①. ① may change direction and dribble either way. X₁ must fight over the screen. X₂ and X₃ give defensive help.

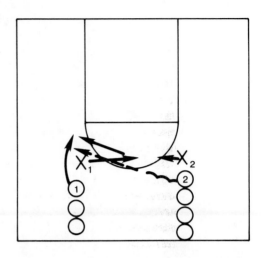

Diagram 23.14 *Guard to guard help-and-recover drill.* ② drives toward middle. X₁ helps stop penetration and recovers to ① when ② picks up dribble. Offensive players go to defense and defensive players go to end of the lines.

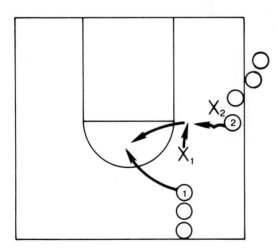

Diagram 23.15. *Guard to forward help-and-recover drill.* ② drives toward middle. X₁ helps stop penetration and returns to ① when ② picks up dribble. Offensive players go to defense and defensive players go to end of lines.

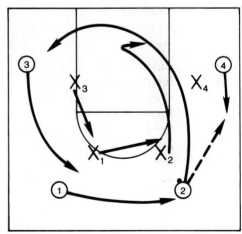

Diagram 23.16 *Shell defensive drill.* Defensive players learn to sag toward the ball, to guard a cutter, and to defense at various positions. Different situations may be presented by the offense. Here, ② passes to ④ and cuts through. ① and ③ rotate. X₂ defenses cutter, then stops in the lane for defensive help if needed.

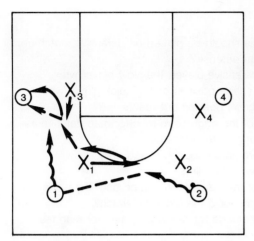

Diagram 23.17 *Shell defensive drill.* Defensive players learn to stop dribble penetration. ② drives middle. X_1 helps stop penetration as ② passes to ①. ① dribbles toward ③. X_3 helps stop penetration and returns to ③ on pass to ③ from ①.

Diagram 23.18 *Shell defensive drill.* Here defensive players learn to defense an offside interchange of offensive players. ② passes to ① and interchanges with ④. X_2 and X_4 must use the proper technique to stay with their respective opponents. After this interchange, ① may pass to ④ and interchange with ③.

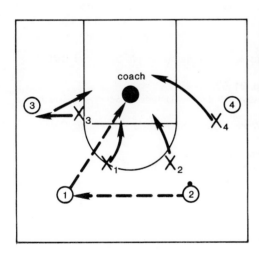

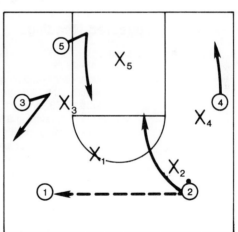

Diagram 23.19. *Shell defense drill.* Coach acts as opposing center in lane. Ball is passed around perimeter and then passed into coach. Defensive players must drop back to "choke off" player (coach) with ball.

Diagram 23.20 *5-on-5 defensive drill.* Offensive players move in any direction with defensive players maintaining proper defensive position. On shot, defensive players must block out and get rebound. Coach should make corrections and penalize defense if offense gets rebound.

Discussion Questions

1. How much emphasis should be placed on defensive match-ups in man-for-man team defense?
2. Which is the best defensive player, the slow player who maintains good defensive position or the quick player who does not maintain good position but reacts well?
3. Discuss the merits of the aggressive man-for-man defense as compared to the sagging man-for-man.
4. What team defensive drills should be used daily, if any?
5. How should screens be handled?
6. If it is impossible for the defender to watch both the ball and the opponent, which should the defender watch?
7. Discuss coaching methods for developing man-for-man team defense.
8. Discuss rebounding from the "help side."

Projects

1. Write a brief paper outlining the differences in defensive positioning in a basket-protection, man-for-man defense and an aggressive, overplay, man-for-man defense.
2. Interview a local coach about his or her philosophy on defensing screens. On defensing a split-the-post maneuver. On defensing the baseline. On defensing a player without the ball.

Suggested Readings

Goetz, Lou. "Push Them Baseline." *Scholastic Coach,* December 1975, pp. 48–49.

Hankinson, *Progressions,* pp. 91–92.

Kloppenburg, Bob. "Progressive Off the Ball Defense." *Scholastic Coach,* October 1978, pp. 22ff.

Mili, Vinnie. "Developing a Winning Defensive Attitude." *Scholastic Coach,* December 1979, p. 36ff.

Stewart and Scholz, *Complete Program,* pp. 229–77.

Tarkanian and Warren, *Winning Basketball,* pp. 198–99.

Wooden, *Modern Basketball,* pp. 275–78.

chapter twenty-four

Zone Defense

Zone defenses differ from man-for-man defenses in that players are assigned a particular area of the court to defense rather than a particular opponent. Foremost attention is focused on the ball and the area of the court to be defensed. All defensive players mass in assigned areas in and around the free-throw lane and shift as a coordinated unit with each movement of the ball by the offense. This team massing and shifting protects the area close to the basket and makes short shots difficult to obtain.

Advantages of Zone Defense

1. It effectively counters the set-pattern offense involving screening and cutting.
2. It affords maximum protection in the area close to the basket, making short shots difficult.
3. Fouls are committed less frequently. A switch to a zone defense when a key player has accumulated several fouls is wise in many cases.
4. It conserves energy.
5. Fast breaks are more easily obtained from zone formations.
6. Most zone defenses strengthen rebounding.
7. It is very effective on the small courts so often used by high school teams.
8. It minimizes fundamental mistakes by a defensive player.
9. It increases chances for pass interceptions and encourages "ball hawking."
10. It is relatively easy both to teach and to learn.
11. The tall, slow player tends to play zone better than man-for-man.

Disadvantages of Zone Defense

1. It is weak against good outside shooting teams.
2. It is susceptible to fast-breaking teams.
3. It allows opponents to overload an area by placing two players in the area guarded by one defensive player.
4. Individual defensive fundamentals tend to be weakened.
5. It is often ineffective against the deliberate game or stall.
6. The offense often can move the ball faster than the defense can shift.
7. The standard zone defense must be abandoned when a team is behind in the score late in the game.
8. Using the zone makes it more difficult to determine individual responsibility.

General Zone Principles

1. *Players must get position quickly.* Most offensive plans for defeating the zone include the fast break. Therefore, zone defensive players must hustle downcourt and into proper position immediately after giving up the ball.
2. *Players must maintain good individual defensive stance.* The rapid shifts necessary to offensive ball movement can be executed more quickly when proper defensive stance is maintained. In addition, correct stance is necessary to prevent offensive drives.
3. *Players should keep hands up in position to deflect passes.*
4. *To be able to handle offensive movement, talk between players is of utmost importance.*
5. *Players must focus their attention on the ball and shift rapidly with each movement of the ball.* No zone defensive player should ever turn his or her back on the ball.
6. When an offensive player cuts through a zone near the ball, *he should be guarded man-for-man until no longer in position to receive the pass.* The defensive player guarding him man-for-man must then release and hustle back to his original position (diagram 24.17).
7. *All players must be rebound conscious.*

Types of Zone Defenses

There are three major zone defenses used by modern basketball teams:

1. 2-1-2 or 2-3 zone
2. 1-2-2 or 3-2 zone
3. 1-3-1 zone

Figure 24.1 Zone players must focus their attention on the ball and keep their hands up in position to deflect passes.

Figure 24.2 *The 2-1-2 zone defense.*

Zone Formations

The three major zone defenses are illustrated in diagrams 24.1 through 24.5.

In the 2-1-2 zone, X_1 and X_2 are usually the defensive guards, X_3 and X_4 are the forwards, and X_5 is the center.

Some philosophical argument exists on whether the 2-1-2 and 2-3 zones are different types of zone defenses or simply the same one. Actually, they are one defense with an adjustment of the number 5 player dependent upon whether the offense plays a player in the foul-line area. If the offense plays in the foul-line area, X_5 moves up toward the foul line. This requires X_3 and X_4 to play a little more tightly on the baseline, thus creating a 2-1-2 formation. If no opponent is at the foul line, X_5 can play back near the basket and allow X_3 and X_4 to move further toward the corners, hence the 2-3 terminology. The shifts are really the same, and the zone is one defense with adjustments.

In the 1-2-2 zone, X_1 is usually the smallest player, X_2 is the second guard, X_3 is the small forward, and X_4 and X_5 are the two tallest players and best rebounders.

As in previous discussion about the 2-1-2 and the 2-3 zone terminology, some philosophical argument exists among coaches as to whether the 1-2-2 zone and the 3-2 zone are the same. Again, the shifts are identical. If the

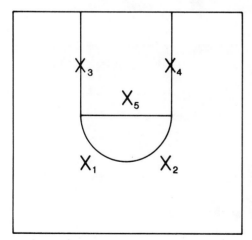

Diagram 24.1 *2-1-2 zone formation.*

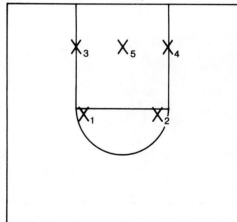

Diagram 24.2 When X_5 moves back under the basket, the 2-1-2 zone becomes a 2-3.

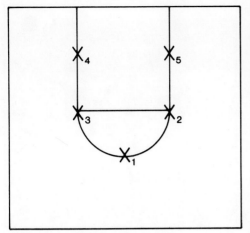

Diagram 24.3 *The 1-2-2 zone.*

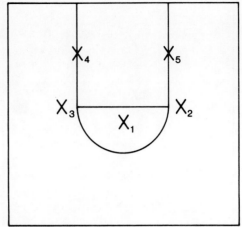

Diagram 24.4 When X_1 moves back and X_2 and X_3 move wide, the 1-2-2 becomes a 3-2 in formation.

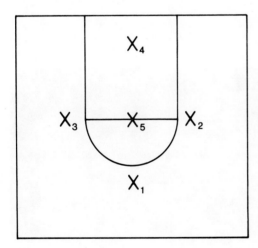

Diagram 24.5 *The 1-3-1 zone formation.*

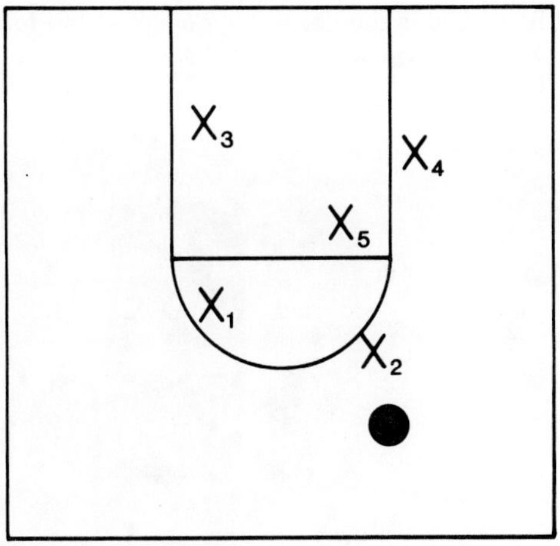

Diagram 24.6 *The 2-1-2 zone with the ball at the guard position.*

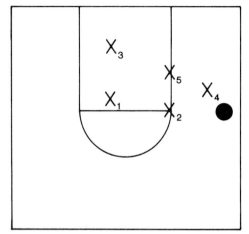

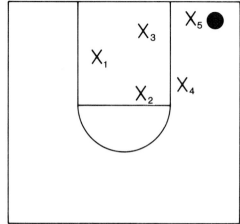

Diagram 24.7 *2-1-2 zone shifting responsibilities with the ball at the forward position.* Some teams do not allow X_4 to come out this far; instead, they "hedge" with X_4 and chase the ball with X_2. This depends a great deal on how good a shooter the opponent at the forward position is.

Diagram 24.8 *2-1-2 zone shifting responsibilities with the ball in the corner.* This assumes that X_4 has moved up to defense the player at the forward position. If not, X_4 would take the corner.

Figure 24.3 *The 1-2-2 zone defense.*

wing players, X_2 and X_3, play tightly along the lane, the defense takes on a definite 1-2-2 formation. However, if a team plays its wing players further away from the lane, either to stop long outside shooting attempts or to increase opportunities for pass interceptions by playing in the passing lanes, the defense can take on a 3-2 appearance. Again, the two are one zone defense with adjustments.

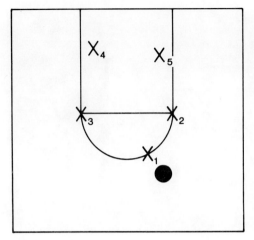

Diagram 24.9 *The 1-2-2 zone with the ball at the guard position.*

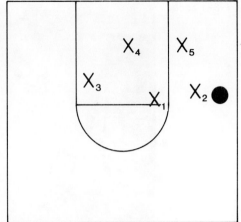

Diagram 24.10 *The 1-2-2 zone shifting responsibilities with the ball at the forward position.*

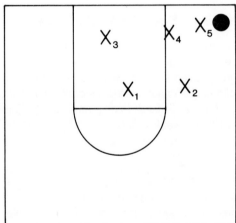

Diagram 24.11. *1-2-2 zone shifting responsibilities with the ball in the corner.*

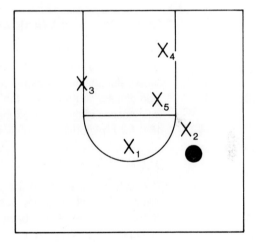

Diagram 24.12 *The 1-3-1 zone with the ball at the right guard position.*

Figure 24.4 *The 1-3-1 zone defense.*

In the 1-3-1 zone, X_1 is usually the smallest defensive player. X_2 can either be the second guard or the small forward. X_4 can also either be the second guard or the small forward, with X_3 and X_5 being the big forward and the center.

Strengths and Weaknesses of Each Zone Defense

Each type of zone has its particular strengths and weaknesses. Since offensive strengths vary, the zone that is effective against one opponent may be unsuccessful against another. For this reason, many teams use more than one type of zone. In addition to the following summary of the major strengths and weaknesses of the various zone defenses, go back to diagrams 16.3 through 16.6 for a pictorial presentation of these weak areas.

2-1-2 or 2-3 Zone

This defense is strong in the pivot area and corners and affords good rebounding strength. It is very weak on the sides at the free-throw line extended. If the X_5 player is played back near the basket, the defense becomes even stronger in the corners but is somewhat weaker at the high-post area.

1-2-2 or 3-2 Zone

This defense is the strongest zone against outside shooting teams and provides excellent fast-break opportunities, especially if the two inside defenders are good rebounders. It is weak in the corners and pivot area, and it is not recommended for use against a good post player.

1-3-1 Zone

This defense is exceptionally strong in the pivot area and is a very sound defense when opposing a high-scoring post player. It is strong at the forward positions, and rebounding strength is good. It is not very strong against good shooting from the guard positions and is very weak in the corners.

Shifting Responsibilities

Diagrams 24.6 through 24.16 delineate shifting responsibilities for the various types of zone defenses.

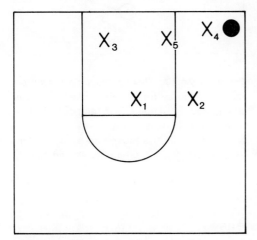

Diagram 24.13

Diagram 24.13 *The 1–3–1 zone shifting responsibilities with the ball in the corner.*

Diagram 24.14 *The 1–3–1 zone shifting responsibilities with the ball in the opposite corner.* Notice that X_4 has corner-to-corner responsibility.

Diagram 24.15 *Shifting responsibilities of the 1–3–1 zone on a skip pass from the corner.* In this case, X_4 cannot cover from corner to corner. Instead, X_5 takes the corner after the skip pass, and X_4 moves to the middle.

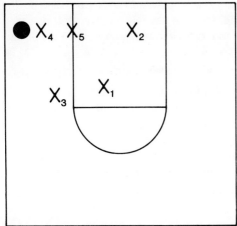

Diagram 24.14

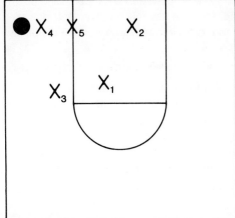

Diagram 24.15

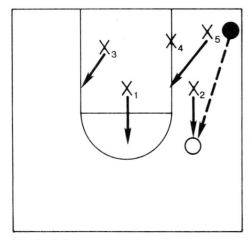 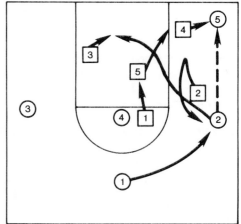

Diagram 24.16 After X₅ defenses the corner, X₅ returns to the middle on the next pass out. X₄ then resumes normal corner-to-corner responsibility. This adjustment is easy to teach and is very important to the success of the 1–3–1 zone.

Diagram 24.17 *Playing the cutter man-for-man until the cutter can be picked up in another zone.* ② *passes to* ⑤ *and cuts. Defensive player* ☐2 *must play* ② *man-for-man a few steps until* ② *is picked up by* ☐5 *. Defensive player* ☐2 *must then release and quickly hustle back into position to pick up* ① *cutting over.*

The Match-up Zone Defense

The match-up zone defense attempts to shift into position to be able to defend each opponent man-for-man, and this shifting into position is referred to as "matching up." It can be rather easy to play and very confusing to the opponent, especially if the offense does not use much movement. However, the match-up defense becomes more difficult to play with increased offensive movement.

Some key advantages of the match-up zone defense are

1. Many opposing teams fail to recognize the defense.
2. Most teams do not have a match-up zone attack.
3. It reduces fouling.
4. It affords good defensive rebounding.
5. A team can hide a poor defender.
6. A team can play zone yet still put pressure on the ball.

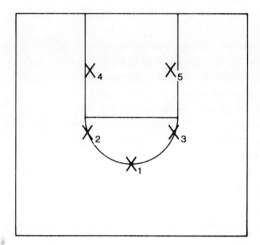

Diagram 24.18 *Initial formation for the 1-2-2 match-up zone defense.*

Match-up Initial Formation

The match-up zone defense begins from an initial zone defense formation or "home formation." This initial formation can be any of the standard zone defenses; however, it is important that a team learn to match-up from only one zone defensive formation. Players can become confused enough when matching from one formation, and attempting to match from more than one is almost impossible.

Basic Match-up Rules

Rules that clearly outline shifting responsibilities must be established for each defensive position of the "home formation." The following are basic rules for matching from the 1-2-2 zone formation (diagram 24.18).

1. Defensive players rotate with the first move by X_1. If X_1 takes an opponent to the right of the defense, X_3 moves up. If X_1 takes an opponent to the left, X_2 moves up.
2. X_3 defends the first player to the left of X_1.
3. X_2 defends the first player to the right of X_1.
4. X_4 defends the low post on the right side of defense. If no low post, look to corner or high post.
5. X_5 defends the low post on the left side of the defense. If no low post, look to corner or high post. Any post player within 10 feet of the basket must be fronted.

Rules to Cover Motion

Matching the offense is simple until the offense begins movement. When this occurs, players must shift opponents. In order to be able to do this effectively, players must understand the rules for defending any offensive maneuver and must have had a great deal of practice against any situation.

Because of the great variety of possible maneuvers by the offense, scouting becomes a premium to the match-up zone team. Knowing what attack patterns the offense might use and having time to practice against these maneuvers is vital to the match-up's success.

Examples of offensive movement and rules for shifting responsibilities are given in diagrams 24.19 through 24.21.

Diagram 24.19 *Matching on a strong side cut.* X_3 takes ②. X_1 covers high post ③, and X_5 takes cutter ①.

Diagram 24.20 *Matching on a cut away from the ball.* X_3 takes ball. X_1 takes ⑤. X_5 picks up ① but stops in lane when ① continues to corner. X_4 now has responsibility for ①, and X_5 has responsibility for ④.

Diagram 24.21 *Matching on a baseline cut.* X_1 takes ball. X_3 fronts ⑤ as X_5 picks up ③. X_5 stops in lane looking at ball and releases ③ to X_4. X_5 now has responsibility for ④.

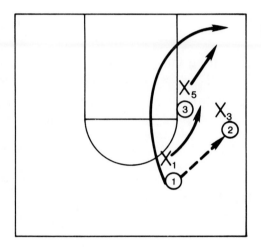

Diagram 24.19

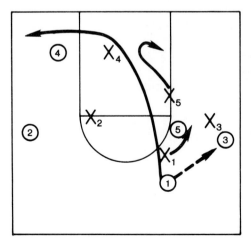

Diagram 24.20

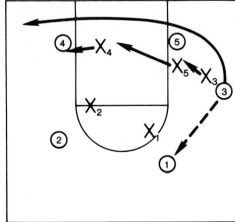

Diagram 24.21

Discussion Questions

1. Is rebounding stronger in a zone or a man-for-man defense?
2. What type of defense does a zone defensive team use when it has to press to obtain possession of the ball?
3. Does a good zone defense conserve energy?
4. Does a good zone defense reduce fouling?
5. Of what importance are breakdown drills in teaching zone defense?
6. How can a zone defense be set up against a fast-breaking team?
7. Should zones be adjusted with each particular opponent?

Projects

1. Write a brief paper discussing defensive rebounding in a zone defense.
2. Write a brief paper discussing the strengths and weaknesses of various zone defenses.
3. Devise two breakdown drills for teaching a zone defense and teach these drills to the class.

Suggested Readings

Ebert and Cheatum, *Basketball*, pp. 165–83.

Gappy, Bill. "Michigan Tech's 2-3 Match-up Zone." *Scholastic Coach*, December 1978, pp. 28–30.

Hankinson, *Progressions*, pp. 97–115.

Hartwig, James. "Camouflaging Your Zone Defense." *Scholastic Coach*, November 1978, pp. 79–80.

McCrea, Dotty. "2-3 Match-up Zone." *Scholastic Coach*, September 1977, p. 62.

Miller, David, and Kobel, Butch. "Beat Motion with a 23X Zone." *Scholastic Coach*, November 1979, pp. 42ff.

Piscopo, Joe. " 'T' Match-Up Defense." *Scholastic Coach*, November 1977, pp. 22ff.

Potter, Dr. Glenn R. "Zone Defense by the Rules." *Scholastic Coach*, September 1979, pp. 34ff.

Summers, Al. "A Junior High School 1-3-1 Zone Defense." *Scholastic Coach*, October 1979, pp. 26ff.

Tarkanian and Warren, *Winning Basketball*, pp. 207–34.

Wendelken, Maureen, and Wendelken, John. "Montclair State's 2-3 Zone Defense." *Pro-Keds Coaches Digest*, 1980, pp. 38–39.

Wooden, *Modern Basketball*, pp. 289–90.

chapter twenty-five

Pressing Defenses

It is absolutely necessary for every basketball team to have some type of pressing defense, mainly for the simple reason that a team must be able to press for the ball when behind in score late in the game. The usefulness of pressing defenses, however, is not limited to this situation alone. Pressing defenses are strategically sound in the following situations:

1. When behind in the score late in the game
2. Against the poor ball-handling team
3. Against the inexperienced team
4. Against the poorly conditioned team
5. Against the methodical, slow-breaking team
6. Against the team with a very outstanding offensive center
7. As a surprise element
8. For game tempo control

Prerequisites for Pressing Defenses

The following essentials are prerequisites for any pressing defense:

1. Desire and pride
2. Hustle and aggressiveness
3. Anticipation
4. Teamwork
5. Speed and quickness
6. Talk
7. Conditioning

Types of Pressing Defenses

Pressing defenses usually are either a type of man-for-man or a type of zone. Occasionally, a combination of the two is used. There are three positions of pick-up for both man-for-man and zone presses—at full-court, three-quarter court, and half-court.

Man-for-Man Press

Full-Court Man-for-Man Press

Since the entire court area must be defended, the full-court man-for-man press demands the utmost in team cooperation for success. Failure of one defensive player to do the job completely voids the work of four others. Constantly emphasize this point when teaching the defense.

Inbounds Pass. After a basket, the defense must first concentrate on the inbounds pass. Pressure must be exerted on every inbounds player in a coordinated team effort to force a bad pass on the throw-in. Every defensive player must pick up an assigned opponent immediately and play in position to see both the ball and the opponent (diagram 25.1). This is the only time when it is absolutely necessary for the offense to make a pass. After the throw-in, the offense may elect to clear the floor for a clever dribbler and allow the dribbler to advance the ball downcourt. Since this pass must be made, proper defensive pressure results in opportunities for interceptions.

The defensive player guarding the inbounds passer may either harass the passer in an effort to prevent an easy throw-in or may drop away from the passer to double-team possible receivers. It may be necessary to overplay the passer to keep the ball away from particular opponents. For example, if the opponent's best dribbler is on the left side of the court, the out-of-bounds player may be overplayed to the left to encourage the pass to a less proficient ball-handler on the right.

When pressure results in preventing a successful throw-in, the offensive team usually resorts to screening tactics to free a player for a pass. Since the pass must be made inbounds within 5 seconds, a simple switch can nullify the effectiveness of a screen.

Downcourt Advancement. After a successful throw-in, most press attacks clear the floor for the good dribbler and let this dribbler advance the ball downcourt. Preventing the dribbler from advancing the ball downcourt can be extremely difficult. The best defensive player should be assigned to this dribbler. The defensive player should continually put as much pressure as possible on the dribbler and should "turn" the dribbler, or make him or her change direction, as many times as possible. Although continual pressure on the dribbler is needed, it is also important that the defensive player avoid

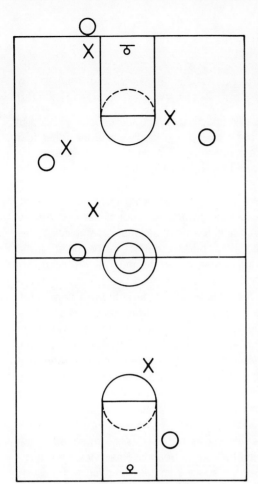

Diagram 25.1 *Full-court man-for-man defensive positioning.*

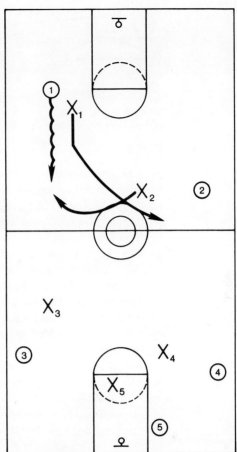

Diagram 25.2 *The switch to pick up the open dribbler. As ① drives by X₁ X₂ quickly moves over to defense ① while X₁ takes ②.*

fouling the dribbler and that he or she be contained and not allowed to dribble by. Excessive fouling ruins any pressing defense, and when a dribbler is allowed to dribble past a defender, the result is an outnumbering situation at the offensive end of the court. If the dribbler succeeds in driving by the defensive opponent, he or she must be picked up as soon as possible by the next nearest defensive opponent. The defensive player guarding the dribbler must then hustle to pick up the open offensive player and complete the switch. Diagram 25.2 illustrates a method of switching to the open dribbler.

Once the dribbler is advancing the ball downcourt, the best tactic for the defense is to wait until he or she picks up the dribble.

Figure 25.1 *Double-team technique.*

When this occurs, the defensive player guarding the dribbler should put on extreme pressure—waving arms and yelling loudly—and the other four defensive players should play in a denial position on their respective opponents. Such harrassment can lead to interceptions and mistakes by the offense.

The offense may use other methods in advancing the ball downcourt. If the forwards and center are breaking back to meet passes, defensive players must stay in position to contest for these passes. A defensive center may tend to be lax in this assignment, but this cannot be permitted. If the center will not press the opposing center, he or she must be replaced with another player who will.

If the offense is using screening tactics to advance the ball downcourt, the defense must have clear assignments in handling the screens. Simple switches usually reduce the value of the screen in these situations. The switch should always be made aggressively and decisively. *Talk* is very important for ensuring coordinated defensive moves against these screens and preventing fouling. If the defense is trailing, use the double-team on all screens on the ball to gain possession. If an offensive player with the ball turns away so that his or her vision of the overall defense is limited, use the double-team again (fig. 25.1).

The full-court press after a rebound is not as easily formed, since the offense does not have to take the ball out of bounds. Basic defensive technique is the same as the press after a score, with the exception of the player responsible for defensive balance. This player must check to be sure no offensive player is cutting downcourt unguarded before releasing backcourt responsibility and hurrying into position. Because of the difficulty in setting up a press after a rebound, the three-quarter court press is used more often in this situation.

Three-Quarter Court Man-for-Man Press

The defensive technique for the three-quarter court man-for-man press is basically the same as for the full-court press. The position of pick-up is from 10 to 15 feet from the midcourt line, as shown by diagram 25.3. Since the defense does not have as much area to cover, it is not as susceptible to the long scoring pass or to other errors as is the full-court defense. It is excellent for use after the opponent rebounds a missed shot, because it does not require as much time to establish defensive positions. If two quick and agile guards are available, this defense can be used to harass the offense into making costly mistakes.

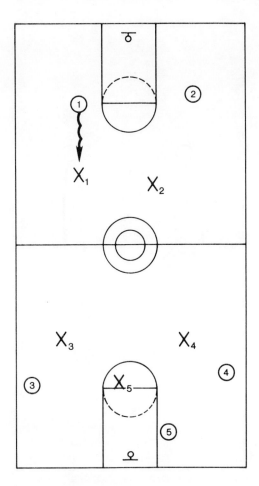

Diagram 25.3 *Position of pick-up for the three-quarter-court man-for-man press.*

Half-Court Man-for-Man Press

The half-court man-for-man press challenges the offense as it attempts to advance the ball across midcourt. This is an excellent defense against the methodical set-play type of team, because it can force the opponents out of their preferred pattern and into unaccustomed cutting maneuvers. The offense that likes to dribble the ball across midcourt uncontested and then call its plays by some prearranged signal can find this defense particularly troublesome. Since this defense does not have as much of the floor area to cover as the full-court and three-quarter court presses, it is stronger in the scoring area. Reduced floor coverage does not require as much stamina and conditioning. The team with little squad depth probably will find this defense more suitable than the full-court press.

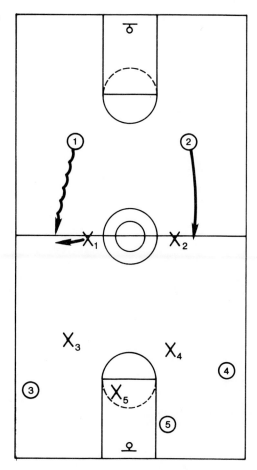

Diagram 25.4 *The half-court man-for-man press.*

As the offense advances the ball across midcourt, the defense should force the dribbler to the sideline (diag. 25.4). Of course, the objective is to force the dribbler to stop the dribble as near to the midcourt corner as possible. Once the offensive player has picked up the dribble and become "dead," the defensive player guarding that player should continually harass with hands and arms in an effort to prevent a good pass. Encourage the lob pass or bounce pass. The other defensive players should guard between their respective opponents and the ball in an attempt to prevent any opponent from being open for a pass. Encourage interception attempts, and thoroughly practice methods for defensing situations that arise from unsuccessful interception attempts (diag. 25.5).

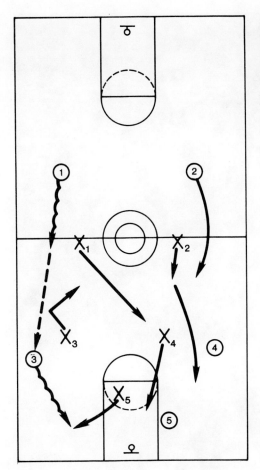

Diagram 25.5 *Defensive coverage for the missed interception attempt.* X₃ attempts interception unsuccessfully. As ③ drives for the basket, X₅ moves to stop the drive while X₄ shifts to defense ⑤. The other defensive players shift accordingly.

Zone Presses

Full-Court and Three-Quarter Court Zone Presses

Most zone presses, whether full-court or three-quarter court, are a variation of one of the following:

1. 1-2-1-1
2. 1-2-2
3. 2-2-1

Figure 25.2 *The double-team situation.* Defensive players should keep arms up to prevent a downcourt pass if possible and should not reach in and foul the ball-handler.

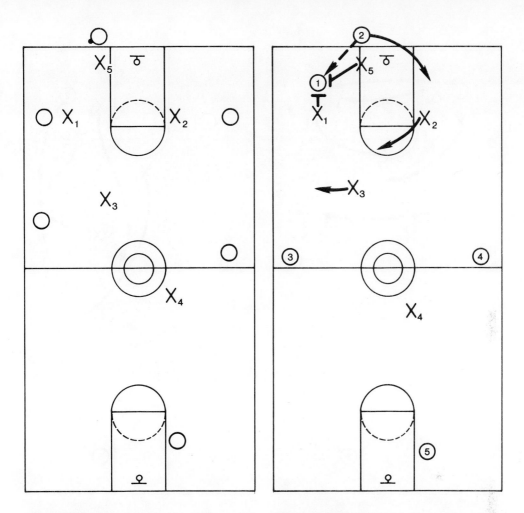

Diagram 25.6 *The 1-2-1-1 zone press set-up with the ball out of bounds.*

Diagram 25.7 *The 1-2-1-1 zone press. As ① receives ball inbounds, X₁ and X₅ move into double team position. X₂ shuts off any pass to the middle, while X₃ prevents pass down the sideline. X₄ protects deep and also looks to intercept any lob pass to ④.*

1-2-1-1 Full-Court Zone Press. The 1-2-1-1 full-court zone press is given in diagram 25.6. X_5 is usually one of the tallest players on the team and is positioned to be able to harass the inbound passer. X_1 is normally the best individual defensive player and is positioned at the left front so he or she can challenge the player receiving the inbounds pass, since the majority of teams throw the ball into that side. X_2 is stationed on the right side of the court and must be a type of defensive player similar to X_1. X_3 is in the "interceptor" position, and X_4 is responsible for the backline defense.

Diagram 25.7 illustrates the double-team situation after the throw-in. As ① receives the basketball, X_1 and X_5 converge to set a double-team. X_3

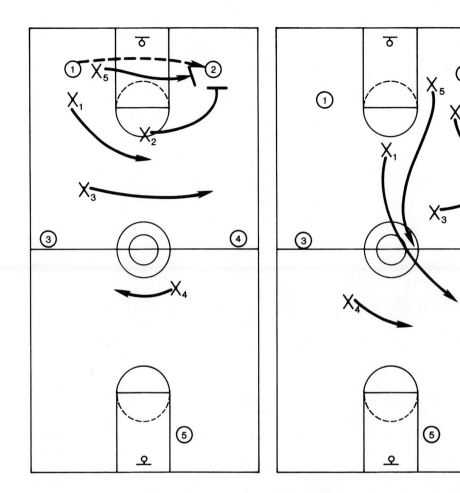

Diagram 25.8 *The 1-2-1-1 zone press.* ① passes to ②. X_5 leaves first double-team to come across court and join X_2 in a double-team on ②. X_1 must shut off any pass to the middle. X_3 rushes across court to prevent pass to ④ down sideline. X_4 continues to protect deep but must now look to intercept any lob pass made to ③.

Diagram 25.9 *The 1-2-1-1 zone press.* When ② passes to ④, another double-team can be formed by X_2 and X_3. X_1 must come across to protect sideline, while X_5 must defense the middle area. X_4 is still responsible for the basket area.

shuts off the pass receiver near the sideline, and X_2 shuts off the middle. X_4 must protect the basket but should be ready to intercept a long diagonal lob pass to ④. Shifting responsibilities are shown in diagram 25.8. If ① succeeds in making the pass to ②, X_2 advances and joins X_5 in another double-team situation. The interceptor, X_3, must quickly move across court to the opposite sideline, and X_1 must shut off the middle area. X_4 moves away to the opposite

Figure 25.3 Most full-court zone presses use one player to press the out-of-bounds passer.

side of the court ready again for an attempt at intercepting any cross-court lob pass.

If the pass is made to ③ or another player downcourt, most zone presses eliminate any future double-team. Instead they pursue the ball downcourt and set up in their normal defensive position. Actually, one of the keys to the success of the zone press is how well a team gets "pursuit" after the ball. Once the ball passes the front line of the defense an outnumbering situation exists and, unless there is great "pursuit" by the defense, the offense gets a very close uncontested shot.

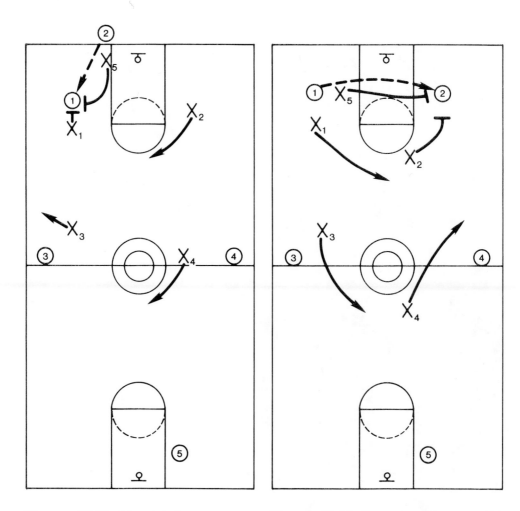

Diagram 25.10. *The 1-2-2 zone press.* Front players have basically the same responsibilities as those in the 1-2-1-1. However, X_3 and X_4 share responsibilities. In this case, X_3 prevents pass down sideline while X_4 protects deep.

Diagram 25.11 *The 1-2-2 zone press.* On pass from ① to ②, X_4 moves up to prevent pass to ④ while X_3 moves back to protect basket.

1-2-2 Full-Court Zone Press. The 1-2-2 full-court zone press is the same as the 1-2-1-1 with the exception of the backline responsibilities. In the 1-2-1-1, the interceptor, X_3, covers from sideline to sideline, and the back player, X_4, is responsible for basket protection. The 1-2-2 zone press allows X_3 and X_4 to share those responsibilities. On the double-team in diagram 25.10, X_3 protects the sideline, and X_4 has basket protection as in the 1-2-1-1 zone press. The difference occurs when the pass is made from ① to ② (diag. 25.11). Then, X_4 moves up and takes the sideline, and X_3 moves back and

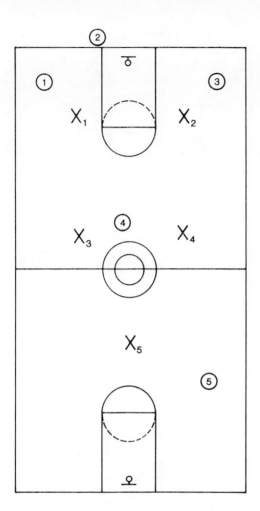

Diagram 25.12 *The 2-2-1 full-court zone press with the ball out of bounds.*

takes basket protection. The 1-2-2 is stronger in sideline coverage than the 1-2-1-1, because X_4 can move up more quickly to cover the sideline area than X_3 can come across. However, the 1-2-2 does not afford as good of basket protection as the 1-2-1-1. Hence, many coaches use the safer 1-2-1-1 press.

2-2-1 Full-Court Zone Press. The 2-2-1 zone press was popularized by John Wooden at UCLA. It does not depend upon a double-team situation as much as the 1-2-1-1 and the 1-2-2 presses. Instead, it depends on harassment of the dribbler by one player with the other players in position to make an interception. Diagram 25.12 shows the basic set-up of the 2-2-1. X_1 and X_2 must be good containing players who can prevent the dribbler from blasting by on the dribble. X_3 and X_4 should be good interceptors, while X_5 must be the "traffic director" and basket protector. It is X_5's job to constantly talk to teammates, telling them of offensive screens or cuts.

Diagram 25.13 *The 2-2-1 full-court zone press after the throw-in.* X₁ *puts pressure on* ① , X₂ *moves to prevent a pass to the middle,* X₃ *prevents a pass down sideline, while* X₄ *is responsible for protecting the mid-court area.* X₅ *protects deep and looks to intercept any long lob pass downcourt.*

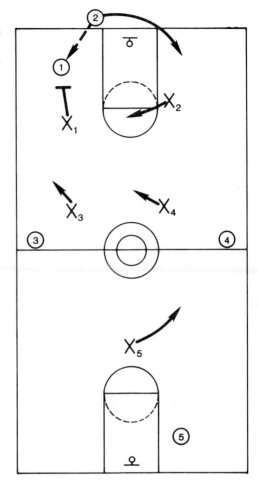

Diagram 25.13 indicates the position of the defense after the initial throw-in. As ① receives the pass, X₁ moves up into a pressure position. X₂ shuts the middle of the court, X₃ defenses the sideline, and X₄ defenses the area near midcourt.

As the pass is made from ① to ② , X₂ moves into a position to pressure the ball, while X₁ shuts the middle, X₄ moves to protect the sideline, and X₃ covers the area near midcourt.

As in the 1-2-1-1 and 1-2-2, once the ball advances by the frontline players, most zone-pressing teams retreat quickly into a better position to protect the basket.

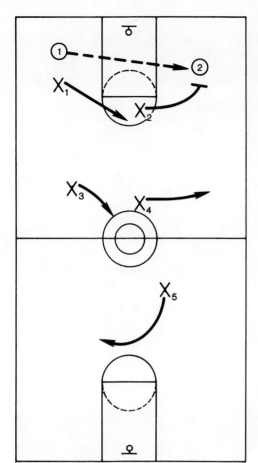

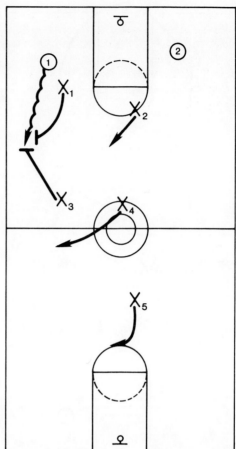

Diagram 25.14 *The 2-2-1 full-court zone press.* ①passes to ②. X_2 moves to put pressure on ②, while X_1 moves to protect middle. X_4 shifts to cover sideline, and X_3 protects midcourt area. X_5 continues deep protection.

Diagram 25.15 *The 2-2-1 full-court zone press with a sideline double-team.* X_3 moves up to join X_1 in double-teaming ①driving down sideline. X_2 moves to protect midcourt area as X_4 moves to sideline. X_5 continues to protect deep and must continually be alert for cross-court passes.

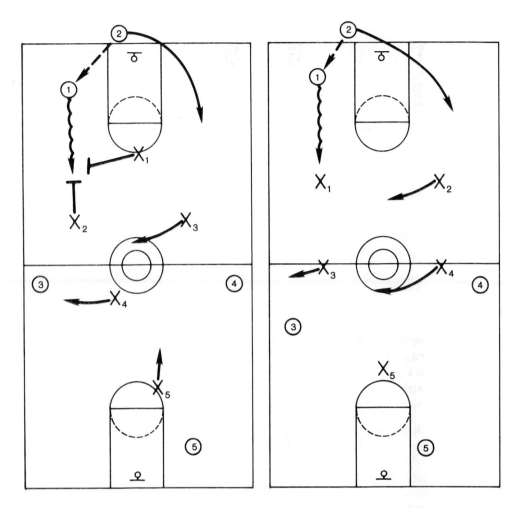

Diagram 25.16 *The 1-2-1-1 three-quarter court zone press.* The basic shifts are the same as in the full-court defense. However, since the defense has more time to get organized, the taller player normally used to press the ball out of bounds can move back to basket protection, and quicker guards can move forward into double-team position.

Diagram 25.17. *The 2-2-1 three-quarter court zone press.* The basic shifts are the same as in the full-court defense.

Three-Quarter Court Zone Presses. Any of the zone presses mentioned here can be used both at full-court and at three-quarter court. The position of defensive pick-up varies, but the shifting responsibilities are the same. Diagram 25.16 illustrates the 1-2-1-1 press used at three-quarter court, while diagram 25.17 shows the 2-2-1 press at three-quarter court.

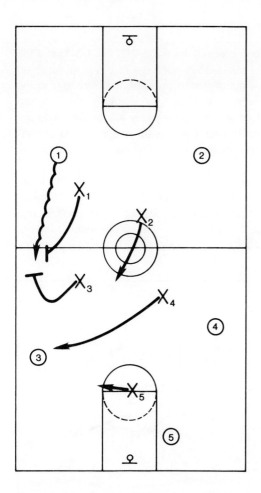

Diagram 25.18 *A midcourt double-team from the 2-2-1 three-quarter court zone press.*

One of the differences between the full- and three-quarter court zone press is in the positioning of players. Since the full-court zone press must be set up very quickly, and since while it is being set up a defensive guard must check for defensive balance, taller players who have cut into rebound position are often placed in the front of the press. Therefore many full-court pressing teams use their center to guard the out-of-bounds player and to make the first double-team. However, the three-quarter court press has a little more time available to set up, and most teams tend to put their center back and their guards up front.

Half-Court Zone Press

The basic types of half-court zone presses are the 1-2-2, the 1-3-1, and the 2-1-2. Since the half-court zone press does not have to cover as large an area as the full-court and three-quarter zone presses, it is stronger in the scoring area and not as susceptible to error. It is excellent against a stalling team, because double-team situations are more easily established, and underbasket protection can be maintained. Every team needs a type of half-court zone press, simply to have another weapon when behind late in the game.

Shifting responsibilities for the half-court presses are basically the same as the full-court zone presses, with a few exceptions. Diagrams 25.19 through 25.26 show the three basic half-court zone presses. Diagram 25.25 illustrates a cornertrap maneuver from the 1-3-1 formation that can produce interceptions.

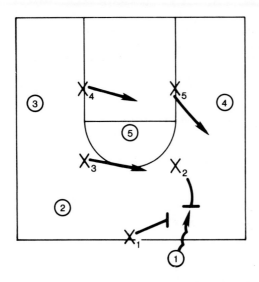

Diagram 25.19 *The 1-2-2 half-court zone press.* X₁ and X₂ double-team ① just past midcourt. X₃ protects the middle, X₅ prevents pass to sideline, and X₄ protects basket.

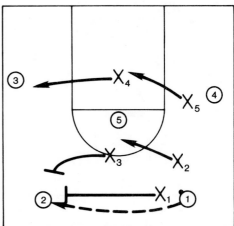

Diagram 25.20 ① passes to ② out of the double-team. X₁ chases and joins X₃ in a new double-team. X₂ protects middle, X₄ moves to protect sideline, and X₅ protects baskets.

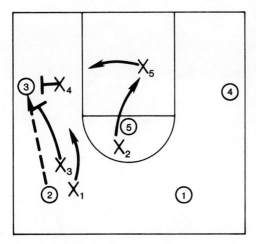

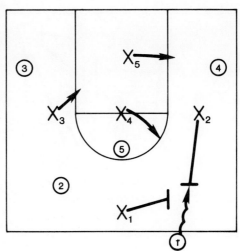

Diagram 25.21 *A double-team at the forward position in the 1-2-2 half-court press.* X_3 and X_4 double-team. X_5 protects low-post area, X_2 moves into lane and looks to go for any cross-court pass. X_1 looks to go for interception on outlet pass to ②.

Diagram 25.22 *The 1-3-1 half-court zone press.* X_1 and X_2 double-team ①. X_4 protects middle, X_5 moves toward sideline, while X_3 moves toward basket.

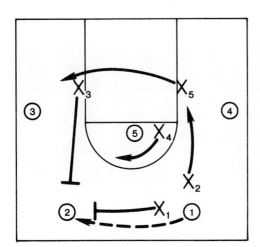

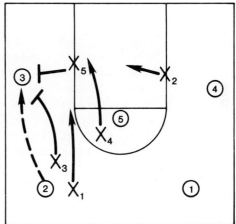

Diagram 25.23 *The 1-3-1 half-court zone press.* ① passes to ②. X_1 chases to join X_3 in new double-team. X_4 continues to protect middle, while X_5 moves to opposite side, and X_2 moves back toward basket.

Diagram 25.24 *A double-team at the forward position from the 1-3-1 half-court zone press.*

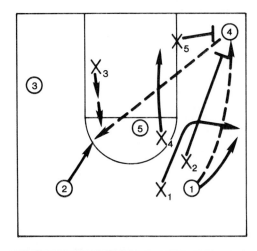

Diagram 25.25 *A corner trap from the 1-3-1 half-court zone press.* X₂ and X₅ double-team. X₁ prevents pass back to ① . X₄ protects under basket. X₃ moves up two steps ready to go for cross-court pass to ② . Corner traps can be devised from any of the half-court defenses.

Diagram 25.26 *The 2-1-2 half-court zone press.* X₃ will be in the double-team on both sides of the court.

The Run-and-Jump Press

The run-and-jump press is a man-for-man press popularized by Coach Dean Smith of the University of North Carolina. It differs from the normal man-for-man press in that it uses a technique called appropriately the "run-and-jump" or the "long switch." In addition, it requires considerable rotation by backline players in the attempt to intercept passes and to cover players who have gotten open by virtue of the run-and-jump technique.

Diagram 25.27 shows the basic run-and-jump or long switch technique. X₁ has put pressure on the dribbler, ① , and has forced a dribble towards X₂. As ① nears X₂, X₂ runs and switches opponents with X₁. Usually X₂ yells a key word such as "switch" or "go" to signal to X₁ to switch opponents. X₁ must switch quickly to ② unless another teammate has rotated up to ② as shown in diagram 25.28. In this case it is X₁'s responsibility to move on downcourt and look for the open player.

The run-and-jump technique could also be described as a surprise switch; in fact, the technique is most effective when the dribbler is caught by surprise. This is a gambling type press, and many times it lets a dribbler get open for an outnumbering situation. However, when played properly, it can be very effective and can lead to many interceptions and mistakes by the offense.

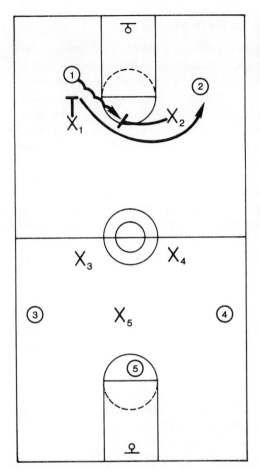

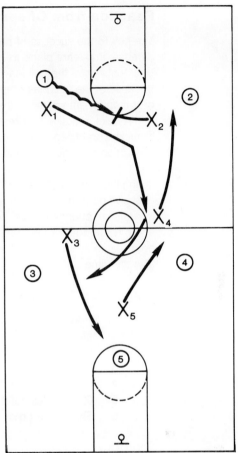

Diagram 25.27 *The run-and-jump, or long switch.* X_1 puts pressure on ① and forces ① toward middle. X_2 runs at ①. X_1 moves immediately to defense ②.

Diagram 25.28 *A rotation from the run-and-jump defense.* As X_2 jumps ①, X_1 moves to pick up ②. However, X_4 has moved up to ②, so X_1 must look downcourt for the open player. In this case X_5 has moved to defense ④, X_3 has moved to defense ⑤, and X_1 will defense ③.

Reaction from Offense to Defense

The key to the success of pressing defenses is the reaction from offense to defense. If a team plans to press, it must begin thinking of its pressing assignments once the ball leaves a teammate's hands on a shooting attempt. Because of the fast play of modern basketball, this quick reaction is needed, or the opponent will move the ball downcourt before a press can be set up.

A quick reaction for pressing cannot be achieved with minimum practice. It must be practiced daily, and it is the coach's responsibility to include reaction from offense to defense drills in the practice plan.

One key method of doing this is to work on team offense and the press during the same drill. Team A may have the responsibility of running the team offensive pattern against a man-for-man defense, then going into some pressing defense after all scores. Team B can be working on man-for-man defense and offense against the press. This creates more of a gamelike situation for both teams and prepares the pressing team for the quick reaction needed at game time.

Discussion Questions

1. How many pressing defenses should be in a team's defensive play?
2. Can a slow team be a good pressing team?
3. Discuss the key coaching points in teaching pressing defenses.
4. How can a man-for-man team handle the good dribbler?
5. Can the full-court press be set up after a missed shot?
6. Should the press receive daily practice?

Projects

1. Select a type of pressing defense and outline methods for teaching it.
2. Interview a local coach in regard to problems associated with teaching pressing defenses.

Suggested Readings

Cavalcante, Cal. "Blitz Press." *Scholastic Coach,* November 1975, pp. 46ff.

Comstock, Marc. "Pressure Defense Without Fouling." *Scholastic Coach,* November 1978, pp. 74ff.

Ebert and Cheatum, *Basketball,* pp. 189–214.

Findura, Thomas. "Freedom and Safety of the Press." *Scholastic Coach,* December 1979, pp. 19ff.

Fockler, Neil. "Pressing Off the Free Throw." *Scholastic Coach,* October 1975, pp. 62ff.

Hankinson, *Progressions,* pp. 92–96, pp. 121–28.

Lawhead, Rich. "2-2-1 Full-Court Zone Press." *Scholastic Coach*, January 1976, pp. 62–66.

Lyons, Paul. "Harvard's Run and Read Defense." *Scholastic Coach*, January 1976, pp. 94–98.

Masters, George D. " '22' Pressure Defense." *Scholastic Coach*, February 1978, p. 92.

Miller, Jim. "Extend Your Pressure by Double-Teaming the Inbounder." *Scholastic Coach*, November 1979, pp. 36ff.

O'Neal, Louise. "Pressure Defense Drills for Girls." *Scholastic Coach*, October 1975, pp. 32–34.

Pelliccioni, Louis. "Press Off a Missed Foul." *Scholastic Coach*, October 1977, pp. 7–10.

Schacht, Charles A. "Full-court Pressure Defense." *Scholastic Coach*, December 1977, pp. 90ff.

Schmidt, James. "The 100 Tiger Defense." *Scholastic Coach*, January 1976, pp. 32–34.

Shogan, Debbie. "Alberta's Combination Press." *Scholastic Coach*, September 1978, pp. 64–65.

Smith, Dean. "North Carolina's Pressure Type Defense." *Scholastic Coach*, September 1975, pp. 22ff.

Stewart and Scholz, *Complete Program*, pp. 177–228.

Tarkanian, Jerry, and Warren, William. "Sideline Influence Pressure Defense." *Scholastic Coach*, October 1979, pp. 28ff.

Tarkanian and Warren, *Winning Basketball*, pp. 196–98, pp. 285–322.

Wendelken, Maureen. "Montclair State's 2-2-1 and 2-1-2 Pressing Zones." *Scholastic Coach*, February 1978, pp. 94–97.

Wooden, *Modern Basketball*, pp. 278–84.

chapter twenty-six

Combination Defenses

Enterprising basketball coaches nationwide have used a variety of combination defenses to combat particular strengths or to take advantage of weaknesses in the offense of opponents. The two most popular of these defenses are the four-man zone, one-man man-for-man and the three-man zone, two-man man-for-man. These defenses are effective against an offense with one or two real scoring threats and weak scorers for the other teammates.

Four-Man Zone, One-Man Man-for-Man

In this defense, four defenders play zone and one defensive player is assigned the opposing high scorer. It is used primarily against the "one-man teams" we all meet occasionally and is an excellent method for defensing the opposing star.

Two methods are commonly used in playing this defense:

1. Box-and-one (diag. 26.1 and 26.2)

2. Diamond-and-one (diag. 26.3 and 26.4)

The box-and-one is stronger at the guard position and weaker at forward, while the diamond-and-one is stronger at the forward position and weaker at the guard and in the corners. The position of the opposing star to be defensed man-for-man determines which of the two defenses should be played. If the opposing star is a guard, your zone does not need strength at the guard position, since the man-for-man player is defensing the star there. Consequently, you select the diamond-and-one. However, if the opposing star is a forward, your zone needs more strength in the guard position,

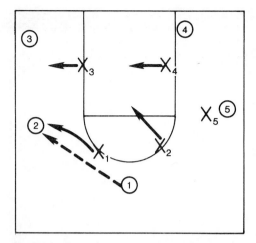

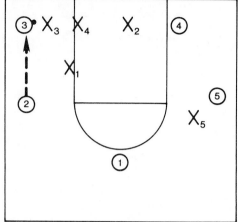

Diagram 26.1 *The box-and-one defense.* X$_5$ guards ⑤ man-for-man while X$_1$, X$_2$, X$_3$, and X$_4$ defense in a box zone.

Diagram 26.2 *The box-and-one defense with the ball in the corner.*

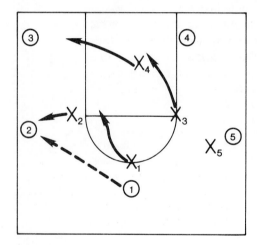

Diagram 26.3 *The diamond-and-one defense.* X$_5$ guards ⑤ man-for-man, while the other players guard in a diamond zone formation.

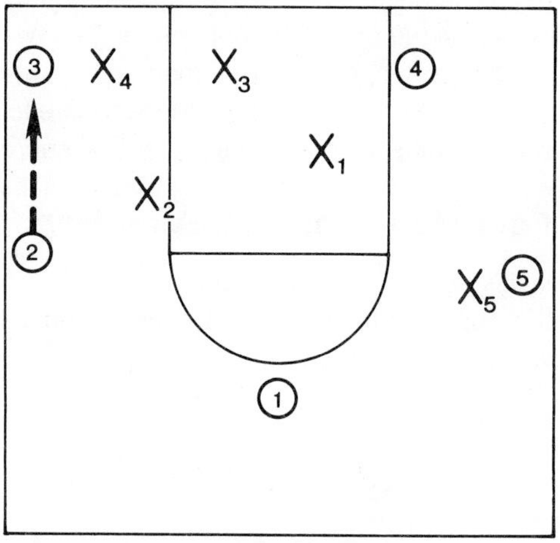

Diagram 26.4 *The diamond-and-one with the ball in the corner.*

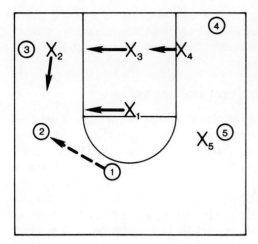

Diagram 26.5 *Another method of using the four-man zone, one-man man-for-man combination defense.* ⑤ *is guarded by* X_5 *man-for-man. The other defensive players set up in a 1–3 formation.*

and the box-and-one is more likely to prove successful. The shifting responsibilities of the zone players in both types of defenses are shown by diagrams 26.1 through 26.4.

Three-Man Zone, Two-Man Man-for-Man

The three-man zone, two-man man-for-man defense is excellent for the team with two top threats, which is so often the case in high school basketball. Three defenders play in triangular zone positions, and two defensive players are assigned to the two top scoring opponents. Diagram 26.6 shows this defense and presents the basic shifting responsibilities of the zone players. The zone shifts are similar to those made by rear line defenders of the 2-1-2 zone defense.

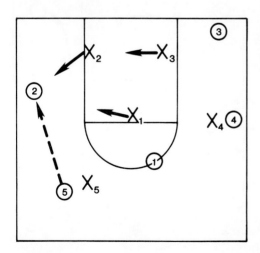

Diagram 26.6 *The two-man man-for-man and three-man zone defense.* X_5 *and* X_4 *guard* ⑤ *and* ④ *man-for-man, while* X_1, X_2, *and* X_3 *guard in a triangular formation.*

Another method for playing this defense is to guard the opposing guards man-for-man and to zone the rear line. The offense often mistakes this defense for a standard man-for-man, especially when the offensive guards are picked up aggressively at the midcourt line.

Other Types of Combination Defenses

Other combination defenses can be played as well. A few teams have used zone tactics on the guards and man-for-man play on the rear line effectively. Occasionally an opponent has an offensive player so weak that four defensive players can play man-for-man, while one defender zones the area around the basket.

Any defense that changes from one type of team defense to another with certain movements by the offense can be classed as a combination defense. Play by a team that sets up in a zone defense and changes to a man-for-man when the offense sets up its zone attack is an example. The reverse— a team playing man-for-man defense as long as the ball is at the guard position and changing to a zone defense on the first pass to a forward or center—can also occur.

It is important to remember that the strengths and weaknesses of the opponent's offense determine the use of combination defenses. They will not prove successful against all opponents, for teams vary a great deal in offensive strengths and weaknesses. It is also important to remember that, while combination defenses may have specific strengths, the strength of a defense may cause glaring weaknesses in other areas of that defense. If these weaknesses are exploited by the offense, the alert coach must be ready to adjust quickly to another defense.

Diagram 26.7 *Rotating the 1–3–1 zone defense into a 2–1–2 zone after the offense has set up in a 2–1–2 formation.* This matches up with the offensive formation and can be troublesome to an offense that does not have much movement.

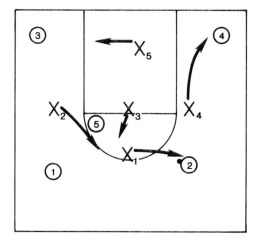

Discussion Questions

1. In a combination defense, should the better defensive players be assigned man-for-man responsibilities or zone responsibilities?
2. Discuss the basic difference between the box-and-one and diamond-and-one.
3. What combination defenses are not presented in this chapter?

Projects

1. By studying various reference materials and talking with local coaches, write a brief paper outlining the advantages and disadvantages of combination defenses.
2. Write a brief paper describing a combination defense not listed in the text.

Suggested Readings

Ebert and Cheatum, *Basketball,* pp. 183–87.
Hankinson, *Progressions,* pp. 115–20.
Kornhauser, Sam. "Triangle-and-Two With a Mousetrap." *Scholastic Coach,* September 1978, pp. 23ff.
Tarkanian and Warren, *Winning Basketball,* pp. 234–38.
Wooden, *Modern Basketball,* pp. 72–74.

part four

Organization and Techniques for Better Coaching

chapter twenty-seven

Practice Organization

Many areas are important to successful coaching in basketball. However, if there is any one area that is more important than the others, it is the area of planning and conducting practices. Through this phase of coaching, players are taught skills that lead to individual improvement, and teams are molded into cohesive offensive and defensive units. Most coaches agree that a player's skill and style in a game is similar to that player's practice behavior. The practice session becomes the foundation for the games ahead, so it is imperative that these sessions be well planned and well conducted.

Why Organize Practice Sessions?

Why is it really necessary to plan and organize practice sessions? A coach—particularly an experienced one—should be able to take the floor and, using his or her judgment, work on the phases of the game particularly needed by the team. Unfortunately this is not always possible. Disorganization can result and inferior learning situations can occur when a coach has not organized a *complete* practice session.

Practice organization is needed primarily for the following reasons:

1. It assures maximum use of the time available.
2. It ensures coverage of all phases of the game. Without thorough planning, you might inadvertently neglect some important phase of the game, which would result in costly mistakes on game nights.

3. It eliminates over-emphasis on any one phase of the game. The natural tendency to overemphasize the offensive side can be curbed and equal time devoted to defense and the other components of the game.
4. It maintains better player interest. Shorter drills are more effective than lengthy ones. Unless practice time is preplanned, drills may become somewhat long and boring to players, and learning may be reduced.
5. It allows for evaluation at the end of the season and aids in planning future seasons. A composite total of time devoted to each phase of the game can be invaluable in determining the reason for individual and team weaknesses. You can make adjustments in practice plans for future seasons to correct these weaknesses.
6. It enables planning drills for maximum results for each participating player. Without proper planning, a drill might have two players playing one-on-one and 8 or 9 players waiting in line for their turn. A well-organized practice has all players working simultaneously.
7. It enables maximum use of assistant coaches.

Types of Plans Needed

The following types of plans are needed for the coach to be able to plan practice sessions properly:

The Master Plan

This is a composite plan of all phases of the game to be covered in practice during a season. By using a master plan and checking it regularly, the coach can be sure that all phases of the game will be covered before the season opens.

The Weekly Plan

The weekly plan is a useful guide to planning daily practice sessions. If you want conditioning to receive primary emphasis during the week, you can draw up the week's daily plans accordingly. If the weekly guide calls for emphasis on offense, you can plan appropriate drills easily for the daily practice sessions.

The Daily Plan

No coach should take the practice floor without a daily practice plan. The plan should include a list of each drill and phase of the game to be covered that day, with the amount of time to be devoted to each drill given.

The master plan should be planned in September and reviewed at the end of each season. The weekly plan should be established in September, and, over the several weeks of practice, it should include everything that is on the master plan. The daily plan should be drawn up daily as determined by a study of the weekly plan and an evaluation of the practice the previous day. Type and post the daily plan in the team locker room so players can see what will be covered in practice that day. Finally, file and evaluate all of your practice plans at the end of each season.

Sample Practice Plans

Master Plan

Conditioning
Fundamentals
    Shooting
    Passing
    Dribbling
    Rebounding
    Footwork
    Individual offense
    Individual defense
Man-for-man offense
Zone offense
Offense for special defenses
Offense for pressing defenses
Fast-break offense
Fast-break defense
Jump-ball situations
Free-throw offense
Free-throw defense
Out-of-bounds plays
Regular team defense
Auxiliary team defense
Pressing defenses
Freeze or stall offense
Freeze or stall defense
Special offensive plays
Strategic situations

Weekly Plan

First Week
Conditioning
Fundamentals
    Shooting
    Passing
    Dribbling
    Individual Defense
Man-for-man offense
Frontcourt phase of the fast break
Regular team defense

Fifth Week
Fundamentals
    Shooting
    Passing
    Rebounding
Fast break (primary and secondary)
Man-for-man offense (transition)
Zone offense (transition)
Freeze or stall offense
Offense for pressing defenses
Strategic situations
Pressing defenses

Daily Plan

First Week
4:00–4:10 Flexibility and warm-up
4:10–4:15 3-line lay-up drill
4:15–4:25 Full-court passing drills
4:25–4:35 Full-court jump shooting drills
4:35–4:40 Dribble tag
4:40–4:45 Defensive footwork drill
4:45–4:55 Explanation of plays one and two
4:55–5:10 Plays one and two (no defense)
5:10–5:20 3-line fast-break drill (half-court)
5:20–5:30 Explanation of regular team defense
5:30–5:35 1-on-1 denial defensive drill
5:35–5:45 Help-and-recover defensive drills
5:45–5:55 Shell defensive drill (emphasis on jumping to ball)
5:55–6:05 Conditioning drills
6:05–6:15 Free-throw shooting

Fifth Week

4:00–4:10 Flexibility and warm-up

4:10–4:15 Full court lay-up drill

4:15–4:25 Individual defensive drills

4:25–4:35 Rapid-fire shooting drill

4:35–4:45 Shell team defensive drill

4:45–5:05 Man-for-man offense/into full-court zone press

5:05–5:15 Offense vs. half-court zone press

5:15–5:30 Offense vs. 2-1-2 zone/into run-and-jump defense

5:30–5:40 Defense for stall offense

5:40–5:50 Strategic situations (Tie score, 1 minute to go, we have ball; Trail by one, 30 seconds to go, we have ball; Leading by two, 20 seconds to go, opponents have ball.)

5:50–6:00 Free-throw shooting

Considerations for Planning Practice Sessions

A number of considerations must be kept in mind in planning practice sessions. Many of these are beyond the coach's control. Nevertheless, they directly affect practice organization. These considerations include:

1. *Time available.* How many hours is the gymnasium available for practice? With the growth of women's athletics, this has become an even more important consideration, since demands on gym time are increasingly competitive. Not only do men's and women's basketball teams need practice time, but so do volleyball, wrestling, gymnastics, and other sports.

2. *Space available.* Is one full court with two goals available, or do you have additional courts and additional goals? Most high school situations have one full court and at least four goals in the gym facility.

3. *Number of players.* 15 or 16 players on a squad requires a different type practice plan than a squad with only 10 or 11 players.

4. *Experience of returning players.* Inexperienced players require more fundamental work and perhaps more drill work than experienced players. If the team is loaded with players returning from the season before, the coach can add more offensive and defensive patterns than would be possible with inexperienced players.

5. *Size of players.* A team with many tall players may need a different type of drill work than a team with many small players. For example, a group of small players may need to press a great deal, and the practice plan should include many

drills and work on pressing defenses. On the other hand, the taller team may find a zone defense better suited, and the practice plan needs to include breakdown drills and team drills to develop the zone defense.

Suggestions for Conducting Practice

1. Keep in mind that coaching and teaching are synonymous.
2. Follow the practice plan with little flexibility. Have a manager time the drill and blow a whistle when it is time to go to the next drill.
3. Players should begin a series of individual stretching and warm-up exercises as soon as they come on the floor.
4. Begin the practice session with warm-up drills.
5. Include considerable amount of shooting practice in every practice.
6. Avoid distractions. The gymnasium floor is a classroom, and any distractions hinder teaching.
7. Do not run overtime. With proper planning, everything that needs to be covered will be covered. You pass the learning stage by going overtime when players are both physically and mentally tired.
8. Plan drills according to the number of participants to get maximum results. For example, if players are working on shooting and 10 players are at the basket, you obviously need more than one basketball. Plan a drill that would use four or five basketballs and avoid players standing around.
9. Make certain players know the purpose of the drill. Players tend to do a better job when they know why they are working on a specific drill.
10. Use competitive drills whenever possible.
11. Emphasize more than one fundamental during a drill. For example, a drill that works mainly on shooting could also emphasize passing and receiving and correct footwork.
12. Use variety in drills. Beginning practice with the same warm-up drill every day, for example, could prove very monotonous and fail to set the proper tone for practice.
13. Make use of your assistant coaches.
14. Provide clean, well-maintained practice equipment for players.

Rules for Practice Sessions

Specific rules or guidelines must be enforced for both players and coaches during the practice session.

Rules for Players

1. Be on time.
2. Hustle from one drill to another. No walking.
3. Stop all activity and talking when the coach blows a whistle.
4. Be enthusiastic.
5. Avoid horseplay and boisterous conduct.

Rules for Coaches

1. Arrive at practice early and stay late to be able to work with individual players.
2. Dress in a sharp coach's uniform. Resist any temptation to come to practice with regular street clothes.
3. Be enthusiastic.
4. Develop a coaching voice. Speak up so all players can hear you when correcting a player.
5. Use as simple terms as possible for better communication.
6. Coach in a positive manner instead of a negative one.

Length of Practice

Most coaches practice an average of two hours on five or six days a week. Although some coaches practice more daily and seven days weekly, I firmly believe that when practice goes beyond two hours, learning ability declines. I also firmly believe that players need at least one day off each week for mental, if not for physical, reasons.

A well-planned practice should enable a coach to prepare his or her team during the two-hour period. At the beginning of the season, practices of one and a half hours are recommended, and, toward the end of the season, practices for an hour and fifteen minutes are probably sufficient.

Practices on the day before and the day after games may need some adjustment in time also. In general, the practice before game day should be hard but shorter than usual. The practice the day after can also be shorter, particularly for the starting players. It is a good idea on days after a game to let the starters go early and to work with the reserve players.

Amount of Scrimmage Needed

During the first two weeks of fall practice, little full-court scrimmage is needed. After that time, two good full-court game-type scrimmages per week are sufficient. After the season gets underway, not much full court game-type scrimmage is needed. Instead, it is better to control all scrimmage to afford better instruction.

Discussion Questions

1. Is it important to organize practice by the minute? Should this schedule be followed precisely?
2. Discuss practice length. Early season. Mid-season. Late season.
3. How many days per week should practices be held?
4. How hard should practices be the day after a game?
5. How much practice time should be devoted to fundamentals? To defense?
6. Should competition or pressure be exerted in all drill work in practice?
7. Discuss criticism of players during practice.
8. What penalty should be imposed for a player who is late for practice?
9. How would you handle fighting among players in practice?
10. How would you handle the player who "talks back" to you when you correct him or her?

Projects

1. By studying various reference materials, outline a practice session for early-season practice. Mid-season practice. Late-season practice.
2. Write to several college coaches requesting copies of their practice plans.
3. Observe an organized practice by a local coach. Write a critique of it.

Suggested Readings

Ebert and Cheatum, *Basketball,* pp. 233–34.
Hankinson, *Progressions,* pp. 252, 272–75.
Stewart and Scholz, *Complete Program,* pp. 314–21, 328–32.
Toomasian, John. "The Pre-practice 100 Shots." *Scholastic Coach,* December 1979, pp. 70ff.
Wooden, *Modern Basketball,* pp. 25–33.

chapter twenty-eight

Charting

Almost all coaches use some type of chart to furnish objective data about each game. Even the keenest of basketball minds cannot accurately retain all the information a chart can give at a glance. Proper charting can measure both individual and team performance and pinpoint areas for work in future practice sessions.

Types of Charts

The types of charts in use today may be grouped as follows:

1. Shot charts
2. Floor-play charts
3. Rebound charts
4. Miscellaneous charts

The Shot Chart

The shot chart is one of the most widely kept charts in basketball coaching and can be of utmost importance if studied properly. It is simply a chart showing who took shots from where during the course of a game and whether they were made or missed. It provides the following information:

1. Number of shots taken by both teams
2. Type of shots taken by both teams
3. Location of shots taken by both teams
4. Shooting percentage of both teams
5. Shooting percentage of individuals on both teams

A knowledge of the number of shots taken by both teams can point to specific offensive or defensive weaknesses that must be corrected. If a team is taking too few shots, concentrating on offensive practice may increase the number taken. If the opponent is taking too many shots, added emphasis on defense in practice may reduce this number. The type of shots taken by both teams may indicate the type of shots to be practiced or defensive adjustments needed. Needless to say, if the opponents are getting too many lay-up shots, the team defense must be improved. If the opponents are getting an excessive number of rebound shots, you need to stress defensive rebounding.

Keeping the Shot Chart

A shot chart on both teams easily can be kept by one individual. Use an outline of the court—mimeographed or purchased in quantity from a professional concern—to mark each shot taken by either team. When a shot is attempted, write the player's number on the chart at the approximate location the shot was taken. If the shot was missed, just write the player's number. If the shot was made, circle the player's number. At half-time or at the conclusion of the game, a coach can survey the chart and find how many shots each player attempted and how many each player made. A completed shot chart is illustrated by figure 28.1.

Floor-Play Charts

What type of information may be recorded by floor-play charts?

1. Assists
2. Interceptions and recoveries
3. Taking the charge
4. Shot blocks
5. Violations
6. Bad passes

Assists, or passes that directly contribute to a score, are important to record, particularly for the good passer's morale. An accurate record of interceptions, recoveries, shot blocks, and those players drawing the charge on a driving opponent is invaluable for helping measure defensive skill.

A knowledge of the mistakes being committed by a team and the individuals committing these mistakes can be an excellent guide in planning practice sessions. If an excessive number of bad passes are being made, you will know to emphasize passing drills. If traveling and dribble violations are being committed, emphasize drills stressing correct pivoting and dribbling technique. Knowing the type of mistakes being made and the individuals making them can be useful in skull sessions when reviewing games. Cautioning the players about these mistakes and the simple knowledge that they are being committed can contribute toward their reduction.

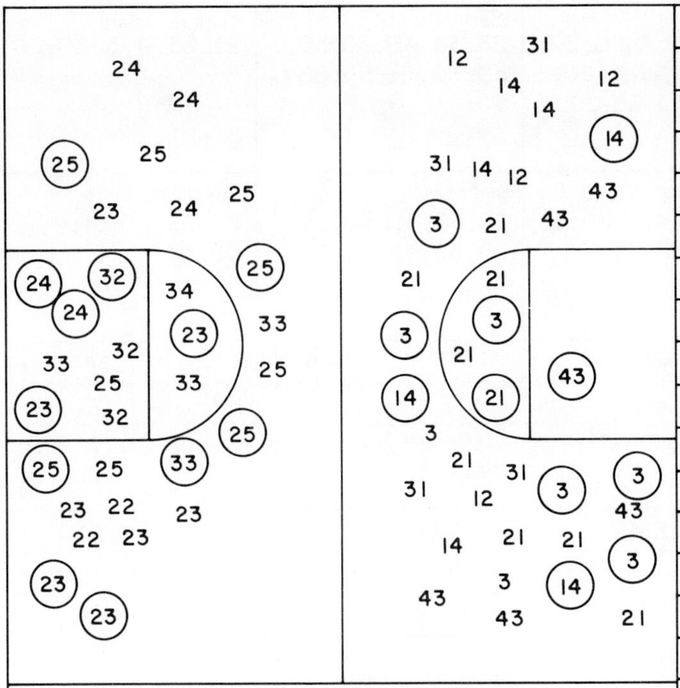

No.	STETSON	FGA	FGM	Perc.
23	Kitchens	8	4	.500
24	Miller	5	2	.400
25	Wells	9	4	.444
33	Gregory	4	1	.250
32	Hearin	3	1	.333
22	Schneider	2	0	.000
34	Dompe	1	0	.000
	Total	32	12	.375

No.	OPPONENT	FGA	FGM	Perc.
3	Williams	8	6	.750
12	Smith	5	0	.000
14	Jones	7	3	.429
21	Rogers	9	2	.222
31	Tillis	4	0	.000
43	Evans	6	1	.167
	Total	39	12	.308

STETSON vs. JACKSONVILLE

at: Deland, FL Date: 2/12/81

Half: 1st

Figure 28.1 *An example of a shot chart.* Note the summary block on the right side.

Keeping the Floor-Play Chart

A simple floor-play chart is shown in figure 28.2. Record floor-play items simply by writing the number of the individual in the appropriate column. These can be totaled easily after the game.

Rebound Charts

Rebound charts provide the following information:

1. Number of offensive and defensive rebounds by each team
2. Number of offensive and defensive rebounds by each individual

Figure 28.2 *Floor-play chart.*

Assists	Blocked shots	Take the charge
4,20,20,4,20,20, 5,50,20,20,5,20, 23,20,53,55,20,21, 23	23,30,40,50,30, 50,30,51,55,53	21,23,4,5,20,21

Interceptions/recov.	Bad passes	Violations
5,21,23,4,5,20,23, 23,55,55,55,30	30,55,4,5,20,4, 23,50,53,51,30	21,23,40,51,4,23, 55,53

No.	Name	A	B	TC	I	BP	V
4	Ramsey	2	0	1	1	2	1
5	Weston	2	0	1	2	1	0
20	McDowell	9	0	1	1	1	0
21	Echols	1	0	2	1	0	1
23	Myrick	2	1	1	3	1	2
30	Mims	0	3	0	1	1	0
40	Maloney	0	1	0	0	0	1
50	Reddick	1	2	0	0	1	0
51	Roach	0	1	0	0	1	1
53	Kaczmarek	1	1	0	0	1	1
55	Montgomery	1	1	0	3	1	1

Insufficient offensive or defensive rebounds can suggest areas of rebounding to work on in practice. If the number of defensive rebounds is not close to the number of missed shots by the opponents, stress blockouts and other defensive rebounding techniques. The reverse would be true if a team is falling down on the offensive boards. Knowing which players on a team are getting the most rebounds can suggest individuals who need additional work in this area and can act as an incentive to future rebounding performances by encouraging competition among individuals on the team.

An accurate knowledge of the leading rebounders on the opposing team may suggest play direction. For example, if their left forward is their best rebounder, initiating plays in his or her defensive area may result in shots being taken while he or she is out on the floor and away from the board.

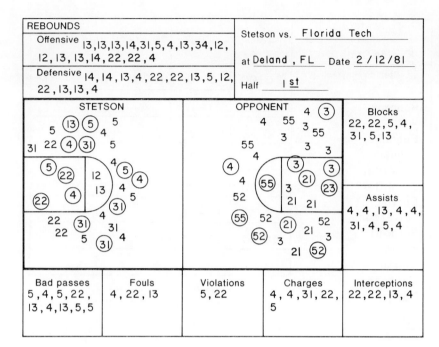

REBOUNDS	
Offensive 13,13,13,14,31,5,4,13,34,12, 12,13,13,14,22,22,4	
Defensive 14,14,13,4,22,22,13,5,12, 22,13,13,4	

Stetson vs. __Florida Tech__

at __Deland , FL__   Date __2 / 12 /81__

Half __1 st__

STETSON

OPPONENT

Blocks 22,22,5,4, 31,5,13

Assists 4,4,13,4,4, 31,4,5,4

Bad passes 5,4,5,22, 13,4,13,5,5	Fouls 4,22,13	Violations 5,22	Charges 4,4,31,22, 5	Interceptions 22,22,13,4

Figure 28.3 *A combined shot, floor play, and rebound chart. The number of the player is placed in the appropriate column and a total is made after the game.*

Keeping the Rebound Chart

Rebounds may be recorded in the same manner as shots and floor play items. Simply write the number of the rebounder in the appropriate offensive or defensive rebounding column.

Miscellaneous Charts

A number of other types of charts are used by many coaches. These include:

1. *Player-combination charts* (fig. 28.4). This chart records each combination of players throughout the game and the time played by each player and combination; it gives a view as to the combination of players achieving the best results. When a player enters the game, write in the player's initial on the line under the name of the player being replaced, along with the score and time remaining.

2. *Officiating charts.* Recording the type of calls made by each official can suggest the type of game to be played. If blocking calls are excessive, you might instruct players to drive a great deal. On the other hand, if charging calls predominate, you might instruct defensive players to jump freely in front of drivers. Few fouls called under the basket may indicate a rougher type of rebounding play.

Figure 28.4 *A player-combination chart.* Note that the first letters of the starting players' last names are placed in the combination column of the top line, with the time at 20 minutes to go in the half and the score 0-0. At 10:03, Sargent replaces Eubanks. (The first two letters of Sargent must be used, since one starting player's name begins with "S.") The chart reveals that when Epting entered the lineup (line 6), Stetson came from one point behind to four points in front, the best combination of the game.

STETSON vs. Florida State	TIME	SCORE	COMBINATIONS					
Stetson Players:	20:00	0 - 0	H	W	E	S		DM
Hancock	10:03	11-17			Sa			
Wells								
Eubanks	3:12	23-25	C					
Schneider	HALF SCORE				29 - 29			
R. Miller								
D. Miller	20:00	29-29	H	W	E	S		DM
Carson								
Jefferson	16:31	35-36			Ep			
Sargent								
Epting	10:30	45-41	C					
Smith	3:02	59-55	H			Sm		
Surface	FINAL SCORE				63 - 59			
Dompe								

Figure 28.5 *Jump-ball chart.* The numbers of the jumpers are written in the first column. A plus or minus is placed in the "tap-control" column to indicate the team controlling the tap. The number of the player gaining possession after the tap is written in the "possession" column with a plus or minus to indicate the team.

JUMPERS STETSON	OPPONENT	TAP CONTROL	POSSESSION
22	5	—	23 +
23	51	—	5 -
31	51	+	5 -
44	33	+	22 +
22	51	—	44 -
31	5	+	22 +

3. *Jump-ball charts.* An accurate record of jump-ball situations may be obtained by the use of the chart shown by figure 28.5. The chart records the players involved in the jump situation, who controls the tap, and who gains ball possession. The numbers of the players jumping are recorded.

4. *Offensive options.* Many teams keep charts that indicate play options that result in shots and scoring, evaluating the effectiveness of their offensive plays on these results.

5. *Defensive mistakes.* A record of mistakes made both by the team defense and by individual defensive players also can help determine areas that need work in practice. Which mistakes to chart depends on the team defense played and must be ascertained by the individual coach. This is a more difficult type of chart to keep, because it requires that someone with considerable knowledge of the team defense maintain it.

Team Statistics

A helpful coaching tool is a record of cumulative statistics compiled from the various charts kept for each game. The cumulative statistics give the coach another objective barometer with which to measure players and to analyze performance. Players enjoy seeing the statistics and also get a certain degree of motivation from them.

Items to keep on the cumulative statistics chart include the following:

Field goal attempts
Field goals made
Field goal percentage
Free-throw attempts
Free-throws made
Free-throw percentage
Rebounds
Rebound average
Assists
Turnovers or ball losses
Interceptions or recoveries
Personal fouls
Charges taken
Time played
Total points scored
Point average per game

General Suggestions

1. Make a thorough study of the information you need and arrive at a sound charting program to obtain this information.
2. Find interested personnel and train them in accurate charting techniques. Proper training in pre-season practice scrimmages results in accurate charting.
3. Study the charts diligently after each game and make the results available to the entire squad.
4. Keep cumulative statistics on all charts and file the charts for future reference.

Discussion Questions

1. How important is charting to the success of a team?
2. What charts are absolutely essential?
3. Is it important to know the location of shots or simply how many shots are made or missed?
4. Discuss how charts should be used at half time and after a game.
5. When is charting needed during practice sessions?

Projects

1. By studying various reference materials, write a brief paper about the type of charts useful in basketball coaching.
2. Keep a shot chart on a game or scrimmage.
3. Keep a rebound and mistake chart on a game or scrimmage.
4. Write a brief paper about the value of charting.

Suggested Readings

Ebert and Cheatum, *Basketball,* pp. 238–41.
Hankinson, *Progressions,* pp. 264, 266.
Samaras, Robert T. "New Dimensions in Statistics." *Scholastic Coach,* October 1976, pp. 12ff.
Stewart and Scholz, *Complete Program,* pp. 321–24.

chapter twenty-nine

Scouting

Two decades ago, those brave enough to be basketball scouts pulled their heads down into their coats and slipped unnoticed through the side door of the gymnasium lest they be caught and shot as spies. How times change! Today's basketball scout is greeted at the door by handclasps, passes to the best seats in the house, and gets free programs and refreshments on the house. Nothing is spared in efforts to make his visit a comfortable one. The scout has become such a respected contributor to the success of a basketball team that his popularity is second only to that of Coach Joe McDokes himself.

The scout's contribution has become increasingly important. Because of the increase in the number of offensive and defensive patterns in modern basketball, a detailed scouting report on each opponent reduces the chances of surprise and allows adequate preparation for each opponent. A particular offensive pattern of course can be better defended if your team has time to practice against it. And you can expect to score more easily against an opponent's troublesome zone if you have had the opportunity to practice against this type of defense. This is but a small part of what a detailed scouting report can reveal that may be used to improve the chances for victory.

The Scouting Report

The detailed scouting report includes the following:

Team Characteristics
Offense
    Team offense (half-court)
    Method for keying offensive plays

Fast-break patterns
Jump-ball plays
Free-throw alignment
Zone attack
Attack for pressing defenses (both zone and man-for-man)
Freezing pattern
Rebounding responsibilities
What defense gives the offense the most trouble?

Defense
Basic team defense
Types of other defenses used
Pressing defenses (Who are best pressers?)
Method of combating screens
Weak areas of team defense
Rebounding responsibilities
Defensive free-throw alignment

General
General condition of team
Experience
Speed
Shooting ability
Rebounding ability
Depth
Teamwork

Individual Characteristics
Offense
Characteristics of each player (height, weight, speed, position, favored shooting hand)
Types of shots and location
Outside shooting ability
Driving ability (Can a player drive both left and right?)
General ball-handling ability
Rebounding ability
Condition
Attitude

Defense
Characteristics of each player (stance, footwork, position)
Rebounding
Eye position (Does a player turn the head to look for the ball?)
Aggressiveness
Talk

Miscellaneous Information
    Type of court (size)
    Type of goals (fan, glass, wood)
    Officiating
    Fan reaction

Reporting on Team Offense

Include every phase of a team's offense in the report: half-court offense, jump-ball offense, free-throw set-up, fast-break patterns, out-of-bounds plays, and other offensive situations.

Observe the type of offense used. Is it a single-post, double-post, or another type? Is the post player a leading scorer? If so, how are feeds made into the post? Does the post pass off to cutters, or does the post player make an effort to score upon getting the ball? Many teams depend on the post player receiving the ball to make their offense effective. This is particularly true of teams who use many split-the-post maneuvers. When a scout notes this, a team can set its defense to prevent the pass from reaching the key offensive player. Of course, the scout also checks the individual abilities of the post player—whether a right-handed or left-handed shooter, whether a variety of fakes are used, and whether or not the post player scores well on tip-ins.

Determine who quarterbacks the offense. If they depend a great deal on one playmaker, plan to keep the ball away from this key player. Determine their better scorers and weaker scorers, their outside shooters, their feeders, drivers—in short, any trait that contributes to offensive play.

Notice the type of screens used in their half-court offense. This is important to adjusting team defense for this opponent. Note any opening tip-off or jump-ball plays, along with out-of-bounds plays from both under the basket and on the sidelines. Knowing special plays the team uses in the last few minutes of play or in "playing for one" is valuable to a coach in planning forthcoming strategy.

Does the team use a fast-break? If so, notice who their key rebounders are and to whom the first outlet pass is made after the rebound. Is the fast-break a controlled break, or is it a helter-skelter racehorse affair? On what occasions do they fastbreak? Do they have a secondary break?

A sometimes overlooked but important point is the type of defense being played against the scouted opponent. If they are facing a 2-1-2 zone defense and are having no trouble attacking it, you can assume that using that type of zone against this team is unwise. On the other hand, the team you are scouting may be having trouble attacking this zone, and, although your team may be predominantly a man-for-man defensive team, you may decide that using a 2-1-2 zone against this opponent is best.

If the team faces a full-court press, make notations on their method of attack. You might find a weakness that would enable the press to be adjusted and used effectively.

What Are the Defensive Weaknesses?

Determine first whether the defense is a zone, a man-for-man, or a combination defense. If it is a zone defense, notice what type and how the zone shifts. Also look for weak spots in the zone and note the height of each zone position. How fast does this zone team adjust from offense to defense? If they adjust slowly, a good fast-break can be their downfall.

If their defense is man-for-man, observe whether it is switching or non-switching, tight or sinking. Do they attempt to prevent passes to the forwards to initiate offensive patterns? Attempt to determine their weakest defensive players and weakest rebounders and center your attack on these players. All of us have seen a team continually drive on a weak defensive player. This may have been due to the scouting report.

Check their method of playing the post. Do they play in front to prevent the post player from receiving the ball, or do they play from the rear? If they play in front, you may find that special plays are necessary to free this post player for a pass. If they allow the post player to receive the ball freely, you may want to include more post plays in the offense.

How much effort do they exert in preventing the outside shot? Many teams sink and allow the outside shot, but strengthen themselves for defensing the drives and close shots at the basket.

Diagram their defensive free-throw setup and their jump-ball defensive play. What type of pressing defense do they use—a man-for-man, a zone press, or both? Do they use a half-court press?

Observe Opponent's Individual Characteristics

A complete scouting report must include a detailed account of the individual characteristics of the opponents. Observe both offensive and defensive characteristics. Record each player's height, weight, position, speed, jumping ability, shooting ability, defensive ability, types of shots, and any other noticeable characteristics. Study and note weaknesses, such as being a "one-way driver," poor dribbling, or poor defensive playing.

For clarification of how to report individual characteristics, note the following sample report:

Joe Smith, #21, 5'11", 165 lbs., guard. Very tough offensively. Best shots: Driving lay-ups and jump-shots from foul circle inward. Right-handed shooter but can drive either way. Excellent driver. Attempts to draw fouls on his drive. Will throw ball up under arm of defensive man to get foul. Seldom if ever passes off on drive. Poor rebounder. Fair defensively. Can be taken to the pivot effectively.

Employing Shot Charts

Use the charts discussed in chapter 28 for scouting opponents, particularly the shot chart. The value of this shot chart and other charts has already been emphasized. However, see figures 29.1 through 29.4 for examples of how the shot chart may be used in scouting a forthcoming opponent.

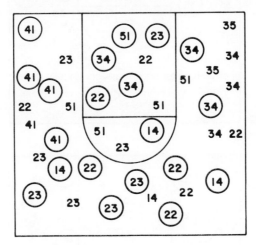

Figure 29.1 This shot chart indicates a very good outside shooting team, virtually eliminating the use of a zone or sagging man-for-man defense against them. Both guards and the left forward must be defensed tightly. However, the right forward seems to be a poor outside shooter and may be played loosely.

Figure 29.2 This shot chart indicates a poor outside shooting team. The number of close successful shots dictates a strong underbasket defense, probably a zone.

Figure 29.3 This shot chart detects a team that has developed the bad habit of running their offense to only one side of the floor. In this example, over 70 percent of the shots were taken on the right side. Defense must overplay this team and force them to go left.

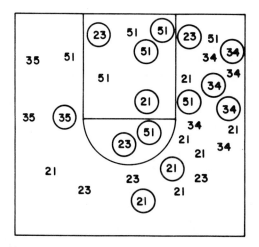

Figure 29.4 This shot chart reveals a "two-man" team. Notice that number 21 and number 34 have attempted 25 of the 34 shots attempted. Of the remaining players, the only made shots were from the underbasket area. This suggests the use of a three-man zone, two-man man-for-man combination defense.

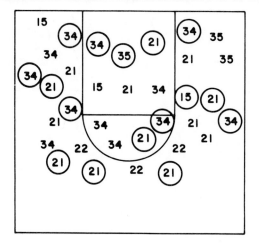

Other Factors Affecting Team Performance

Factors other than those of actual play should also be noted. The type of court, goals, backboards, ball, officiating, and crowd reaction may have a psychological effect on a team. Knowing these factors ahead of time may help prevent the players from becoming discouraged for related reasons. For example, if your team is accustomed to a rectangular-type backboard and the forthcoming opponent's court has the fan-shaped type, you might try to obtain a court with fan-shaped boards for a few workouts before facing this opponent. True, the goals are the same size and the type of backboards *should* make no difference. But it's hard to tell that to a group of basketball players whose shots fail to fall. They are ready to blame it on anything from the water boy to the wind velocity.

Scouting Hints

1. A more detailed report can be compiled if more than one scout can cover the opponent. One scout can compile the charts, while the other scout can watch the offensive and defensive patterns.
2. Arrive early and observe individuals during warm-up.
3. Compile the report immediately after the game while it is fresh in mind.
4. Scout the opponent several times if possible.
5. Study the scouting report thoroughly and use its information in planning for the opponent. Use skull sessions and work on the practice floor against the patterns learned from the report.
6. File scouting reports for future reference.

Discussion Questions

1. Some coaches say they do not scout opponents. What is your reaction to this?
2. Discuss the use of the scouting report in preparing for an opponent.
3. How can a scout best be trained?
4. What can a scout observe during warm-up?
5. How can a scouting report be used from one season to the next?

Projects

1. Scout a local team and write a detailed scouting report.
2. Interview a local coach in regard to his or her use of scouting.

Suggested Readings

Hankinson, *Progressions,* p. 302.
Wooden, *Modern Basketball,* pp. 55–57.

chapter thirty

Game Strategy

Changing a team defense at the proper moment, making a substitution quickly when needed, calling time-out to stop an opponent's rally, and setting up a last second shot to win a game all are a part of *game strategy*. The ability to make the proper strategic decisions from the beginning to the end of a hotly contested basketball game separates great coaches from ordinary ones. A team with inferior personnel often has been able to defeat a superior opponent simply through use of clever strategy. An effective use of correct strategy requires a coach to have a thorough knowledge of the game and its various offensive and defensive strategies, as well as the ability to remain mentally alert throughout every minute of the game.

Routine Game Strategy

A number of strategic observations and decisions must be made in every game and in each half of every game. These include the following:

1. Recognition of opponent's defense
2. Recognition of opponent's offense
3. When to substitute
4. When to call time-out
5. When to adjust the defensive game plan
6. When to adjust the offensive game plan

Recognition of Opponent's Defense

Among the first things to check at the begining of each half is the type of team defense the opposition is playing. Watch closely to determine whether it is a man-for-man, zone, or combination. It is good strategy to begin the game with a play designed to determine the type of defense you are facing. A play that sends a cutter through the heart of the defense usually does the trick.

Recognition of Opponent's Offense

Be sure to check on your opponent's offense during the early part of a game as well as its defense. Is it a single-post? A double-post? Are they using a passing game? Check any special plays they may be running, such as out-of-bounds and jump-ball plays. Ascertain whether they are fast or slow offensively, whether they shoot outside well, who their better scorers are, and whether or not they have a poor scorer from whom you could "slough off" and double-team their post player or prevent the pass from reaching the post player.

After you have surveyed their offense thoroughly, you may find that only a few minor adaptations may be needed in your defense. You may have one of your slower players guarding a faster opponent or a short player guarding a taller opponent, and a simple switch of defensive assignments may solve the problem. On the other hand, if you determine the opponents are poor outside shooters, you may want to use a zone defense. If they are poor ball-handlers, you may decide on a full-court press. Constant study of the opponent's offense is necessary in every game in order to make the right adjustments.

When to Substitute

Substitions are necessary for a number of reasons. The following are the most common reasons:

1. To rest players
2. Because of excessive fouling
3. Because of repeated mistakes
4. Because of "off" nights
5. To convey information to the team
6. Because of an offensive or defensive change by the opponents
7. To maintain discipline
8. To maintain morale
9. For last-second strategic situations

A coach must know thoroughly the strengths and weaknesses of the players in order to be able to substitute correctly. Remember that substitutions should be made to *strengthen* chances for victory. In general, do not break up a winning combination if the game is going well.

When to Call Time-Out

The following are the most common reasons for calling time-out:

1. To make changes in game strategy
2. To stop rallies or "hot streaks" by opponents
3. To correct offensive and defensive mistakes
4. To adjust to surprise moves by opponents
5. To allow players to rest

Using the Time-Out Period to Full Advantage

1. When a time-out is called, make sure players hustle to their bench. Time is limited and should not be wasted.
2. Players should huddle, and talking should be done in an organized manner, with one person speaking at a time. Demand everyone's strict attention.
3. Discuss mistakes being made and suggestions for correction. Clearly explain any necessary changes in game strategy. Answer strategic questions, such as why the opponents are getting the fast-break, why the opponents are getting so many offensive rebounds, or who is being guarded by a weak defensive player.
4. Depending on the manner of play and the situation, give the necessary words of encouragement or reprimand.
5. Save at least two time-outs for the last few minutes of play. Call no more than one time-out during the first half unless absolutely necessary.
6. If you can tell that your opponents are in poor physical condition, call time-outs sparingly against them. You'll wear them down quicker than ever.

When to Adjust the Defensive Game Plan

A team's defensive game plan can be adjusted any time the opponent is scoring too easily against your defense. This could happen at any time during the game and several times during the game. If a team plays only one type of defense, adjustments in that defense must be made. If a team plays more than one type of defense, it may be necessary to change defenses completely. The important thing is to make the adjustment quickly and before the offense has done too much damage.

When to Change the Offensive Game Plan

A coach must be constantly aware of changes or adjustments the opposing team makes in its defense during the game. The opponent may be playing a man-for-man and suddenly change to a zone. The coach must recognize this quickly, convey it to the team, and run the correct zone offense. The game plan might be to attempt to fast-break the opponent; however, they may be combining special fast-break defensive techniques with a ball-control offense to prevent fast-break attempts. Consequently, you may find your team playing too hurriedly and making numerous mistakes. It may be necessary to change the offensive emphasis to a more controlled type of game. Foul situations, time remaining to play, who's ahead in score, substitutions, and injuries are some of the many reasons the offensive game plan may need adjustment.

Special Strategic Situations

A number of strategic situations may not occur in every game, but they do pop up throughout a season, requiring the coach to be well versed in the correct combatative strategy. Several of these strategic situations are discussed in the following sections.

Defensing the Big Center

Fortunately, a team usually does not have to face a high-scoring, big opponent in every game. However, special defensive strategy must be employed when facing such a tall player.

As elementary as it is to state that the big center cannot score without possession of the ball, this fact is the key to defensing that player. Once the big center gets the ball underneath, preventing a shot from this high-percentage area is virtually impossible. Consequently, the defense must be designed to stop the big, fast player from receiving the ball.

The following defenses restrict ball possession by the post player, and, therefore, are recommended techniques for defensing this major threat:

1. The 1–3–1 zone defense
2. The 2–1–2 zone defense
3. The "sagging" man-for-man defense
4. The box-and-one combination defense
5. The full-court press

Any of these defenses can prove effective against the high-scoring big center. Most involve keeping a defensive player in front of the center to prevent the center from receiving the ball. When using the full-court press, the object is to force ball-handling errors prior to getting the ball into position to pass into the big center. The full-court press can also cause the offense to set up its alignment so far from the basket that a pass in to the post player is difficult.

Defensing the Fast Break

The key to a successful fast break is the speed with which the outlet pass is made after a rebound. Thus, strategy designed to stop the fast break begins with delaying the outlet pass. The best method of preventing the quick outlet pass is pressing the rebounder and the outlet pass receiver. Force the rebounder to be cautious with the outlet pass or to take a dribble. Play so close to the outlet pass receiver that the rebounder fears an interception. This gives the other members of the team sufficient time to retreat into proper defensive positions.

When opposing the fast breaking team, designate two players to check defense on every offensive play. One can take deep defensive position, while the other can press the outlet pass receiver. If two players do not remain back on defense, the opponent will undoubtedly get many 2-on-1 and 3-on-1 situations, which are quite hopeless if reasonably good ball-handlers are executing the break. When two players are kept back for defense, odds favor that at least one other player can retreat fast enough to get into defensive position.

The most successful strategic maneuver against the fast-breaking team is the use of ball-control or "slow break" tactics. The fast-breaking team loves to run and, when forced to play a slower game, can become nervous and overeager. Once they do gain possession, they tend to run and shoot as quickly as possible—in the majority of cases, too quickly. This over-eagerness to break often causes the fast-breaking team to take hurried and wild shots with no board strength and to make more fundamental mistakes. If fast breakers did not dislike facing slow-breaking opponents, they would not try to force the slow-breaking team to play a faster game. I have often seen a slow-breaking, methodical team, greatly inferior in talent, upset a fast-breaking team by refusing to run with them.

Let's also look at the type of defense to be employed when the fast-breaking team succeeds in getting the 3-on-2 outnumbering situation down-floor. The 2-man vertical defense (diag. 30.1) is the best method for delaying the fast break until help can arrive from other members of the defensive team.

Diagram 30.1 *Vertical fast-break defense.* X₁ stops penetration by ①. X₂ defenses ② as pass is made by ①. X₁ immediately drops to pick up ③. Defense depends on a third player hustling downcourt to pick up ① on any return pass.

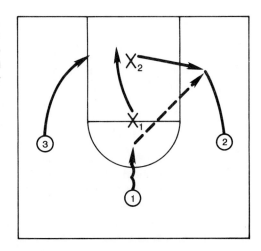

Defensing the Slow Break

One axiom that makes sense to many coaches is *don't play your opponents' game; force them to play yours.* This is an important point to remember in mapping basketball strategy, particularly for the fast-breaking team who faces a methodical, slow-breaking team. But it is very difficult to force a slow-breaking opponent to play a different type of game.

The fast-breaking team must try to force the slow-breaking team to speed up play. Therefore, some type of full or half-court pressing defense must be used. A full-court man-for-man press may prove successful. If not, changing to a zone press or some type of half-court press is sound strategy. Keep in mind that the pressing defense can gamble more with a slow-breaking team. This is because the methodical team does not count on taking advantage of errors that might be made by the pressing defensive team.

If pressing tactics are unsuccessful, emphasize the importance of *obtaining good shots once the team gets the ball.* Attempt to run if possible; however, do not run helter-skelter down the court and shoot the bad shot. If the ball-control team keeps the ball for a minute before shooting and the fast-breaking team throws it at the basket within 5 to 10 seconds after gaining possession, the fast-breaking team is playing directly into the hands of the slow-breaking team. The fast-breaking team will find themselves playing defense for a minute while their methodical opponent is playing defense for only 5 to 10 seconds! Throughout a game, this can amount to the fast-breaking team being forced to play defense over *three-quarters* of play.

Attacking the Star

Quite often your opponents will boast of one player who is considered their star, and you will be faced with the problem of defensing this player. Specific methods of defense have been covered; however, it is wise to have a battle plan for such an opponent that not only includes special defensive emphasis to stop this player, but an offensive plan directed at him or her as well. Many stars refuse to play defense. In fact, some coaches feel that placing a tough defensive assignment on their top scorer is too much of a burden. They believe that the star's scoring effectiveness can be reduced this way. For this reason, direct your attack at the star to make this player play defense or give up an easy shot. In defense the star may commit more personal fouls than normal, possibly fouling out of the game.

Build defensive plans for the star player around reducing the number of times he or she gets the ball. The fewer the scoring opportunities, the less effective the player. If you are using a man-for-man defense, assign your best defensive player to the star and make sure the defensive player overplays and denies passes to the star. Once the star does receive the ball, the defensive player must exert constant pressure, and the other players must be ready to help. In a zone defense, the zone must constantly let each other know where the high-scoring player is so he or she can be properly pressured.

Defensing Individual Weaknesses

Because basketball requires the mastery of so many fundamentals, it is doubtful that even the most polished player has mastered them all. There are always individual weaknesses, and, by careful observation, a coach can detect these weaknesses and adapt defenses to take advantage of them.

Possible individual weaknesses are too numerous to even attempt to list. A poor dribbler could be pressed into losing the ball often. A poor passer could be rushed after becoming "dead" (finished with the dribble). A good outside shooter who is a poor driver could be pressed. A player's speed determines how close the defense should play. If a player is a good outside shooter but slow, the defense should guard tightly. If the player is a poor outside shooter, regardless of speed, the defense should drop off and help clog the area around the basket.

Many players are guilty of being "one-way drivers." They establish the undesirable habit of driving only to the left or to the right. Once you detect the habit, the one-way driver is very easy to defend. A few seasons ago, I saw a one-way driver score 35 points in the semifinals of a state tournament. In the finals he was held to 6 points by the defense overplaying him to his preferred driving side. He refused to drive the opposite way. When you know relatively little about your opponents, it is good strategy to play right-handers a half-step to their right and left-handers a half-step to their left. If one does drive the other way, change the defensive plan on that individual. However, if the player proves to be a one-way driver, there is no logic in playing straight away and allowing that player four or five drives before overplaying to one side.

Occasionally drivers are found who do not pass off on their drives. In this instance, defensive players can pick up the player with little fear of the driver passing off to someone else.

Post players often shoot with only one hand. When you notice this, have the defense play this pivot player accordingly. If predominantly a right-handed shooter, play to the left side and prevent the right-hand shot, and the opposite for left-handers.

The few individual weaknesses pointed out here are selected only to stimulate thought as to the many possibilities the alert coach may be able to use to advantage.

Playing for One

"Playing for one" simply means a team goes for one last shot prior to the end of a period. This strategy often means the difference between victory and defeat in a close contest, particularly for teams who play quarters. The plan is to take the shot so near the end of the period that the opponent does not have an opportunity to rebound any missed attempt and go down and score. The shot should be taken when 5 to 8 seconds remain in the period. This provides ample time for a chance at an offensive rebound if the shot attempt is missed. However, it does not leave enough time for the opponent to rebound the ball and take it downcourt into scoring position.

Last-Minute Strategy

The last few minutes of play are crucial to the outcome of a basketball game. The coach must be a very alert, poised, and know what quick strategic action to take. One coaching mistake during this part of the game can result in quick defeat. During these last few minutes, a coach must determine when to freeze, when to press, when to run special plays, when to substitute for specific strengths or weaknesses, and other strategic decisions. These last few important minutes of play make it wise for the coach to have saved at least two time-outs. Using time-outs correctly late in the game can mean the difference between winning and losing.

When the game enters the last minute of play, coaching decisions are more crucial than ever. In general, if the score is tied inside the last minute, offensively most teams play for one. Defensively, it is extremely important that the players know not to foul in this situation. If a team holds a one-point lead during this last minute of play, no shot should be attempted unless it is an unmolested lay-up. On the other hand, if a team trails by one or two points, the defense must be overly aggressive in an effort to obtain ball possession.

There are two schools of thought in regard to playing for one in the latter part of a game. For many years, virtually all teams would play for one by holding the ball until approximately 10 seconds remained in the game, calling time-out, and then setting up a last-second play. In recent years, however, many teams have gone to another philosophy, that of not calling time-out but rather having a prearranged play for the situation. The theory is that by not calling time-out the defense is not given any opportunity to adjust and the offense is given an advantage.

Regardless of how alert a coach may be or how much knowledge a coach may have of the game, a team cannot function at its best in the last part of a game unless it has practiced these last minute situations. Prior to the beginning of the season, the daily practice plan should include some work on last-minute situations, using the clock.

The following are examples of situations to set up in practice, 2 minutes to play, team trails by 3; 1 minute to play, score tied; 10 seconds to play, down by 2; 4 minutes to play, leading by 6. Practice each with and without ball possession.

Numerous other late-game situations can be set up in practice. When players have faced these situations in practice regularly, they are far more prepared and confident when they meet these situations in actual game play.

Last-Second Plays

Diagrams 30.2 through 30.6 show plays that can be used in the last few seconds of a game. Review your prepracticed plays during the last-second time-outs, and, when play begins, these plays might bring victory. It is far better to use a prepracticed play than for the coach to grab a chalkboard and try to dream up a play in the excitement of a time-out with 10 seconds to go in a close game.

Diagram 30.2 *Special last-second play.* ① passes inbounds to ② coming off screen set by ③. ④ cuts off ⑤ yelling for the ball. ⑤ breaks up to receive pass from ②. ⑤ looks to pass to ③ on a backdoor move. If ③ is not open, ⑤ drives for the basket.

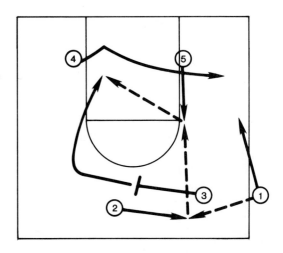

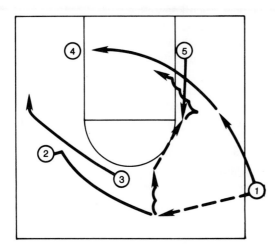

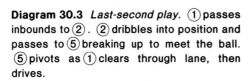

Diagram 30.3 *Last-second play.* ① passes inbounds to ②. ② dribbles into position and passes to ⑤ breaking up to meet the ball. ⑤ pivots as ① clears through lane, then drives.

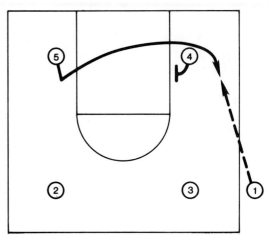

Diagram 30.4 This is a good play to use when only two or three seconds remain to play. ① passes directly to ⑤ cutting off screen set by ④. It is important that ⑤ be the team's best outside shooter.

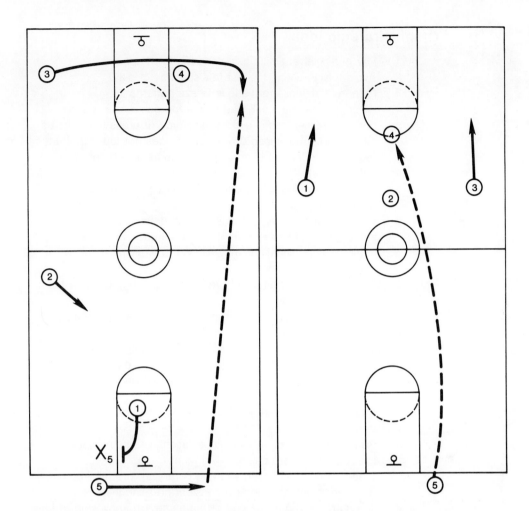

Diagram 30.5 This is a good play to use when the ball must be advanced full-court and only two or three seconds remain to play. ⑤ fakes the pass and then runs the endline. ① steps up and attempts to draw the charge from X_5. If no whistle, ⑤ throws the ball to the right corner to ③ who cuts off screen set by ④. It is important for ⑤ to pass the ball to the corner before ③ gets to the corner.

Diagram 30.6 This is another play to use when the ball must be advanced full-court and only two or three seconds remain to be played. ⑤ throws downcourt pass to ④, who attempts to deflect ball to either ①, ②, or ③ for a shot.

Other Strategic Ideas

1. Pay particular attention to defensive match-ups.
2. Avoid fouling during the last few seconds of play.
3. Prepare a defense for various freeze patterns.
4. When you have a small lead late in the game, use a semi-press. A semi-press is a containing type of press that retreats as the ball is advanced downcourt; it does not foul, but it does require the offensive team to use up some time before being able to score.
5. If you are arguing with the referee, can you be thinking about game strategy?
6. When using changing defenses, if one defense does not work in the game, get away from it but come back to it later. Different game situations may allow it to work far more effectively the second time.
7. Use some type of full-court press when playing against a team with a high-scoring center.
8. Use ball-control tactics when playing against a fast-breaking, run-and-gun team.
9. If you are planning to run a special play during the last few seconds of the game, it is wise to mention the play to a referee and to the timer so you can be certain they do not make a mistake.
10. Rear screens are very effective against any type of overplay defense.
11. Be alert for "situation type" substitutions late in the game.
12. Press the mediocre ball-handling team.
13. When a team has trailed you and is rallying; (a) call time out; (b) change defense; and (c) consider pressing them.
14. If you are behind at the end of the game; (a) know who to foul if you have to foul; (b) look for the charge on an offensive cutter; (c) contain the player with the ball and call out "5 seconds" if that player holds it; and (d) deny passes to players without the ball.
15. If you are ahead at the end of the game: (a) keep your poise; (b) make the easy pass; (c) never hurry but be quick; (d) shoot nothing except the unmolested lay-up; and (e) cut or drive to the basket under control.
16. If a defensive opponent gets three fouls, take that opponent into the post area.

17. If you are being guarded by a big player, play a great deal on the outside.
18. Head faking is the best way to get fouls on an inside player.
19. Begin each game and each half by taking the ball inside. This is wise for two reasons: (a) percentage power shots, and (b) forcing fouls on the opponent, thereby getting into the one-and-one foul situation quicker than they do.
20. Avoid fouling the shooter.

Discussion Questions

1. How can a coach quickly determine the type of offense being run by the opponent? The type of defense being run?
2. Discuss strategic reasons for substitution.
3. How many time-outs should be saved for the latter part of a game?
4. What effect does controlling tempo have on a fast-breaking team?
5. Discuss strategy for attacking a slow-breaking opponent.
6. How often should last-second plays be practiced?
7. If your team obtains the ball with 10 seconds to play and a tie score, should you call time-out?
8. Discuss catch-up strategy.
9. Is it ever wise to hold the ball and play for a last shot when trailing?
10. With the score tied in the last few seconds, is it better to drive or to shoot the open jump shot?

Projects

1. Compile at least five plays for use in the last minute of play.
2. Write a brief paper about the value of time-outs late in the game.
3. Observe a game and write a critique of game strategy by a selected team.

Suggested Readings

Brown, Bruce "Self-Substitution System." *Scholastic Coach,* October 1979, pp. 70ff.

Chaney, John. "Inside Defense Against the Stall." *Pro-Keds Coaches Digest,* 1980, pp. 6–7.

Crawford, Larry. "Getting the Clutch Two-Pointer." *Scholastic Coach,* October 1975, p. 17.

Ebert and Cheatum, *Basketball,* pp. 236–38.

Haklin, Joe. "Beat the Stall with a 10-Point Plan." *Scholastic Coach,* November 1978, pp. 6–8.

Hankinson, Mel. "Defensing the 4-Corner Game." *Scholastic Coach,* November 1979, pp. 38ff.

Hankinson, *Progressions,* pp. 257–59.

Hartwig, James. "Last-Minute Strategy: When the Game Is On The Line." *Scholastic Coach,* October 1979, pp. 50ff.

Healey and Hartley, *Basketball Offenses,* pp. 220–43.

Jenkins, Red, and Wootten, Morgan. "Late-Game Situation Winners." *Scholastic Coach,* October 1977, pp. 70ff.

Pelliccioni, Louis. "Scramble Drills." *Scholastic Coach,* October 1978, pp. 88ff.

Stewart and Scholz, *Complete Program,* pp. 327–74.

West, *Basketball My Way,* pp. 137–63.

Wilk, John F. "Tempo Control," *Scholastic Coach,* October 1978, pp. 86ff.

Wooden, *Modern Basketball,* pp. 62–66.

chapter thirty-one

Auxiliary Coaching Responsibilities

The head coach has a number of responsibilities besides actual floor coaching. Assistant coaches, managerial responsibilities, squad selection, purchase of equipment, trip organization, tournament preparation, summer programs, player motivation, and public relations are all important facets of a successful basketball program. The coach has to devote attention to all of these areas for a well-rounded approach to team success.

Assistant Coaches

Assistant coaches are an invaluable part of a quality basketball program, because they enable it to be far more comprehensive. They should be used in virtually all phases of the program, including floor coaching, input in decisions during a game, conditioning, and relations within the community. Proper use of assistant coaches not only ensures a more comprehensive basketball program, it ensures the assistants' personal growth as well. Few assistant coaches want to remain assistants, and the opportunity for them to improve their coaching skills is an important responsibility of the head coach.

You need considerable planning and communication to get full value from your assistant. Their exact responsibilities—what they will do in practice, what input will be expected of them, what role they will play in discipline, and a host of other responsibilities—must be planned well in advance and properly communicated to them.

Tasks that can be assigned assistant coaches include:

1. Helping plan practice sessions
2. Off-season conditioning
3. Individual instruction
4. Supervising one team during 5-on-5 play in practice
5. Scouting opponents
6. Supervision of managers
7. Supervision of charting
8. Game suggestions
9. Trip planning
10. Bulletin boards
11. Locker room cleanliness
12. Academic planning and grade checks
13. Publicity
14. Banquet planning
15. Game programs
16. Ball boys or girls
17. Film study and evaluation
18. Speaking engagements
19. Recruiting (college coaches)

Obtaining an assistant coach can sometimes be a challenge in itself. Though a large number of schools provide at least one assistant, many—particularly smaller schools—provide none. Getting a volunteer assistant coach is the answer in these situations. There are usually several young people in the school or community who are interested in coaching and are eager to contribute their time—particularly if they have an opportunity for growth and proper recognition.

The selection process for an assistant coach is vital since you obviously want a responsible person who can add to your success rather than detract from it. Solicit applications and study the credentials of each applicant. Carefully check the references of the most qualified and conduct personal interviews with a selected few.

The following are qualities to look for in an assistant coach:

1. *Loyalty.* There is simply no quality more important. A disloyal assistant coach can wreak havoc on a basketball program and can even cause the head coach to lose his or her job.
2. *Knowledge of the game.* An assistant coach cannot make an appropriate contribution to the program unless he or she has sufficient knowledge of basketball. Although you, the head coach, should not expect a young assistant to posses as much knowledge as you do, you can expect that assistant to have enough basketball knowledge to be able to help plan practice, teach fundamentals to individual players, and scout opposing teams.

3. *Personality.* An assistant coach must have a pleasant personality, meaning he or she must be friendly and have a positive attitude. A surly, complaining person is detrimental to the program.
4. *Ambition.* The assistant coach must be ambitious and eager to move upward in basketball. The ambitious assistant works harder, studies the game more intensely, and is more willing to be of assistance to the head coach. The head coach should encourage ambition and afford guidance when an assistant is ready for advancement.
5. *Initiative.* The assistant coach should look for opportunities to help the program rather than sit around and wait for instructions from the head coach.
6. *Enthusiasm.* A good assistant coach helps generate enthusiasm for the program and conveys optimism and excitement to those with which he or she works. An enthusiastic coach creates a desire to learn among players and makes them far more willing to work to improve.

Squad Selection

All students should have the opportunity to try out for the team, but of course you want the best for the squad. Methods for try-outs and final selection of team members are the sole responsibility of the coaching staff and should be done with total fairness to all candidates.

Students can be invited to try out for the team by announcements on bulletin boards, in school newspapers, and over the school loudspeaker system. Reviewing a large number of candidates requires two or three days if the coaching staff is to fairly assess each candidate. However, in established programs, those trying out for the varsity team are usually either returning players from the previous year's varsity or junior varsity team members. New candidates are usually younger players who are vying for a junior varsity berth.

A number of considerations are important to final squad selection:

1. Height
2. Quickness
3. Shooting ability
4. Experience
5. Potential
6. Physical condition
7. Coachability

You cannot help but use considerable subjective judgment in selecting the final squad. Part of the coach's job is the ability to observe players closely and "instinctively" know who's better than whom. However, whenever possible, use as much objective data as you can. An accurate record of statistics during practice sessions and scrimmages can provide this objective data. This way the coaching staff can determine at a glance the better scorers, better rebounders, better ball-handlers, better free-throw shooters, and better defenders. Having such information is vital to final squad selection, particularly to the selection of a starting line-up.

Managers and Support Personnel

Several well-trained managers are needed for the complete basketball program, and other support personnel must be obtained particularly for help at game time.

At least three managers should be trained to participate in the program. They are usually easily found through posting signs on the bulletin boards at school asking for managerial assistance. Although they may not have the physical skill to actually play, many young people want to get involved in a good basketball program.

It is good to have managers in each class. By doing so, the senior managers can train and help supervise the sophomore and junior managers. Once a good managerial program is established, it is fairly easy to maintain by responsible senior leadership.

The main thing a coach must do with his or her managerial program is to clearly establish the managers' duties. The duties that can be assigned to them include the following:

Pre-Season

1. Meet with coaches to discuss responsibilities
2. Inventory equipment
3. Train younger managers
4. Prepare forms and charts needed for meetings and practices
5. Make certain all equipment is ready for practice to begin
6. Assist with the pre-season conditioning program

Practice

1. Help ready practice uniforms and equipment
2. Make certain floor is clean
3. Have basketballs and special equipment on floor prior to practice
4. Post practice schedule
5. Time practice schedule during practice

6. Keep charts during practice
7. Store all equipment after practice
8. Make certain locker room is clean after practice
9. Launder practice uniforms
10. Turn out all lights
11. Post practice times and notify players of any change

Home Games

1. Have basketballs on floor for pre-game warm-up
2. Game ball and towels to officials
3. Ready game uniforms
4. Have oranges, Cokes, or similar refreshments for halftime
5. One manager should be assigned to visiting team
6. Get charts to coaches after game
7. Secure equipment after game

Road Games

1. Help pack travel bags
2. Pass out travel itinerary to players
3. Assist with charting
4. Have oranges, Cokes, or similar refreshments at halftime
5. Leave dressing room clean
6. Collect equipment on return

Post-Season

1. Inventory all equipment
2. Meet with coaches regarding duties for spring practice
3. Assist coaches with banquet preparation

Support personnel needed for games are ticket sellers, gate keepers, a scorer, a timer, a public address announcer, statisticians, and janitors. In most situations the athletic director employs most of these personnel. Regardless of who does the actual assignment of duty, responsible adults should have most of these positions. This is particularly true for the timer. Visiting coaches complain at any minor error made by a timer, and no student should be subjected to this pressure.

Students should, however, be trained as statisticians. In order to do an accurate job they must attend a number of practices and chart several scrimmages. Statistics are so important in analyzing a game, and players are so aware of this importance, that accurate statistics are absolutely essential. Inaccurate statistics are very upsetting to players and undermine the value of keeping the charts.

Purchase and Care of Equipment

The following are factors important to the purchase and care of equipment:

Purchase

1. Inventory all equipment at the conclusion of each season.
2. Put together list of equipment needed for the following season immediately upon completion of the inventory.
3. Invite suppliers to bid on equipment needed. Consider the lowest bid, of course, but try to give preference to local merchants, particularly when they can provide greater service in the future.
4. Place orders in early spring to assure delivery in early fall prior to practice.
5. Never place an order without a school purchase order or without available funds from another source.

Care

1. Instruct players on the care of equipment. Uniforms should never be thrown on the floor or any equipment handled in a sloppy, careless manner.
2. Practice uniforms should be washed daily and game uniforms either washed or drycleaned after each use.
3. Basketballs must be cleaned regularly.
4. Keep all uniforms and equipment under lock and key. Basketball equipment should be kept in a separate bin from other athletic equipment, so only the head basketball coach or assistants have access. It does no good to purchase quality equipment and take meticulous care of it only to have it lost or stolen.
5. Remember, the more care given to equipment the longer it lasts—and the more funds available for additional equipment.

Trip Organization

The amount of organization for trips depends on distance involved and whether it is an overnight trip. The majority of trips for high school teams are not overnight and involve travel after school and return immediately after the game. Usually college teams stay overnight on trips and often play more than one game on the trip.

The following are key areas for organization for trips:

1. *Traveling squad.* Post the traveling squad several days in advance. If the entire squad will not make the trip, it is unfair to wait until the day before to tell a player he or she is not going to go. Give travel itinerary to each person, with copies to appropriate school authorities so the team can be contacted if need be.

2. *Equipment.* Make all arrangements for uniforms and equipment that will be needed on the trip. Some coaches have players pack their own uniforms and shoes, while other coaches assign this task to managers. I prefer to have players pack their own uniforms, because I believe this helps them develop responsibility. Managers will need to take basketballs, towels, first-aid kit, and a "spare parts" bag containing an extra uniform, socks, supporters, shoe laces, and miscellaneous equipment. This extra bag covers any equipment forgotten, lost, or stolen.

3. *Travel dress and regulations.* Instruct players on how to dress for trips, proper travel conduct, and any rules that will be enforced. Do this verbally in a team meeting, then give it to them in writing so that there can be no misunderstanding. Few coaches require players to wear coats and ties today, but most still want their players to look "dressy" on trips. Primary rules that need to be discussed include being on time, loud noise in motels, curfews, and use of telephones in rooms.

4. *Mode of transportation.* Determine the method of team travel shortly after the schedule is made for the next season. If buses or vans are to be used, be sure to make reservations with proper authorities to avoid conflicts with other school organizations. If the trip is to be by plane, reservations need to be made and tickets purchased as soon as possible. Purchasing airline tickets nine months in advance can sometimes save thousands of dollars over purchasing them two months or so in advance.

5. *Lodging and meal arrangements.* Both lodging and meal arrangements can be made in advance, but, of the two, it is far more important to have your lodging arrangements tacked down first. Sometimes you can save money by waiting to make meal arrangements until the team actually arrives at its destination. As soon as the schedule is complete, contact several motels in the cities where overnight stay is needed. Team lodging needs should be outlined and prices requested. You can save a considerable amount of money by doing this several months in advance and by contacting several motels.

One thing that sometimes can become a problem if not handled properly is the trip home after a game. A coach often receives requests by players to ride home with parents or friends after a game. This is a potentially dangerous practice that can result in liability to the coach and school. The best rule is to require all players to return home together. This practice is not only safer but helps build team morale.

Tournament Preparation

One of the greatest parts of a basketball season is the set of tournaments at the end of the season. Records are thrown out, and winning and losing teams enter on an equal basis. Losing teams see a new opportunity for accomplishment, and the vast number of upsets each year add interest and excitement to the season's end.

Tournament participation creates new situations for the coach to handle. First, a team usually is somewhat tired at the end of a grueling schedule and needs some rest if at all possible. Assuming several days exist between the last regular game and the first tournament game, try to give at least two days off from practice to help tired legs and mental attitudes.

Preparation for the opening game begins with getting a scouting report on the first opponent and working on the practice floor for this opponent. If your team has faced the opponent during the regular season, a scouting report should already be available. If you are facing a new opponent, several telephone calls to coaches who have faced them may be necessary for sufficient scouting information. If a game film on the new opponent is available, it will be extremely helpful.

As a team advances in the tournament, it's easy to get scouting reports on potential upcoming opponents by just observing them in tournament play. Two scouts are needed in these situations; one for each team. If a winner becomes obvious, both scouting coaches can concentrate on the winning team. After scouting each opponent, the staff should analyze the information and present it to the team.

Whether or not a team practices on days of tournament games depends on the coach's personal preference and on how tired the team may be. I prefer to take my team on the floor on the day of each tournament game, walk through the opponents' offense and defense and our plan of attack, and then allow our players to shoot for 10 minutes. This type of light practice perhaps has more of a psychological usefulness than a strategic one. Going to the gym gets the players out of the motel room and gives them a break in what otherwise could be a long, monotonous day. I strongly feel that players should rest their legs on game days, but too much lying around watching television in a motel room can make them listless and less aggressive at gametime.

Tournament play requires a great deal of supervision. If the players are staying in a motel, bed checks must be enforced and loud boisterous conduct not permitted. Daily activity must be watched carefully, because players on their own may not be able to resist trooping downtown on hard concrete which tires the legs. One pitfall is lack of supervision of a team *after* they have won the championship. I have seen many coaches become lax in this situation and allow their players to stay up all night, celebrating and often doing considerable damage to motel property. This is inexcusable, and the responsibility for preventing this rests solely on the shoulders of the coach. Winning is important and should be enjoyed, but never at the expense of others!

Developing Summer and Feeder Programs

Successful high school basketball programs operate virtually year-round. Therefore, a coach must spend some time organizing programs for summer play. In addition, a coach must spend time looking into the recreation programs and junior high programs that feed players into the high school.

Summer coaching involves a definite program that enables individual work on fundamentals, strength training, and some scrimmage work. It is best to operate the summer program at night, since many players have daytime jobs.

The amount of involvement a coach may have in a summer program varies from state to state, because of different high school association rules. Some states allow coaches a free hand to work with their players in the summer, while other states forbid summer work completely. It is important that the coach follow the rules explicitly.

If rules do *not* allow coaching in the summer, give each player a detailed program for individual development at the end of the season, and make arrangements for players to report their progress to you.

Although association rules may forbid direct coaching, they usually allow play in leagues established by various recreation organizations for the summer months. Nothing forbids a coach from working with a recreation department in giving advice on how to organize such summer programs.

Feeder programs are probably more important than summer programs. The better young players are grounded in proper basketball fundamentals, the better players they will be in high school. A high school coach should work closely with the local recreation departments to develop winter basketball leagues for the upper elementary school ages. The coach should also meet with junior high coaches, develop their friendship, and help them in any way possible. Many junior high school coaches welcome properly offered assistance in basic basketball techniques.

Figure 31.1 Many players attend basketball camps on college campuses in the summer. These camps not only help increase skill, they can be very motivating as well.

Motivating the Teenage Athlete

One of the most important roles a coach must play is that of a motivator; in fact, the ability to motivate separates the great coaches from the ordinary ones. It is not enough for a coach to have a thorough knowledge of basketball and its techniques, he or she must be able to motivate players to give their best efforts at all times.

A number of things contribute to player motivation. The following are some of the most important:

1. *Organization.* Players can recognize disorganization in a program, and this adversely affects their efforts. Well-planned practice sessions in which all players are kept busy in useful drill, a competent coaching staff all of whom are involved in the teaching process, and off-season programs designed for optimum player development reflect the type of good organization that contributes to player motivation.

2. *Discipline.* Players respond to discipline; in fact, discipline is absolutely required for consistent motivation. Discipline must be realistic and must be exerted firmly and fairly. Few players resent the type of discipline needed to bring forth their best efforts, but many do resent the lack of it that causes them to remain in the shadow of mediocrity.

3. *Praise.* It is simple human nature to enjoy being praised, and athletes are no different from anyone else. The wise coach looks for areas to praise in each athlete. When a player is praised for doing something well, his or her usual reaction is to attempt to do it even better the next time.

4. *Criticism.* Although criticism can be used as a motivating force, coaches must be careful in how they do it. Never criticize to cause embarrassment to a player. Singling out one player and showering him or her with a torrent of negative words only tends to embarrass that player and may result in a lesser desire to achieve. Criticism done in a positive manner has far greater motivating power. Let's look at two examples, both involving a player who has made a bad pass. The negative criticism: "John, you are the worst passer I have ever seen. I've seen elementary kids pass better than you. Keep up passes like that and you may not even be on this team." On the other hand, the positive criticism: "John, you are too good a passer to make a careless pass like that. You know I cannot put up with careless passes, particularly from a player like you who has good passing ability." It is easy to recognize the approach with the most motivating force. Criticism does have its place in coaching, but care must be taken in using it.

5. *Learning environment.* Clean, well-painted gymnasiums and locker rooms, classy practice and game uniforms, clean basketballs, and coaches in neat uniforms are all parts of the learning environment that can help develop pride among players and motivate them to greater effort. No one likes to dress in a shabby dressing room, practice on a dirty floor with dirty basketballs, and be coached by a person in street clothing.

6. *Goal setting.* Individual and team goals are very powerful motivating forces. Goals provide daily incentives for players and give them specific measurable objectives.

   It is important that goals be demanding—goals that bring out 100 percent effort in trying to attain them. Goals also must be realistic, however. For a college team that did not win a game last season to set the NCAA Championship as its goal would be unrealistic. Players would know the goal was unrealistic and would derive no motivation from it. However, the team could set a realistic goal of a winning season, and this could serve to motivate them a great deal.

Players need guidance by the coaching staff to establish both individual and team goals. Individual goals should be established in private conference between coach and player. The coach knows each player's potential and can guide him or her privately toward making realistic goals.

A second team forward might have the following individual goals for a coming year:

Gain 10 pounds
Be able to tip out on the rebound machine at 10'2"
Make the starting line-up
Shoot 50 percent of field goal attempts
Shoot 70 percent of free-throw attempts

Team goals should be established by the entire team at a team meeting after considerable discussion. A team might set the following goals for the season:

Win at least 18 games
Win the conference championship
Team field goal percentage of 48 percent
Team free-throw percentage of 70 percent
Out-rebound opponents by an average of six rebounds
  per game
Defensive average of 45 points per game

Public Relations

Coaches are in the public eye probably more than any other teachers in the school system. It is important for coaches to recognize this fact and to be careful to represent the school well at all times. This requires good public relations in a number of key areas:

1. *Administration and faculty.* A successful program requires the cooperation of the administration and faculty. Conscious efforts to work closely with the principal, athletic director, and members of the faculty can pay rich dividends. The principal or athletic director controls the funds available for the basketball program and has final voice in policy changes. A friendly, cooperative coach has a far better chance for additional funds or favorable policy decisions than an arrogant, unfriendly one.

2. *Parents of players.* This is a very touchy area. Almost all parents feel their sons and daughters have the ability to be in the starting line-up, and many voice these opinions very strongly to the coach. Although a coach cannot satisfy

everyone, maintaining close contact with parents and being open and honest with them does help them understand the status of their son or daughter on the team. Group meetings with parents, visiting them in their homes, and involving them in team projects helps develop the needed rapport between coach and parent.

3. *Community.* Most school teams have a following of local fans who are genuinely interested in their team. These fans often are ready to lend both financial and other assistance, provided they are cultivated properly. Virtually all fans enjoy being in contact with the coach, and many of them will become directly involved with the program when asked. As stated earlier, the coach is always in the public eye and should constantly be conscious of being friendly with the public, watching his or her dress and appearance, and properly representing the school and team within the community.

4. *Media.* Publicity is extremely important to the development of a quality basketball program. Players enjoy personal and team publicity, and the right kind of publicity can be very motivating to them. However, this publicity cannot be obtained without the cooperation of the news media.

Coaches should be cooperative and courteous to the media at all times. They should be readily available for interviews and should be eager to provide the media with information about the team, players, and schedule.

Many coaches seem to resent the media and tend to avoid them if they can. Often these coaches claim they have been "misquoted," or they resent a writer who has written negatively about them. Misquotes and negative articles are simply a part of sportswriting, and a coach is hurt mainly by overreacting to them.

Basketball Coaching As a Profession

Basketball coaching can be a very rewarding profession. It is one of the few professions that makes a contribution to the development of young people. For the individual who genuinely loves the game of basketball and sincerely likes to work with young people, basketball coaching can be the best of professions.

Coaching can be a very exciting life. The basketball coach is constantly in the limelight, instantly recognized throughout the community, and treated with a great deal of respect by students and adults alike. The thrill that comes with competitive action during game play is almost a one-of-a-kind experience.

There are definite disadvantages to recognize. Basketball coaching can be an unstable life—for two reasons. One, the successful coach is sought by other school systems and tempting offers can change your life, sometimes drastically. Two, coaching success, unfortunately, is measured by wins and losses, and some school authorities are eager to dismiss coaches at the end of a losing season. Both situations mean that the coach usually moves on to another community.

Another disadvantage of basketball coaching is the long hours required to do the job right. In virtually all high school situations, the coach must teach a full load of classes during the school day and then devote several hours to coaching after school. Add to this the hours of planning, travel, scouting, and the study of game films and one can easily see that a coach works more hours than almost anyone else in the school system.

Despite the long hours, basketball coaching is not a particularly high paying profession, with the exception of those few coaches who reach the top. Although remuneration should never be the sole reason for choosing a profession, the aspiring coach should know prior to entering the profession just what to expect financially. A young coach often enters the profession with a great deal of enthusiasm, and, as his or her family grows and money pressures increase, moves out of coaching to accept a higher paying position in the school system or to enter private business. Many dedicated coaches, however, budget their funds quite well and are able to remain in the profession throughout their careers. So many of these coaches have made invaluable contributions to hundreds of young lives.

For the coach who aspires to reach the top of the profession, I make the following suggestions:

1. *Be a constant student of the game.* The game continues to change and new techniques come into it almost yearly. Basketball coaching is a never-ending process of learning.
2. *Attend coaching clinics whenever possible.* You may pick up only a few points from each clinic, but each little thing you learn can be worthwhile. Fortunately, there are many good clinics around the country featuring lectures by some of the game's greatest coaches, and it is easy to attend several clinics each year.
3. *Make as many contacts with top high school and college coaches as you can.* Ask them questions, write to them for information, and offer to work for them in their summer camps. Virtually all college coaches have summer basketball camps and are looking for young junior and senior high school coaches to work for them. Many assistant coaches in college have obtained their jobs by working in college camps, doing a good teaching job in them, and getting recommendations from the coach directing the camp.

4. *Attend college games and professional games as often as possible, observing various offensive and defensive strategies.*
5. *Work the year-round in learning the game and coaching your players.*
6. *Never be afraid to apply for a higher position.* Head coaches are never offended at receiving an application from a young, talented coach who can provide strong references. You may not get the job, but the coach may remember your application and consider you the next time a vacancy occurs.
7. *Never let money enter into your decision to accept a higher position.* Many assistant coaches in college make less than many high school coaches, yet the college assistant moves on into a head college coaching position far more often than does the high school head coach. The young coach must be willing to make financial sacrifices in order to move into a position that will provide opportunities for even greater advancement in the future.

Discussion Questions

1. Discuss questions that should be asked an applicant for an assistant coaching position.
2. How can an assistant coach receive proper recognition in the program?
3. Should a coach accept gifts from sporting goods sales representatives?
4. Should players pack their own equipment for trips or should this be done by managers?
5. A team is to face an opponent in the first round of a tournament that they have defeated twice easily. How can a coach motivate players for such an opponent?
6. One of the team's better players does not want to participate in the summer program. Should this affect this player's standing in the fall?
7. Discuss techniques you have seen coaches use that have served to motivate their teams.
8. The principal is a former basketball coach. He calls you to his office and tells you that your team should fast-break more. How would you handle this?
9. How should a high school coach go about trying to get a college job?

Projects

1. Your staff consists of you and two assistants. Make up a job description for each position.
2. Make up a trip itinerary for a two-game trip.
3. Write a paper on motivating the athlete.
4. Write a news release about your team's upcoming game.
5. Make up a personal resume that you could use in applying for a job.

Suggested Readings

Ebert and Cheatum, *Basketball,* pp. 231–36.

Hankinson, *Progressions,* pp. xiv–xix, 264–66, 296–301.

Kindall, Jerry. "Motivation: Last Year's NCAA Champion Coach Tells All." *Coach and Athlete,* April 1981, pp. 36–38.

Stewart and Scholz, *Complete Program,* pp. 10–23, 321–24, 339–40, 352–54.

Wooden, *Modern Basketball,* pp. 19–25, 33–35, 40–43, 45–47, 57–61.

glossary

Approach step A defensive step used when the defensive player moves into proper position as the opponent receives the ball.

Assist A pass that directly results in a score.

Backboard The rectangular or fan-shaped board behind the goal that often is used for banking shots.

Backcourt The half of the court that is farthest from the offensive basket.

Backdoor An offensive cut along the baseline when a player is being overplayed by the defense or when the defense turns to look at the ball.

Ball fake Faking a pass in one direction and passing in another.

Ball-you-opponent principle A man-for-man defensive principle that requires defensive players to be constantly aware of the location of the ball and their respective opponents and to maintain a position between the two.

Baseball pass A pass thrown with the same basic technique used in throwing a baseball. The baseball pass is usually employed for long downcourt passes.

Baseline The end line running under the basket from sideline to sideline.

Basket The goal.

Blockout The positioning of the defensive player in such a manner as to prevent the offensive player from going to the basket for a rebound. Also referred to as box out.

Bounce pass A pass that strikes the floor before it gets to the receiver.

Box-and-one A combination defense in which four players play zone and one player plays man-for-man. The zone players set up in a box formation.

Center A position usually played by the tallest player on the team.

Change of direction Changing cutting direction in an effort to elude a defensive opponent.

Change of pace An offensive technique, usually used by the dribbler, in which speed is reduced then quickly increased to evade a defender.

Charging Running into a player who is stationary.

Chest pass A pass made with two hands that is initiated from the region of the chest.

Clear out An offensive technique in which a player close to a teammate with the ball cuts away from that player so that the defensive opponent cannot help out on any drive attempt.

Control dribble A low dribble used when the dribbler is closely guarded.

Control offense An offense that does not allow a quick shot.

Controlled fast break A fast break that emphasizes taking only the good shot.

Controlling the boards Gaining a majority of the rebounds.

Cross-over step The first step of a one-on-one drive when that step is made toward the side of the pivot foot.

Cut A quick move by the offensive player, usually toward the offensive basket.

Diamond-and-one A combination defense in which four players play zone and one player plays man-for-man. The zone players set up in a box formation.

Double dribble A player continuing to dribble after touching the ball with both hands.

Double-post A type of team offense in which two players play in the pivot area near the basket.

Double screen A screen set by two players.

Double-team A defensive tactic of using two players to guard the opponent with the ball.

Dribble Bouncing the ball on the floor with one hand or tapping it in the air. The dribble ends when both hands touch the ball.

Drive A quick dribble toward the basket in an effort to score.

Dunking Slamming the ball down through the goal.

Fake switch A man-for-man defensive technique in which a defensive player fakes a switch to another opponent but remains with the original assignment.

Fast break A situation in which the defensive team gains possession of the ball and moves into scoring position so quickly that its members outnumber the opponents.

Filling the lanes Cutting players into the three hypothetical lanes necessary for a 3-on-2 break situation.

Flip pass A pass made with one hand when exchanging the ball at close range.

Floor balance A term used to describe the necessity of offensive players maintaining sufficient space from each other to avoid excessive defensive help, to allow for proper offensive rebounding, and to afford at least one player in position to stop the opponent's fast-break.

Forward A position that requires both shooting and rebounding ability and usually played by one of the taller players. The forward usually plays near the sideline and toward the corner near the offensive basket.

Four corners A delay game in which a player is stationed in each corner of the frontcourt and the remaining player dribbles in the area near the top of the circle.

Free throw An unguarded shot from the free-throw line that is the result of a foul by the opponent.

Freezing the ball Withholding the ball from play without any effort to score; a tactic often used late in a game in an effort to protect a slight lead.

Fronting the post Guarding the post player in front rather than between that player and the basket. It is a defensive tactic often used to keep a good post player from obtaining possession of the ball close to the basket.

Give-and-go Passing the ball to a teammate and cutting hard to the basket for a return pass.

Goal tending Touching the ball or basket when the ball is above, on, or within the basket.

Guard A position usually played by the smaller players. It requires good ball handling and passing as well as the ability to shoot from the outside.

Head fake A one-on-one offensive maneuver used near the basket in which the player simply fakes with the head and ball in an effort to throw the defensive player off balance. Also called a ball fake.

Help-and-recover A man-for-man defensive technique by which a player guarding an opponent near the ball can help defend the ball and yet return to the original assignment when necessary.

Help side The side of the defensive court in which the ball is not located.

High post An offensive player who plays near the free-throw line.

Hook pass A pass made with the passing arm fully extended, similar to the hook shot.

Hook shot A shot taken with the shooting arm fully extended away from the body. The hook shot is usually initiated with the back to the basket.

Individual defense Position, footwork, and the various defensive techniques needed by an individual in playing defense.

Individual offense Shooting, passing, dribbling, cutting, and other movements an offensive player can use in an effort to score.

Jump ball The situation involving joint possession, in which the official tosses the ball into the air and two opposing players jump in an effort to tap it toward a teammate—also referred to as a toss up.

Jump shot A shot taken after the shooter has jumped into the air.

Lay-up shot A shot taken close to the basket, usually with one hand.

Low post An offensive player who plays near the basket.

Man-for-man defense A team defense in which each player is assigned a specific opponent to guard wherever this opponent may go in the offensive pattern.

Man-for-man press A pressing defense in which each defensive player is assigned a specific opponent to guard.

Match-up zone defense A defense that combines zone and man-for-man defensive principles.

One-handed push pass A pass made with one hand that is initiated from the side of the body and pushed toward the receiver.

One-on-one The situation in which one offensive player tries to score against one defensive player.

Outlet pass A pass made after a defensive rebound.

Overtime An extra period played to break a tie score.

Passing game A half-court offense that functions on rules rather than set plays.

Perimeter player An offensive player who plays outside away from the basket and not in the post area.

Peripheral vision Also referred to as split-vision, or the ability to see to the side while looking ahead.

Pivot Footwork that enables the ball handler to move one foot while keeping the other in the same position on the floor. Also a position on the court near the basket where the tallest player is usually stationed.

Pivot area The area close to the basket where the center usually plays.

Pivot player A player who plays close to the basket. Also called a post player.

Playing for one The strategy of playing for one shot prior to the end of a period.

Point guard The guard who has most of the ball-handling and playmaking responsibilities.

Post player A player who plays close to the basket. Also called a pivot player.

Pressing defense A forcing type defense in which the offense is picked up farther away from the basket than normal. The press may be half-court, three-quarter court, or full-court.

Rear screen A screen set to the rear of a defensive player.

Rebound A missed shot attempt.

Retreat step A defensive step used to guard an opponent driving to the basket.

Reverse dribble The dribble technique in which the dribbler changes direction by making a complete 180-degree turn so that the body protects the ball as the dribble continues.

Run-and-jump press A type of man-for-man press in which defensive players switch opponents in an effort to surprise the offense.

Sagging defense A defense that drops back toward the free-throw lane area to jam the area close to the basket. A sagging defense is very effective when playing against a strong post player.

Screen   A legal maneuver used by the offense in an effort to free a player for a shot at the basket. The screener stands in such a position that the opposing defensive player cannot get to the player in position to shoot.

Screen-and-roll   An offensive technique in which the screener pivots on the inside foot and cuts to the basket. The screen-and-roll technique is used to combat the switching defense.

Screen away   A screen set for a player away from the ball.

Second guard play   A very popular play in basketball in which one guard passes to a forward, cuts through, and the forward hands off to the second guard coming around.

Shot chart   A chart that shows what players took shots, from where, and whether these shots were made or missed.

Shuffle offense   A continuity offense that requires each player to be able to play all positions.

Single-post   A type of team offense in which one player plays in the post area.

Slide step   A defensive step used to guard an opponent moving laterally or obliquely across the court.

Speed dribble   A high dribble used to advance the ball downcourt quickly when no defensive player is harassing the dribbler.

Split-the-post   A three-player offensive maneuver in which the ball is passed to a post player and two players scissor off the post for a possible pass.

Spot up   Moving to an open spot when a defensive player moves to help a defensive teammate.

Spread offense   A man-for-man offensive pattern in which players are spread around the circle with no player in the post area. The spread offense can be used as a regular offense or a stall offense.

Staleness   A mental attitude of a player or team characterized by sloppy, sub-par play and a decline in enthusiasm.

Stall   An offensive technique in which a team makes little effort to score. It is usually used by a team late in the game in an effort to kill the clock. The stall is similar to the freeze.

Strong side   The side of the defensive court in which the ball is located.

Switch   A maneuver used by the defense to combat a screen and make possible a change of defensive assignments.

Switch dribble   The dribble technique in which the dribbler changes dribbling hands by crossing the ball in front of the body.

Tandem-post   An offense with a high and low post.

Tease offense   A delay game in which all players are stationed in the third of the frontcourt near the ten-second line.

Ten-second line   The midcourt line past which the team in ball possession must advance within 10 seconds.

Three-on-two   A fast-break situation in which three offensive players attack two defensive players.

Three-second-lane The offensive free-throw lane in which no offensive player can remain for more than three seconds at a time.

Tip-in A quick one-handed tip of a missed field goal try that results in a score.

Trailer An offensive player who comes downcourt after teammates have tried to score on a 3-on-2 situation. The trailer can be available for an outlet pass for a quick shot or to cut through for a lay-up or a rebound.

Traveling Taking more than one step with the ball without dribbling. Also referred to as "walking."

Turnover Any loss of ball possession.

Two-on-one A fast-break situation in which two offensive players attempt to score on one defensive player.

Violation A rules violation that results in loss of the ball.

Weave A type of offense involving close exchanges of the ball. The weave may be a three-player, four-player, or five-player maneuver.

Wheel offense A continuity offense that requires each player to be able to play all positions. It differs from the shuffle offense in that a double screen is set for the first cutter instead of a single screen.

Wing player A player who plays near the sideline and even with the free-throw line.

Zone defense A team defense in which the defensive player is assigned an area on the court to guard.

Zone press A pressing defense in which each defensive player is assigned a specific area of the court to defend.

index